A Prince of

Flora Annie Webster Steel

Alpha Editions

This edition published in 2024

ISBN 9789362098825

Design and Setting By

Alpha Editions

www.alphaedis.com

Email - info@alphaedis.com

Contents

PREFACE

"The fiction which resembles truth is better than the truth which is dissevered from the imagination," said the Persian poet Nizami, in the year 1250.

It remains true, however, to-day. So I give no excuse for this book. It is not one which will appeal to the man in the street. Nevertheless I make the attempt to give the character and the times of the Prince of Dreamers with a glad heart. It is as well that the twentieth century of the West should know something of the sixteenth century in the East.

So many of my *dramatis personæ* once lived in the flesh and spoke many of the words imputed to them in the following pages, that it will be shorter to designate those who are purely imaginary puppets.

To begin with Mirza Ibrahîm and Khodadâd. For obvious reasons it is always safer in historical novels to draw the out-and-out villains with imagination. The death of the latter, however, together with the curious privileges of the Târkhâns are part of the truth which is stranger than fiction.

For Âtma Devi I have also no warranty; Indian history does not concern itself with womenkind. But dear Auntie Rosebody's Memoirs[1] have supplied me with my sketch of the Beneficent Ladies, while, of course, the story of Mihr-un-nissa, who in long after-years did, under the name of Nurjahân, become Prince Salîm's wife, and, as such, did undoubtedly add to the honour and glory of his reign as Jâhangîr, is purely historical; even to the chance meeting in the Paradise Bazaar.

Pâyandâr Khân, the Wayfarer, is so far possible that the heir to the throne of Sinde, who bore that name, suddenly lost his senses in consequence of some direful tragedy, disappeared into the desert, and was no more heard of. The crediting of him with hypnotic powers is offered as an explanation of many marvels which are constantly cropping up in Indian story and legend.

It has been suggested to me that for those to whom the word Mogul is mixed up with tobacconists' shops and packs of cards, a brief outline of the dynasty called by that name might be advisable.

It was founded, then, by one Babar, poet, knight-errant, perfect lover, who is, without doubt, the most charming figure in all history. He sacrificed his life in 1540 for his son Humâyon, that most unfortunate of kingly adventurers from whose opium-soddened hands the thirteen-year-old boy, Akbar, took an uncertain sceptre. In him the glory of the Moguls culminated. After him three more kings were worthy of the title "Great," and then by slow degrees the dynasty dwindled down to one Bahâdur Shâh, a feeble old man, who after defying us at Delhi, died miserably in exile.

Akbar was cotemporary of Queen Elizabeth, and his rightful place is among the great company of dreamers--Shakespeare, Raphael, Drake, Galileo, Michelangelo, Cervantes, and half a hundred others--who in the sixteenth century arose (and God alone knows why or whence) to place the whole world, spiritual and temporal, under the sway of imagination for the time.

I have chosen as my period in Akbar's life that time of glorious peace before the abandonment of the City of Victory, Fatehpur Sikri, which he had built to commemorate the birth of his son.

The reason for this abandonment is unknown, though scarcity of water was certainly one of the factors in it.

One thing is clear, the step must have meant much to Akbar; must have involved the giving up of many cherished dreams. And it is equally clear that his whole policy changed from the day he left what was the embodiment of his own personal pride, his own personal outlook on the future. Evidently he felt himself faced by some necessity for supreme choice, and having made it, he kept to the course he had chosen undeviatingly.

I have presumed to find this necessity in the bitter disappointment caused to him by his sons.

This at any rate is history, and with a man of Akbar's temperament it is impossible to overestimate the effect of knowing that his natural heirs were unworthy, incapable indeed, of carrying on his Dream of Empire.

Whether the diamond which plays its part in these pages is the one now called the Koh-i-nur, or whether it was the stone afterward known as the Great Mogul, or whether it was yet a third one, who can say? The history of Oriental gems is often too mysterious even for fiction. But there is a legend that Akbar possessed such a lucky stone, and it is certain that William Leedes remained to cut gems in the Imperial Court when his companions John Newbery and Ralph Fitch left it.

Finally, if competent critics feel inclined to cavil at the extraordinary aloofness of Akbar from his surroundings, I can only bid them remember that he was literally centuries ahead of his time, and assert that in this very aloofness lies the only claim of any soul to be remembered above its fellows.

The two friends whom he chose to be friends--out of the millions of men he governed--fittingly go down with him through those centuries, a trio; Akbar the dreamer, Birbal the doubter, Abulfazl the doer, who between them made of the Great Mogul a king of kings.

CHAPTER I

"Hush! The King listens!"

The sudden sonorous voice of the court-usher echoed over the crowd and there was instant silence.

The multitude sank, seated on the ground where it had been standing, and so disclosed to view the rose-red palaces of Fatehpur Sikri, the City of Victory, rising from the rose-set gardens where the silvery fountains sprang from the rose-red earth into the deep blue of the sky.

Akbar the King showed also, seated on a low, marble, cushion-covered pedestal beneath a group of palms.

He was a man between the forties and the fifties with no trace of the passing years in form or feature, save in the transverse lines of thought upon his forehead. For the rest, his handsome aquiline face with its dreamy yet fireful eyes and firm mouth, held just the promise of contradiction which is often the attribute of genius.

So, as he sate listening, a woman sang.

She stood tall, supple, looking in the intensity of her crimson-scarlet dress, like a pomegranate blossom, almost like a blood-stain amongst the white robes of her fellow musicians. The face of one of these, fine, careworn, stood out clear-cut as a cameo against the glowing colour of her drapery, and the arched bow of his *rebeck* swayed rhythmic ally as the high fretful notes followed the trilling turns of her voice:

Gladness is Gain, because Annoy has fled
Sadness is Pain, because some Joy is dead
Light wins its Halo from the Gloom of night
Night spins its Shadow at the Loom of light.

The Twain are one, the One is twain
Naught lives alone in joy or pain
Except the King! Akbar the King is One!

Birth sends us Death, and flings us back to Earth
Earth lends us Breath, and brings us fresh to Birth
Love gives delight----

"Hush! The King wearies!"

Once again the sonorous voice of the court-usher following a faint uplift of the King's finger brought instant obedience. The singer was silent, the crowd remained expectant, while the hot afternoon sun blazed down on all things save the King, sheltered by the royal baldequin.

He raised his keen yet dreamy eyes and looked out almost wistfully to the far blue horizon of India, which from this rocky red ridge whereon he had built his City of Victory showed distant, unreal, a mere shadow on the inconceivable depth of the blue beyond.

Jalâl-ud-din Mahomed Akbar, Great Mogul, Emperor of India, Defender of the Faith, Head of Kingdoms Spiritual and Temporal! Aye, he thought, he was all that so far as the Shadow went. But in the Light? What of the Light beyond, wherein Someone--Something--sate enthroned, King-of-Kings, Lord-of-Lords? What was he *there*?

He rose suddenly, and the crowd rising also swept back from his path tumultuously, as the waters of the Red Sea swept back from the staff of Moses, to leave him free, unfettered.

There was no lack of power about him anyhow! He stepped forward, centring his world with the swing of an athlete--a swing which made the bearers of the royal baldequin jostle almost to a trot in their efforts to keep the Sacred Personality duly shaded; and then he paused to look thoughtfully into a pool that was fretted into ceaseless rippling laughter by the fine misty spray which was all that fell back from the clear, strong, skyward leap of the water in the central fountain. Was that typical of all men's efforts, he wondered? A skyward leap impelled by individual strength; and then dispersion? When he died--and death came early to his race--what then?

He stood absorbed while the crowd closed in behind the courtiers who circled round him at a respectful distance. Beyond them the fun of the fair commenced; bursts of laughter, a hum of high-pitched voices, the tinkling of wire-stringed fiddles, the occasional blare of a conch, with every now and again the insistent throbbing of a hand drum, and a trilling song--

"*May the gods pity us, dreamers who dream of their godhead*"

And over all the hot yellow sunshine of an April afternoon in Northern India.

"The King is in his mood again," remarked one of the courtiers vexedly. He was Mân Singh, the Râjpût generalissimo, son of the Râjah Bhagwân Singh who had been Akbar's first Hindoo adherent, who was still his close friend and soon to be his relative by marriage. The speaker was in the prime of life, and the damascened armour seen beneath a flimsy white muslin overcoat seemed to match his proud arrogance of bearing. The courtier to whom he spoke was of a very different mould; small, slender, dark, with the face of a mime full of the possibilities of tears and laughter, but full also of a supreme intelligence which held all other things in absolute thrall. He gave a quick glance of comprehension toward his master, then shrugged his shoulders lightly.

"He sighs for new worlds to conquer, *Mirza-rajah*," he replied, with a faint emphasis on the curious conglomerate title which was one of the King's quaint imaginative efforts after cohesion in his court of mixed Hindus and Mahommedans. "You Râjpût soldiers are too swift even for Akbar's dreams! With Bengal pacified, Guzerât gagged, Berhampur squashed and the Deccan disturbances decadent, His Majesty is--mayhap!--busy in contriving a new machine to turn swords into wedding presents."

He gave an almost sinister little bow at this allusion to the coming political marriage of the Heir-Apparent, Prince Salîm to Mân Singh's cousin; a match which set the adverse factions in the court by the ears.

Mân Singh laid his hand on his sword-hilt and frowned.

"If Birbal could speak without jesting 'twere well," he said, significantly. "Those bigoted fools"--he nodded toward a group of long-bearded Mahommedan preachers--"may howl about heretics if they choose, but we Râjpûts know not how to take this mixed marriage either; for in God's truth the Prince is not as the King, but an ill-doing lout of a lad--so Akbar has no time for moods. He needs skill."

Birbal gave another of his comprehending glances toward his master, another of his habitual slight shrugs of the shoulder.

"Perchance he wearies of skill! The doubt will come to all of us at times, Sir soldier, whether aught avails to check the feeblest worm Fate sends to cross the path! But ask Abulfazl there, he stands closer in council to Akbar than I."

There was a slight suspicion of jealousy in his tone as he turned toward a burly, broad-faced, clean-shaven man whose expression of sound common sense almost overlaid the high intellectuality of his face.

"What ails the King?" he answered, and as he spoke his light brown eyes, scarce darker than his olive skin, were on Akbar with all the affection of a mother who glories because her son has outgrown her own stature. "Can you not see that he fears death?"

"Death!" echoed Mân Singh, hotly. "Since when? There was no fear of death in Akbar when he, my father, and I--each guarding the other's head--rode down that cactus lane at Sarsa when the spear points were thick as the thorns!--nor when at Ahmedabad he sounded the *reveille* to awaken his sleeping foes--though they outnumbered him by four to one--because it was not regal to take them unawares--nor when----"

Abulfazl laughed, a fat chuckling laugh which suited his broad open face: "Lo! I shall have come to thee, stalwart and true, when I run short of incidents for my poor history of this glorious reign. Yet none knows the Most Excellent's reckless bravery better than I. But 'tis to his dream he fears death, Mân Singh,--his dream of personal empire that is bound up with this thirst-stricken town, founded for the heir of his body! And this fear of the force of fate comes upon him at the Nau-rôz[2] always, since both father and grandfather died ere they were fifty; and Prince Salîm----"

"Curse the young cub," broke in the Râjpût angrily, "what of him now?"

"Only the old tale," replied Shaikh Abulfazl gravely, "drunk----"

"Oh! Let the young folk be----" interrupted Birbal bitterly, as he passed on. "'Tis God gives us our sons; not we who make them. Mayhap some of us might have found better heirs through the town crier!"

Abulfazl looked after him pityingly. "It wrings him too, with Lâlla, his son, ever in the Prince's pocket. Such things are tragedies, and I thank heaven that my father----"

"If Abulfazl has time for gratitude to his Creator"--broke in a voice polished to the keenest acerbity--"can he not find a better subject for it than mere man, even though the man *be* his father?"

Abulfazl turned in perfect good-humour on his bitterest enemy, the rival historian Budaoni, who, as opponent-in-chief of all reforms, still wore a beard, while his green shawl and turban showed him an orthodox Mahommedan.

"Not so, *Mulla-sahib*," retorted the Shaikh carelessly. "I will leave the remark as a *Shiah*[3] sin for you to chronicle in your *Suni*[4] fashion."

So saying, he also passed on to stand beside the King, and, as Birbal had already done, strive to rouse him from his dreams.

"My liege!" he said, "the deputation from the English Queen----"

For an instant Akbar looked at him, resentfully; then the despotic finger raised itself, and Abulfazl fell back to join Birbal in failure.

From behind in the circle of the courtiers came an airy laugh.

"Will you not try, Oh! most learned! to rouse him with religion, since politics and art have been given *congé*, or shall I, as pleasure, fling myself into the breach?" said an overdressed noble with a handsome evil-looking face as he bowed ornately to the group of long-bearded Mahommedan doctors who held themselves together in contemptuous condemnation of all things.

"Where God sends meditation, Mirza Ibrahîm, He may haply send penitence also," replied their leader, the Makhdûm-ul'-mulk. "For that, we men of God wait with what patience that we can."

"I would we could rouse him," murmured Birbal, standing apart, "the generalissimo said true. He has need of all his skill--and yours, Shaikh-jee."

"Mine has he ever," replied Abulfazl, simply; and it was true. No lover was more absorbed by his mistress than he by Akbar and Akbar's fortunes. He was obsessed by them.

So as they stood, those two faithful friends and counsellors of the one man whom they held dearest upon earth--yet in a way unfaithful, distrustful of each other because of unconfessed jealousy--there came to them close at hand throbbing through the hot yellow sunshine that seemed to throb back in rhythm, the sound of an hourglass drum, and a high trilling voice--

"*May the gods pity us, dreamers who dream of their godhead.*"

"It is Âtma," muttered Birbal to himself. "What seeks the madwoman now?" And he strode back to where on the outskirts of the circle of courtiers some disturbance was evidently going on.

"Let her pass in an' she will," he called to the ushers, angrily. "When will men learn that fair words fight women better than foul ones. I will dismiss her."

"Bards of a feather flock together," sneered Budaoni, alluding to Birbal's own minstrel birth. Abulfazl who was close behind his enemy turned on him courteously.

"Mayhap he and my brother Faiz, Hindu and Unorthodox poets-laureate, being disappointed of a worthy colleague from your sect *Mulla-jee*, are seeking one--amongst women!"

There was a laugh, and Budaoni turned aside scowling, with a murmured "May God roast him!" It was his favourite wish for the unorthodox.

Meanwhile a red dress showed through the bevy of protesting ushers and the next moment a group of three persons was standing before Birbal. One the woman who had sung, the other the *rebeck* player whose fine careworn face had shown cameo-like against her glowing colour, the third an old man almost hidden by his big drum.

The woman was past her first youth, but she was still extraordinarily handsome, and her dark eyes, full of some hidden thought, looked defiantly into Birbal's.

"I am the King's bard--the King's champion," she said in a low rapid voice, "I have come to sing to him."

Birbal bowed with a half-disdainful sweep of both hands.

"Those who know Âtma Devi as the daughter--the *daughter* only--of her dead father, may disclaim her right of succession. Birbal does nothing so--so unnecessary! Akbar has no need of your pedigrees to-day, madam! The King listens to no one--not even to your servant! Let the lady pass out again, ushers!"

For an instant Âtma hesitated. Then her eyes sought the *rebeck* player's and Birbal's followed hers instinctively. There was nothing unusual in the musician's thin face save its excessive pallor; in that he looked as if he had been dead for days. For the rest he was clean shaven to his very scalp, and wore no headdress; nor much of dress below that either. Birbal's swift downward glance paused in a moment at something attached to a skein of greasy black silk which the man wore, talisman fashion, about his throat.

What was it? A stone of some sort roughly smoothed to a square, and of a dull green uneven texture like growing grass. No! it was like leaves--like the rose leaves in a garden, and those faintly red specks were the roses. Yes! it was a rose garden. How the perfume of it assailed the senses, making one forget--forget--forget--

"Oh! rose of roses is thy scent of God?
Speak rose, disclose the secret!" "Foolish clod,
Who knows discloses not what's sent of God."

The quaint old triplet seemed afloat in the air and Âtma's voice to come from beyond something that was eternally unchanged, inevitable.

"Has the seedling no need of the root; does the flower not nurture the fruit?" she chanted, her eyes still upon the *rebeck* player.

Birbal looked at her, caught in the great World-Wisdom which poets see sometimes in the simplest words.

"She says truth," he murmured to himself. "She says truth!" Then with a light laugh he turned to Abulfazl. "Shall we let her pass? At least she can do no harm."

"Nor any good," broke in Mân Singh hotly; "and it will but strengthen her madness! What! a woman to claim a Châran's[5] place--to give her body to the sword?--her honour to the dust for the King's? Psha! Bid her go back to her spinning wheel!"

Abulfazl smiled largely. "Lo! even Râjpût manhood lives in the woman for nine long months--none can escape from the dark life before birth. Yea! let her pass in, Birbal--she can do no harm."

"Nor good," persisted Mân Singh stoutly.

Birbal's shoulders moved once more. "I would not swear," he answered airily, "since Akbar is not of the common herd. Go then, good mad soul, and sing thy pedigrees, and you,"----he paused pointing at the quaint green stone. "What call you that, musician?"

The *rebeck* player paused also, keeping his eyes downward submissively.

"They call it smagdarite, Excellence. It comes from Sinde."

"Sinned or no sin," echoed Birbal gaily, "the devil is in it. But 'tis a good name. Pass on Smagdarite! Stay"--here the old man half-hidden by his drum essayed to follow--"whom have we here? Old Deena the drum-banger! In what vile stew of Satanstown didst spend the night, villain?"

Thus apostrophised, Deena's comically wicked, leering, old face hid itself completely in a salaam behind the drum, and came up again puckered with pure mischief.

"That is a question for the virtuous Lord Chamberlain, Mirza Ibrahîm," he replied, demurely.

The sally was greeted with a boisterous laugh, and Mirza Ibrahîm--whose fine clothes dispersed a perfect atmosphere of musk--scowled fiercely. For Satanstown, as ultimate exile of all the bad characters of the city was in his charge, and report had it that he pursued his duty of inspection with more than usual assiduity.

"Sit thou here then, by Smagdarite," continued Birbal, recovering from his laugh, "and drum from a distance, lest thou be utterly damned for deserting honourable company. Hark! she begins!"

Âtma had by this time sunk to the ground beside the King. Her flimsy scarlet skirts curved about her like overblown poppy petals. Her dark eyes, full of fire, were fixed on the unconscious figure so close beside her, and, under the slow circling of her lissome forefinger the little drum held in her left hand was beginning to give out an indescribably mysterious sound like the first faint sobbing of air before an organ pipe breaks into a note.

From the distance, almost unheard, came the muffled throbbing of old Deena's drum, and the thin thread of the *rebeck*, light yet insistent like a summer gnat; both kept to the same stern delicacy of rhythm.

The singer's voice, high and clear, rose on it almost aggressively--

Hark! and hist!
To the list
Of the kings who have died
In their pride,
To the wide,

      wide,
      world.

MÎRUN-KHÂN!

Lo! He dreamt he was King!
But he died
In his pride
To the wide,

      wide,
      world.

SO HIS SON SULÎMÂN

Dreamt the dreamings of kings
Till he died
In his pride
To the wide,

wide,
world.

SO THE DREAM WAS JEHÂN'S!

And he dreamt he was king
Till he died
In his pride
To the wide,

    wide,
    world.

The rhythmic background broke with the singing voice into troubled triplets, and the King's slack hands gripped in on themselves. Was he listening?

Now the tale of the Kings who have died

    In their pride
    Is many, and many beside.
    But the dream is the same,
    So it came----

The pliant forefinger's whirling gave out a continuous boom like distant thunder amongst hills. Deena's drum throbbed a *réveillé*, the *rebeck* thrilled like a cicala--

TO KUMÂN

And he dreamt he was King

    In the wide,
    wide,
    world----

"Enough!" The word came swiftly as Akbar turned with a frown. "The end, woman? The end?"

There was a pause; then from the very dust of his feet rose her reply:

"There is none to the dreaming of kings!"

"There is none--to the dreaming--of kings," he echoed slowly, and his eyes scanned her face curiously as he raised her from the ground. "Who art thou, woman?" he asked suddenly; then as suddenly dropped the hands he held, and said coldly: "Give her gold for her song." But once more a fresh feeling came to make him add: "Nay! not gold--let her choose her own reward--what wouldst thou, sister?"

His face, grown soft as a woman's, looked sympathetically into hers; she stood before him abashed by the quick tie that seemed to have sprung up between them, unable to realise the chance that was hers.

"Quick step!" cried Mân Singh brutally. "See you not the Most-Gracious waits? What shall it be? Gold, fal-lals, dresses--the things for which women sell their souls?"

She turned on him like a queen.

"The women who nurture such heroes as Râjah Mân Singh mayhap so sell them; but I----" here her recognition of opportunity swept trivialities before it, she drew herself up to her full height and faced both King and court, her voice ringing like a clarion.

"I claim my father's office!" she cried. "Listen, O King-of-Kings! He gave you faithful service when you came to take the crown of India. What to him was Hindu or Mahommedan? He was the King's herald! Akbar was the King! His eldest son--my brother--died to save the honour of the Râjpût chief he served before you came! And little Heera--son of his old age, begot *for you*, died ere his baby tongue had ceased to trip in challenging the world--*for you!* Lo! I have kissed the words to steadiness upon his childish lips when father grew impatient! Why was I not the son? Hid in this dustlike body lies the spirit of my race. Is it my fault that in the dark months of my mother's womb, Fate made me woman, as she made you man? Give me my father's office, O my King, and if my tongue forgets one word of all my father's lore, or if I fail in guarding the King's honour, treat me as woman then--but not till then."

The dying fall of her words left the court amazed, almost affronted. Here was a claim indeed! A claim foreign to the whole conservative fabric of Eastern society--which heaven knows had already suffered shock enough at the King's reforming hands!

But Akbar took no heed of the looks around him; he was deep in that problem of Sex which was one of the many to claim his quick interest at all times.

"The spirit of thy race is in thee, sure enough, O sister," he said slowly. "Manhood is in the woman, as womanhood is in the man--do I not know the latter to my cost? So take thy gift. Thou art the King's Châran from this day. But hearken! If thou failest in thy task, I treat thee not as woman--but as man."

He turned away, dismissing her with an autocratic wave from sight, even from thought. "Ushers!" he went on, raising his voice in command, "Sound the advance! I go. And my Lord Chamberlain, bid the travelling Englishmen attend me in the Diwani-Khas. Abul! your arm; I would speak with you about this queen--this woman who has stretched her hand out over the seas to meet mine." He gave a quick joyous laugh and stretched out his own--the true Eastern hand, small, fine, but with a grip as of wrought iron in its slender, flexible fingers. "By God and his prophets I seem to feel it here--a woman's hand close clasped to mine."

A fanfaronade of trumpets, shawms, and drums drowned his words, as with a waving of plumes, a blinding glitter of gold and jewels, the royal cortège of Akbar the Magnificent swept on its way.

"One moment!" cried Birbal to Mân Singh who awaited him impatiently, "I must find Smagdarite first."

But both the *rebeck* player and Âtma Devi had gone. Only old Deena remained drumming softly; a fitting accompaniment to the murmurs which rose around him, as the immediate *entourage* of the King disappeared.

"Yet one more insult to Islâm," muttered the Makhdûm-ul'-mulk spitting fiercely ere he spoke.

"And to honest men!" asserted a jealous old Turk who was suspicioned of having drowned more than one young wife on the sly, "for what is woman but ultimate deceit and guile?"

"What?" echoed one whose calling could best be described as court-pandar; "Why a means for man's making money withal; though the King's virtue steals many a penny out of my pocket. I tell you he is no King--and no man. Would either spend his moneys on duty instead of pleasure?"

Ghiâss Beg, the Lord High Treasurer, laughed uneasily. "The money goes nevertheless. Tôdar Mull as Finance Minister is for ever cutting down state revenues, and the King's private charities----"

"To say nothing of the civil list for five thousand women within the palace walls at whom he never looks," put in Mirza Ibrahîm sarcastically.

"Five thousand and one, my friend," laughed a man with a sinister face, "since there will be a pension now for Âtma Devi, King's Châran, unless

Mirza Ibrahîm prefers to provide for her himself. I caught a lewd eye appraising her many charms."

The Lord Chamberlain frowned. "I was but following the lead of Khodadâd Khân, who hath the quickest sight of any in India for a pretty woman."

"King's pensioners belong to the King," replied Khodadâd of the sinister face, "and I meddle not with Majesty."

"So Majesty meddles not with me," remarked Ghiâss Beg, "and leaves me my quail[6] curry and my saffron *pillau*, it is welcome to starve an' it likes on one meal of pease-porridge a day!"

And as he rolled off, good-natured, hospitable, he felt in the heart which lay beneath his fat stomach a pang of regret that the King, in so many ways a prince of good fellows, the best shot, the best rider, the best polo player, the best all-round man and sportsman in his kingdom, should be so marvellously out of touch with his court.

But the princes, his sons, were, thank heaven, different!

CHAPTER II

For the Lord our God Most High
He hath smote for us a pathway to the Ends of all the Earth.

      *   *   *   *   *

And some we got by purchase
And some we had by trade
And some we found by courtesy
Of pike and carronade.

--KIPLING.

Elizabeth, by the Grace of God, etc.... To the most invincible and most mightie prince Lord Yelabdim Echebar, King of Cambaya Invincible Emperor--etc.

The great affection which our Subjects have to visit the most distant places of the world, not without good will and intention to introduce the trade of all nations whatsoever they can, by which meanes the mutual and friendly traffeque of marchandise on both sides may come, is the cause that the bearer of this letter John Newbery joyntly with those that be in his company, with a curteous and honest boldnesse, doe repaire to the borders and countreys of your Empire, we doubt not but that your Imperial Maiestie through your royal grace will fauvurably and friendly accept him.

And that you would doe it the rather for our sake, to make us greatly beholden of to your Maiestie; wee should more earnestly and with more wordes require it if wee did think it needful.

But by the singular report that is of your Imperial Maiesties humanitie in these uttermost parts of the world, we are greatly eased of that burden and therefore wee use the fewer and lesse words, onely we request that because they are our subjects they may be honestly intreated and received. And that in respect of the hard journey which they have taken to places so far distant it would please your Maiestie with some libertie and securitie of voiage to gratifie it, with such privileges as to you shall seeme good; which curtesie if your Imperiall Maiestie shal to our subjects at our request performe, wee, according to our royall honour will recompence the same with as many deserts as we can. And herewith we bid your Imperiall Maiestie to fare-well.[7]

The polished Persian periods of the translation--the original of which, drawn from its brocaded bag, lay before the King--fell mellifluously from Abulfazl's practised lips; the final cadence of the farewell holding in it a certain sense of finality.

Some of the audience yawned; surfeited with the magnificences, the festivities of this New Year's Day, both minds and bodies were attuned to sleep in the present, not to dreams of the future.

Outside the wide rose-red arches of the Hall of Audience; a rose-red sunset was flaring in the west. Over the wide plain of India the growing shadows were obliterating the familiar life of millions on millions of men.

So there was silence; a second, as it were, of breathing space. Then, suddenly, a gong struck, echoing through the arches and over the purpling plain beyond them, in rolling reverberations.

One of the three Englishmen who stood in worn doublets and hose awaiting the reply to their Queen's letter shivered slightly. It sounded to him like the knell of some doom. Whose? Theirs, or the King's, who, with face suddenly alert, rose, and standing, looked down the central aisle. The assemblage rose also, more or less alertly, and all eyes followed the King's.

So, cleaving the hot evening air, which seemed the more heated by reason of the fierce blare of many colours, the dazzling glitter of gems which came with that sudden uprising, the sound of boys' voices singing a wild, wavering chant was heard. Then far away down the pathway of Persian carpeting two tiny babyish figures showed, heading a procession of lighted tapers. Boy and girl, they were naked save for the wreaths of roses with which they were bound together, and for the filmy gossamer veil, spangled with diamond dewdrops, which, just reaching their foreheads in front, trailed behind them on the floor. The first footsteps of the following choristers almost touched it, as they advanced slowly, twelve of them in single file, each bearing a massive golden candlestick containing a flaring camphor candle. The smoke of these drifted backward, lit up by the white light to fantastic curves, and rested like a pall over the procession.

The Englishman who had shivered, crossed himself devoutly as he stepped back to let it pass. He felt as if some corpse lay there, lifted high above the world, shrouded by that trailing fume of light.

And now the wailing chant of the "Dismissal of Day"--discordant to English ears--steadied to something vaguely reminiscent of the Kyrie in Palestrina's Mass of Pope Marcellus, as the procession formed itself into a semicircle about the throne, the two tiny figures, girl and boy, tight hand-clasped, solemn, wide-eyed, standing together at the King's very feet.

Come Night! Our day is done
Keep thou the Sun
Safe in the West
Lulled on thy breast
For day is done.

Our light its course has run
The West has won
Lo! God's behest
Is manifest
Our course is run.

His Might and Right are one
Plaint have we none
Come darkness blest
Give us thy Rest
Our day is done.

The words fell lingeringly, and with the last, each chorister bent toward his taper and softly blew it out, the tiny children drew the gossamer veil over their faces and, bending to kiss each other, turned, still solemn, wondering, wide-eyed, to head the retreating procession which passed, silently and in shadow, whence it came.

Was it merely the swift extinction of those twelve brilliant tapers symbolising the Hours-of-Light which brought a sudden sense of darkness to all the pomp and magnificence? Or was it only because outside the rose-red arches the sun's last rim was just disappearing beneath the western horizon? Or on that memorable evening when the English grip first closed upon India did some shadow of future fate fall to intensify the solemnity of the Dismissal of Day?

It may well have been so.

"Read that portion again," came Akbar's resonant voice in the pause which ensued, "which says '*with more wordes we should require it.*'"

If there was pride in his tone there was arrogance in most of the faces around him. Their owners had already prejudged the case, and were ready with denial. On Akbar's, however, was only the quick curiosity with which he met all new things, and a not unkindly personal interest for the three adventurers whose bold blue eyes gave back his curiosity unabashed, and whose worn doublets, shabby and travel-stained, appealed directly to one who, like Akbar, was desert-born and hardly bred.

"'*We are greatly eased of that burden and therefore wee use the fewer and lesse words.*'"

The phrase seemed to satisfy, and Akbar held up his despotic forefinger.

"Your names," he said briefly, adding to the clerkly figures who sate in their appointed places on the floor at the extremities of the small semicircle centred on the throne, the equally despotic word, "Write!"

"John Newbery, merchant," replied the tallest of the three, who was also unmistakably the leading spirit. As he spoke he made an obeisance which showed him not absolutely unversed in Eastern etiquettes.

"Your home?" put in Akbar quickly. There was a half-defiance in the answer:

"Aleppo. My purpose is trade." Something in the face, however, belied the latter profession for it showed the restless energy of the born wanderer to whom gain of gold is as nothing to gain of experience and of power.

"Is there then not trade enough in the West?" came the swift question.

"Trade and to spare mayhap, your Majesty," replied John Newbery, "but not enough for Englishmen. We live by trade."

A faint stir of distaste rose from amongst the nobles, and Mân Singh muttered under his breath. "A Râjpût lives by his sword--would I had it in some wames I wot of!"

"And you?" continued the King, turning to the next adventurer. He was shorter, broader, and had an open face, matched by his bluff, frank manner.

"I am one Ralph Fitch by name, may it please your Majesty, citizen and trader of London town."

The answer passed the muster of Akbar's mind, and he repeated the same question to the third traveller.

Older by some years than his companions, his whole appearance suggested a more courtly breeding than theirs.

"May it please your Majesty," he said, dropping on one knee, "if indeed that be the proper form of addressing the mighty Jelabdim Echebar, Emperor of Cambay, I am one William Leedes, a jeweller. Native of England, educated at Ghent and Rotterdam. I have cut gems for royalty"--

his eyes fixed themselves on the almost rough translucence of a huge diamond which Akbar wore ever in his turban as a fastening to the royal heron's plume, and then he paused to draw something from his breast-- "like this, my liege."

He held out betwixt finger and thumb a small rose-cut diamond. Even in the growing dusk of the Audience Hall it showed its hundred pinpoints of light welded into one bright flash, and a low guttural "wâh" of admiration ran through the immediate circle round the throne. Akbar took the stone between finger and thumb also, and as he looked his eyes clouded instantly with dreams.

"A hundred suns where there is but one," he said, absently; "'tis like a many-sided life!" Then he held the jewel out toward Birbal, the young Princes, Abulfazl, Budaoni, and others of the inner court who were craning over to see it.

"'Tis better cut," he went on, "than the little one Pâdré Rudolfo showed us. Where did you learn the art?"

"At the fountain-head, my liege," replied William Leedes; "of old Louis de Berguein's son at Ghent."

"And you could cut such gems here?"

"Given the stones. 'Tis diamond cut diamond----"

"In all things!" interrupted Akbar, with a sudden smile. Then he turned to John Newbery.

"And what do you bring us in exchange?" he asked.

"Gold; and all that gold brings with it," was the ready reply.

Akbar shook his head. "We have gold and to spare already! Purse-bearer! Set forth the immortal money that they may see we lack it not."

In the brief pause, during which an old courtier stiff with age and brocade fumbled in a netted bag and set out a row of coins on an embroidered kerchief, Akbar sate silent, fingering the vellum of the Queen's letter, absorbed in thought.

"All is prepared, Most Excellent," petitioned the purse-bearer.

"Read out the legends, O Diwân!"

In obedience to the order Abulfazl, stepping forward, raised the first huge disc which contained a hundred pounds worth of pure gold, and read aloud from about the plain stamped semblance of a rose, these words:

I am a golden coin
May golden be my use.

So from the obverse, where it encircled a lily, came this couplet:

Golden it is to help
The seeker after truth

The Englishmen looked at one another. Their coin of the realm, despite its stamp "Defender of the Faith," held no such sermons.

So from the next largest disc worth just one half the *s'henser* came these words:

I am a garment of Hope
May hope be high.

and from the obverse:

God in His pleasure
Gives without measure.

"May it please your Most Excellent Majesty," interrupted John Newbery readily, "we ask but this; that following the divine example, your Majesty at your pleasure may grant our request without measure."

Akbar glanced round his court tentatively, first toward his sons. The eldest, Salîm, a big, handsome lad who looked years older than his age-- eighteen--was asleep. Prince Murâd the next, tall, lanky, cadaverous, sate sulky, indifferent. The youngest, Danyâl, a mere boy of some twelve years, was carelessly munching sweetmeats. The King's glance shifted with a sigh to Birbal's face.

"Wanderers are always beggars," quoted the latter warningly.

"Has Akbar's purse no penny left as alms?" came the instant answer.

"If this slave's opinion be asked, as Keeper of the Most Excellent's regalia," spoke up Ghiâss Beg boldly, "I must protest against the jeweller."

Akbar's sudden laugh seemed almost an outrage on that decorous assemblage. "Sure Akbar's crown can spare a gem or two? What dost thou say, O Abulfazl?"

As he spoke, he sought the wide-open, tolerant, far-seeing eyes of the man on whom, more than on all the others, he was dependent for the capable grip on possibilities which changed dreams into realities.

The eyes narrowed themselves for the moment, their gaze concentrated on that somewhat forlorn-looking group of three, awaiting the verdict.

"They come, Most Excellent," he said slowly, "by their own showing from a nation of traders. 'Tis your Majesty's axiom--a true one--that where trade flourishes justice must lie, seeing that the greater principle of mind is needed for the control over the lesser principle of gold. Yet, ere your Majesty decides, it were well that these traders be made acquainted with your Majesty's law, which while yielding due profit to the dealer, denies to him greed of unearned gain; the law demands fair, frank dealing from both parties to every contract of sale." He turned to the trio, adding courteously, "Doubtless it is also the law of your land, and of your Queen; since the fame of the justice of both has echoed here to the East?"

The three wanderers looked at each other dubiously, and Ralph Fitch muttered under his breath, "Ours is *caveat emptor* and it works well."

Then John Newbery pulled himself together and made bold answer:

"We need no such law, for England while she trades free, trades fair. And by that just fame of our country and of our Queen we engage to do naught unbecoming of either----"

"And to abide by my laws," put in Akbar sharply.

"And to abide by such laws!" echoed John Newbery, adding to himself, "so long as they may last."

There was a pause. Once more Akbar's hand--that true Eastern hand, loose-knit, double-jointed, small, yet with sinews of iron--fingered the Queen's letter. At all times his mind went forth joyfully to any new thing, expectant, he scarcely knew of what; and this vellum, warming under his finger-touch seemed to grow responsive.

It was like a woman's hand. Aye! it was a woman's hand stretched out as a Queen's, to him as King! Stretched out across the sea; that dim mysterious sea which he had seen once, long years before, of which he had so often dreamt since, seeing himself standing with the ebbing tide at his feet and calling across the receding waters....

Calling for what?

For reply--always for the reply that never came!

"Write," he said suddenly, "write: Who injures them injures me, Akbar the Emperor. They have safe conduct so long as they remain in my realms."

John Newbery gave almost a laugh of relief. His part was played. The rest lay with Providence--and Commerce! England had gained a foothold in India. Let her see to it that she kept it. Aye! and more than kept it.

"There is yet one more petition," said Abulfazl hastily, as the King made as if he would rise. "The envoy from Sinde waits to bring the accession offering of the new ruler to the feet of acceptance."

Akbar sank back amongst his cushions resignedly. The province of Sinde was a perpetual thorn in his side. Sooner or later he felt it must be delivered from the tyranny of its hereditary rulers, but a Tarkhân was a Tarkhân, that is someone whom even a king would hesitate to touch, someone hedged round by strange privileges and high honours. Still annexation must come in the sequence of civilisation, so what mattered it if Bâzi committed suicide in a fit of drunkenness, if Payandâr Jân his son-- poor "Wayfarer in Life" by name indeed!--had gone mad and disappeared in the Great Desert, or whether Jâni Beg or any other of the ill-doing royal house of Târkhâns had seized the reins of government.

It was a farce from beginning to end. His sympathies lay, if anywhere, with the Wanderer who had sought escape, so men said, from hereditary iniquity in the wilderness. From what? If rumour spoke true from terrors almost too horrible to be told.

So he sate indifferent while the envoy, a slight man with flowing black hair and beard, and curious dull eyes, read out from a gold-leaf besprinkled paper that Bâzi had taken the baggage of immortality from the lodging of life, that Payandâr having poured the dust of his brain into the sieve of perplexity and so removed the known into the unknown, Jâni Beg placed his unworthiness on the steps of the Throne of Virtue.

He did not even look up when the reading ceased and Birbal advanced to perform his duty of taking the missive in its brocaded bag and handing it to the throne.

But a quick exclamation roused him.

"What is it?" he asked, for Birbal stood staring at the envoy.

"Nothing, Most Excellent!" was the hasty reply, but the speaker still stared at the envoy's throat. Was it--or was it not--a smagdarite of which Birbal had caught a glimpse beneath brocaded muslin? His curiosity prevailed.

"I wait, sire," he added suavely, "for the virtuous name of this accredited of Kings."

The envoy's hand went up to his throat; he bowed gravely.

"Sufur-Dâr Khân of the Kingly House," he replied.

For the life of him Birbal could not resist another low swift question.

"And of the talisman he wears?"

The dull dark eyes held the alert ones.

"A common stone called smagdarite. If it pleases the Favoured-of-Kings, this Dust-born-Atom-in-a-Beam-of-Light resigns it."

Ye Gods! A rose-garden indeed! Birbal's bodily eyes saw the slender dark hand holding out the lustreless green stone, but his mind was lost in colour, beauty, perfume. Rose-leaves twined themselves into his brain, they sought his heart, their scent bewildered his soul, and faint and far off he seemed to hear a singing voice--

Who would have Musk of Roses must not touch the Rose.
Its scent is secret; only Heaven knows
How the sweet essence of a spirit grows.

"What now!" came Akbar's full imperious voice. "Must the King wait while Birbal dreams?"

The rose garden disappeared, for Birbal, taking it, thrust it hastily into his bosom, and then advanced toward the King with the brocaded bag.

"It is accepted," said the latter impatiently, signing away the offering, "the audience ends. Birbal, your arm. I lack air. This place is stifling."

The Englishmen awaiting the Lord Chamberlain to conduct them to suitable lodging looked round the fast-emptying Hall-of-Audience with the sort of stupefaction which follows on accomplishment.

"If we lose grip," said John Newbery suddenly, "'twill be the fault of metal."

"Mettle," echoed William Leedes almost sadly. "There is mettle here and to spare already, God knows. Yet must it go, since it is not of English making."

Ralph Fitch looked at him dubiously. "We be Christian men, comrade, and these but Pagans. Moreover, our commerce----"

John Newbery gave a loud laugh. "The pike and carronade for my choice, my masters! But cheer up, friend! We will do the cutting of India whilst William Leedes facets yonder pigeon's egg Echebar wore in his turban."

The jeweller looked up quickly. "Lo! I could not an' I would! There is something of steady radiance in it that would defy my tools."

So they followed their guide, catching a glimpse as they passed through the courtyards of two figures standing under the Great Arch of Victory and looking out over the purpling Indian plain. It was Akbar's favourite evening resort, and to-night he had his favourite companion, Birbal.

It was growing chill already under the massive masonry of the palaces, but it was still warm out in the open where the blistering sun had scorched all day long into the very heart of India--that dreaming heart hidden away under the wide arid levels, under the calm content of its multitudinous peoples.

The little dancing lights of the long line of booths and shops which edged the whole twenty miles from Fatehpur Sikri to Agra had already begun to glitter. The stars were lower in the sky, and only in the West, Venus hung resplendent. A haze of heat and dust from the lingering steps of homing cattle lay in quaint streaks, still faintly tinted with gold, over the distant country, and hung whiter, more obscure, and mingled with the smoke of the city, about the base of that mighty mountain of wide measured steps which recedes up and upward, climbing the low ridge of rocks until it finds pause in the vast platform whence--as springs no other in the wide world--the tall Arch of Victory thrusts itself skyward exultantly.

"'*Hafiz!*'" quoted the King suddenly. "'*No one knows the secret! Why dost ask what happens in the Wheel of Time?*' But we do ask it, Birbal! How many years is it since we two have sought the rose-essence of truth and found nothing but the scentless leaves? And yet 'tis here! I feel it, I know it!"--he touched his forehead lightly. "Strange to hunger so, after what is hidden in me, myself!"

Birbal shook his head. "What is self, my master? Purûsha gazes upon the Dancer Prakrîti, but by and by his eyes will tire of her disguises----"

"And then," interrupted Akbar, eagerly, "what then? When the object is gone, what of the subject? Answer me that, thou cold Kapilian! Nay! Birbal! I cannot believe it so. It strikes a chill to my very marrow. 'Tis warmer beneath the shelter of All-pervading Âtman holding both mind and matter in tenacious grip. Yet even that is cold to my hot life."

He turned slightly, and let his eyes follow the inlaid marble lettering of the legend which he himself had ordered to be set round his great Arch of Victory.

Said Jesus, on whom be peace: The world is a bridge, pass over it, but build no house there. Who hopes for an Hour, hopes for Eternity. Spend the Hour in Devotion. The rest is unknown.

"Aye! but a bridge to what?" he murmured. "Could I but know what lies before me--before this land!" His eyes embraced the darkening plain, and questioned vainly the reddening flush behind the departed sun. "We hope--that is all--hope for an hour--hope for eternity!--an eternity for ourselves and for our children!"

Those far-seeing eyes turned to rest lovingly on the red towers of Fatehpur Sikri. "No! I will never give it up. Birbal--it is my city of dreams-- the heritage of those who shall come after me--the birthplace and the death-place of the holder of an empire that is deathless. Water? Lo! what is water? 'Man,' says Pâdré Rudolfo the Jesuit, 'doth not live by bread alone.' Neither does he live by water."

"Natheless, sire!" put in Birbal drily, "it hath a trick of being the birthplace of most things; and the last report of the engineers is unfavourable. There is not even a dampness at three hundred feet!"

"Then we must make an aqueduct from the river--the Ganges, an' thou wilt--even from Holy Himâlya," answered the King gaily. "Akbar is not to be let or hindered by aught save Death--and even so"--he glanced with his winning, affectionate, almost womanish smile, at the man beside him-- "thou dost not forget the promise that whoever of us finds freedom first shall come back--with news."

"I have not forgotten, Master," replied Birbal. "Yet who should want my poor ghost--if I have one?"

Akbar's face lit up with curiosity, almost with credulousness.

"A ghost! By my faith, Birbal--which only God Himself knows since I sway like any weathercock!--a ghost is what we need! Someone to tell us fairly, squarely----" Then he smiled. "Didst see one but now when thou stoodst staring at the Sinde envoy like a fretted porcupine?"

Birbal paused. He had almost forgotten the incident. "Nay, I saw no ghost," he said slowly, and his hand sought his bosom as he spoke.

Then his face paled, for he could feel nothing there. The Garden of Roses had gone.

CHAPTER III

Oh! fathers who have sung I sing

      With woman's lips

Yet shall your sword hold honour for the King

      Till my blood drips

To cover failure with red blazoning,

Of set defiance, deathful-triumphing

      Ohé the King

      Challenge I bring

      Ohé the King, the King!

The huge silver hilted, cross-handled sword she had been holding--its point skyward--smote the stone at her feet as the wild chant ended, and the clang of the tempered steel rang out over the roof as Âtma Devi, turning to the north, the south, the east, the west, repeated her challenge. She had put on her father's silvered coat of mail, and her long black hair bound with a silver fillet about the brows, made her look like some Valkyrie of the West, ready to avenge the slain.

A water-bright ripple of laughter came from the door opening on to the small square of roof, and Âtma turned toward it fiercely to see a pink and yellow lollipop of a woman, respectability, in the shape of a thick white *burka* veil,[8] flung at her feet, leaning against the door lintel and watching her amusedly.

Her fierce frown faded. "Yamin," she said slowly, "What dost thou here?"

Siyah Yamin, pampered darling of the town, sank down, like a snake coiling itself, amid circling billows of soft scented satin and jingling fringes of silver and pearls. She was a small woman, extraordinarily graceful, extraordinarily beautiful, with a tiny oval innocent-looking face on which neither pleasure no pain left any mark whatever. From the crown of her head to the sole of her feet she looked, and was, prepared at all points for her trade; a dainty piece of confectionery ready to satisfy any sensual appetite.

"Here?" she echoed, and the one word showed her a passed-mistress in polished elocution. "Didst fancy I would stay in Satanstown because his Majesty the Monk chose to lump me with other loose livers and exile us beyond his city's walls? Not I!" Here the water-bright laugh rang out derisively. "Lo! many things have happened since Siyâla played with Âtma--what a bully thou wast in those days to poor little me; and thou lookst it now, thou sister of the veil!--for did we not drink milk together out of one vessel and under one veil, see you, before I drifted to the temple--and so hitherward? Yea! leaning on thy sword so--why! thou lookst beautiful! Could but some of my men see you----"

"Peace, woman!" said Âtma sternly. The tall cross-hilted sword held point downward formed a support for her elbow as she rested her head on her hand and gazed thoughtfully at Siyah Yamin.

"Thou hast not changed much, Siyâla," she said, more softly.

"Come! that is more like," laughed the little lady. "Those were merry old days! A pity thou didst not come with me to the temple, Âtma! Better anyhow than widowhood ere womanhood began."

"Peace, child!" repeated Âtma sternly. "What canst thou know of that high fate which makes of womanhood something beyond itself--but I waste words. Wherefore hast thou come?"

Siyah Yamin pouted her pretended sulkiness. "Because from my roof yonder--lo! how well we have kept the secret that thou didst not know the Companion-of-the-Court was thy next neighbour!--it hath been such fun, Âtma! beguiling the beadles whom his Monkey Majesty----"

"Have a care, Siyah Yamin!" interrupted Âtma hotly--"the King----"

Siyah Yamin coiled herself to closer laughing curves. "The King!" she echoed, "Oh yea! Âtma and the King--the King and Âtma!"

The woman hidden within the sword-bearer shrank back and paled.

"Well! What of Âtma and the King?"

"Naught! Naught!" laughed the little lady, "but I have heard of thy success to-day. What is there that Siyah Yamin does not hear? So when I saw thee from my roof up yonder with the old man's armour and the sword--frown not sweet sister, it becomes thee mightily--I just caught up my veil, and ran downstairs (for we have many entrances see you, and this tenement of yours is one of them) to offer thee congratulations--since if the King cast even the wink of an eye on a woman that is something! And they *say* he raised thee by the hands!"

The hot blood surged into Âtma's face. "And if he did, what then?" she asked.

Siyah Yamin rose, and yawning took up her veil. "Touching comes before tasting," she replied airily, "even with Kings. And so, having offered my gratulations on good luck--farewell."

Âtma stood frowning at her. "Thou playest a dangerous game, Siyâla; if the King discovers that thou--the darling of the town--hast set his rule at naught----"

Siyah Yamin burst into a perfect cascade of laughter. "Fie on thee, Âtma! and me a married woman, veiled, secluded, a perfect cupola of chastity!" Wrapped in her white burka, all one could see of the devilry within, was two eyes brimming over with malignant mischief.

"Married!" gasped Âtma, "what man has dared----?"

"Aye! He is brave," assented the courtesan, "and I love him--as much as I love most! And he is the best-looking of them all--is Jamâl-ud-din."

"Syed Jamâl-ud-din of Bârha?" echoed Âtma incredulously.

The veiled head nodded. "Yea! He is Syed, and set on his religion. So I said the Creed and he gave me one of the eight marriages--I forget which. These Mahommedan ceremonials are not awe-inspiring like the Seven Steps and the Sacrificial Fire; lo! even with no man, but a dagger, that gave me shivers. Thou wilt come and see me, Âtma. It is pleasant up there. We have joined four roofs. Ask for the Persian *bibi* from Khorasân and if needful give the password--'Kings-town.' Rage not, virtuous beloved! 'Tis better anyhow to live under Akbar than under Satan!"

So with a tinkling of silver and pearl fringes she passed upward.

Âtma stood for a while lost in thought, then rousing herself in quick impatience, put aside the sword in its appointed corner, removed her hauberk, laid it on the ground in front of the sword and on it set the two lamps which all night long kept watch and ward over the weapon, placed between them the death-dagger of her race, and so, her new-come evening task finished, went toward the parapet of the roof and, leaning her arms on it, looked out over the fast-fading horizon of India.

In her dark eyes still lay some of the unrest, the resentment which, since her father's death, had made the townsfolk call her mad: for those words with which the King had gifted to her the Châranship, "I'll treat thee not as woman, but as man," had curiously enough brought home to her all the limitations of that womanhood.

How little she could do--except die--for the King's honour. Still the roof was no longer voiceless. The challenge had rung out from it once more, obliterating the sad echoes of that last dying effort of the old man. She looked round as if listening for that feeble whisper.

No! It had gone. She was the Châran now! and the edge of the death-dagger was keen enough for woman's flesh; she might yet join the great and noble company of the self-immolated.

Her heart stirred in her at the thought of their deeds enshrined in old bardic verses that had been handed down from father to son from generation to generation.

They were in her keeping now at any rate, and she must not forget them.

So, half-kneeling by the low parapet, her chin resting upon her crossed arms, she said them over to herself rough, rude, almost unintelligible, yet still instinct with fire, with courage, with defiance.

She lingered lovingly over one: that tale of how the young ten-year-old Heera when his father was treacherously slain and his master falsely accused of high treason to his suzerain, was sent forth by his mother to seek his father's body in the wilds, and having found it, to take the death-dagger from the bleeding corpse, and so, all travel-stained and weary, his young face blistered with tears, to appear before the hasty tribunal and give the champion's cry--

It is a lie!
I, Heera, I
I take the lie!
Ye Bright-Ones see me die!
Avenge the lie!

And thus by his death force upon the conspirators a full inquiry. So she knelt dreaming, her chin upon her hand while the glow of the set sun faded from the sky.

Yet with all her dreaming she was very woman, and in every fibre of her being she still felt the touch of the King's hands upon hers.

Such hungry hands! Dimly, in her sexless soul, she recognised that quality in them. What did they want? Not womanhood certainly. But who wanted that? No one. Motherhood was one thing and widowhood was another, but sexual womanhood was nescience.

With a sigh she rose to fetch her Dharm-shastra and read her nightly portion from its pages, choosing it at random, so many *slokas* this way or that way from the one on which her eye fell first. Yet despite this superstitious selection, she was learned beyond the learning of most women, beyond even that of many learned men, for her father had taught her as he taught his sons--all save the Sacred Text, that privilege of Brahmanhood. The limitation, however, left Âtma smiling, since her widowhood outweighed for her the repetition of many *gayatris*.

By it she gained a privilege greater than her brothers. By its very virginity she became their ancestress, the ancestress of all her race. That voluntary yielding up of sex brought her eternal motherhood, because through her renunciation those heroes had found life everlasting.

Her barren breasts--sucked of no child's lips--had nurtured them--nurtured them all!

Shiv-jee, Râjindar, half a hundred others, were all her children. Aye, it was her hands which had sent little Heera into the wilderness to do his duty. His childish face full of tears of courage was hers!--was hers!

There was no death; nothing but unending life that "cannot slay that is not slain." So to her, as she sate reading the Sacred Book came spirits innumerable, until in the vast multitude of men, her own womanhood was lost.

A low knock came to the door. Holding the light by which she had been reading in her hand, she rose and went toward it.

"Who enters?" she asked, and started at the reply.

"It is I, Birbal. Open, my sister. I come from the King."

He stood within the threshold unfolding the shawl with which he was enveloped, and disclosing his keen face lit by a satirical smile.

"A good password, by all that's holy," he said airily. "Nay! frown not, sister, I am of thy tribe."

"True," she replied gravely. "My father spoke often of Maheshwar Rao"--she gave Birbal's tribal name with intent--"and said that could he but learn not to jest----"

The faint laugh, the little shrug of the shoulders came, unfailing as ever.

"Were the world less amusing, sister," he said, "Birbal might have more chance!" He passed lightly to the parapet, and sate on it dangling his legs "Padré Rudolfo, the Jesuit, hath it," he continued, "that I am the fool who saith 'There is no God'; but Birbal propounds no such proposition. He hath an open mind. His very errand here this night, my sister, shows--shall we say credulity? I come, sister, for thy *rebeck* player. I need him."

"Wherefore?" asked Âtma quickly.

Birbal's mouth quivered cynically. "Shall I say the King desires him, sister? Nay! I will not lie. I want him, because of a talisman stone he wears around his neck. He called it smagdarite. I wish to see it again."

"A stone?" echoed Âtma surprised, "what stone? He wears no talisman, for sure."

Birbal's feet came down the roof in sudden excitement. "He wears none! Better and better! Tell me where he lives, sister. I would see for myself. Come! quick, the night goes on, and it is time the King's Châran was abed."

He looked at her in frank mockery and she flushed slowly.

"If it be not for harm," she began, "he is but a poor player."

"Harm!" he echoed impatiently. "If what I think prove true, it is not likely Birbal would harm one possessed of--smagdarite! Out with it, sister. I have tramped from well to water, and water to well, these two hours seeking the Sinde envoy, but it comes ever from each clue that he has gone--disappeared beyond the city. So I bethought me of smagdarite and thee. Come! where lives he?"

"I will take my lord thither," she said evasively. "Nay! 'tis no trouble; he lives--he lives here in this very house."

She raised the light above her head and passed down the stairs. It was a many-storied tenement house, that circled round a central stair, and then broke away from it and wandered in labyrinthine passages to return once more to the same flight of steps; or was it another and she was purposely deluding him?

On and on they went through the dark silence, going down and down.

"He is in the cellars," she said, pausing at a corner to show with her lamp a flight of smaller, steeper steps. "He is so poor, he cannot pay. Have a care! the steps are broken!"

They stood before a small low door at which Âtma knocked. There was no answer. "Wayfarer!"[2] she cried softly. "O! Wayfarer!"

Still no answer.

"I have a key," she said, and drew one from her bosom. Birbal followed the light into the dark room. In that hot climate a cellar is no bad place wherein to live, and this one struck pleasantly cool, deliciously scented as by a thousand roses in blossom.

Birbal was conscious of a sudden elation. He was on the track assuredly! The next instant he was standing beside a string bed on which lay, wrapped in a white sheet, the figure of the *rebeck* player. The clear, fine profile turned upward almost as if he lay dead, and he did not stir when Âtma touched him on the shoulder.

She gave a vexed sigh. "It is the Dream-compeller," she said, "he takes it at times, and lies like a log, and then----"

But Birbal, eager in his quest, had drawn the sheet aside, and now started back with a swift exclamation. For, on the drugged man's breast was no talisman; but, upturned as his, there lay the most beautiful face surely in the whole wide world. It was that of a girl apparently not yet in her teens, yet still close on womanhood; perfect, delicate, pure, like some scented lily. Her breath coming and going regularly exhaled the perfume of a thousand flowers.

"'Tis Zarîfa--his daughter," explained Âtma softly. "She is a cripple utterly. Naught shows of her scarcely save her face, but when her eyes are open, one forgets." She gathered the sheet together so as to hide all that should be hidden. Only that perfect face remained asleep upon the Wayfarer's breast.

"Does he give the Dream-stuff to her also?" asked Birbal, feeling his voice unsteady. Poet, artist, to his finger-tips, the sight before him stirred him in every fibre, bringing with it a sense of half-remembered dreams.

She shook her head. "He sends her to sleep first with flower essences. She is like a deer for scent--a rose makes her unconscious, and then they sleep, and sleep, and sleep."

Slumber seemed in the air. They stood beside the low string bed, silent, almost drowsy. Âtma roused herself with an effort.

"He promised he would not; but they must have been given money to-day," she said regretfully. "There is no use waiting, my lord--they will sleep for hours--perhaps days."

"Days?" he echoed interrogatively.

She passed her hand over her forehead again. "It seems as if it were days. Then, when he goes out, I carry Zarîfa up to my roof. She is so light. There is nothing of her but the face. Yet she sings like a bird."

Birbal's hand went out to the lamp Âtma held and turned its light full on her face.

"You are but half-awake yourself, sister," he said gravely. "And it is all hours of the night. See, I will wait until I note your light pass on the uppermost stair, lest danger lurk for you in the dark."

He waited for her to lock the door, then standing in the dark archway watched her twinkling light circle the stairs, then disappear, circle again higher up and disappear, until he judged from the failure of the twinkle to return that she had reached her roof. And, as he watched his mind was busy.

Who was this man? And did he really possess the art which some deemed magic, but which he, keen rational thinker, found to be inextricably mixed up with the whole problem of life? What was it that all the great ones of the earth had possessed? What gave them their power, their influence? What was it, for instance, which made his own clear-seeing eyes fall at times before those dreams in Akbar's? What was it, what?

His whole life was one ceaseless questioning; and finding no answer, he jested at the very question itself. What was reality? Not surely the death-like profile he had just seen, the death-like form with that flower-face upon its breast.

He was turning to go when a burst of half-sober laughter rose close beside him and a voice answered tipsily.

"Ts'sh, Dhâri, thou art not safe yet in Siyah Yamin's paradise, so lurch not, fool, lest the watch seize thee! Take my arm, lo! I am steady."

A sound as of confused tumbling against the wall belied the assertion.

Every atom of blood in Birbal's body seemed to leap to his hands in anger, for he recognised the voice. It was that of his only son, his spendthrift son Lâlla--the son of so much promise, so many regrets. And the other was his boon companion Dhâri--another bad son of a good father--Tôdar Mull the man whose financial skill had saved the Empire from the oppression of bribery. Where then was the third of this precious trio of young rakes? Where was the Heir Apparent, Prince Salîm? Not far off, that he would warrant!

Slipping off his shoes, he followed up the stairs, keeping at a respectful distance to be beyond reach of the lurches, yet close enough to hear the password given at the closed door, not far he judged from Âtma's square of roof. Allowing a decent interval he knocked again and briefly saying "Kings-town" found himself admitted to an inner, scantily-lit staircase which, however, showed a brilliant light at its end.

A minute more and he stood looking with a curious amusement at Siyah Yamin's paradise. The jade had taste! Here on the highest roof in all the city she had set a terraced garden open only to the stars. The little coloured lights, edging the rose beds and the tiny splashing fountains, scarcely sent their diffused radiance higher than his knee. It did not reach the edge of the trellised walls, and above that was night; cool, quiet, night. A liveried servant salaamed to him profusely, then returned to his solitary game of cards. A white Persian cat rose, hunched up its back and clawed viciously on the Persian carpets laid along the paths, then yawned showing its needle. like teeth. From a confused heap of silks and satins under an awning came loud snores, but at the farther end of the far roof there was wakefulness; for a half-tipsy, wholly-discordant voice made itself heard singing a song--

Why am I drunken, fools? Because I sup
The wine of love from out the bosom's cup
And the soft scented tresses of dark hair trip up
My fuddled feet.

Because my wine-stained mouth has found her lips
Too close for kisses, so their nectar drips
To brain and heart, and body, in slow sips
Of passion sweet.

"His Royal Highness, the Heir Apparent," murmured Birbal, cynically as, looking half-mechanically to the sit of his turban, he went forward. Time was when love--but never wine--had tempted him also; *this*, however, was flagrant disobedience of the King's orders and he must see to it. Siyah Yamin was the town's darling, but even she had her limits and must confine herself to them.

He smiled sardonically, thinking of the torrent of words he was about to face, since she, likely, would be the only one with her wits about her.

And he was right!

As he set aside the silken curtains which hid the interior of her painted pavilion from sight, he found the place half-full of drowsy girls and sodden revellers; but she, raising herself from her cushions on her elbow, greeted him instantly with shrill jest.

"The King himself! Oh! the honour! Nay, 'tis not the King, but the King's Counsellor. Sir! I would rise," she continued pointing and making a graceful wriggle of apparent effort, "but that my treasure, my lover, my husband, lies dead-drunk at my feet."

Birbal gave a quick glance at the prostrate figure among the cushions.

"Yea!" she continued, her baby face at strange variance with her words, which came, clipped hard and fast with defiance, from her soft-parted lips. "'Tis Syed Jamâl-ud-din, of Bârha, sure enough. A good soldier to the King though at this present somewhat overcome with love for poor me and liquor; as indeed is the Prince of Proprieties yonder. Ah! Most Revered! Oh! Most Excellent of Heirs Apparents! rouse thee to greet this Select Emissary of a Fateful Father."

Prince Salîm, a big, heavy looking lad, stared stupidly at the newcomer, his cup arrested at his lips.

"What'sh devil he coming here for?" he muttered fiercely. "That's what I wan'ter know. What'sh a devil----" Then his ferocity subsided amid a titter from Siyah Yamin.

"Heed him not, Birbal, Prince of Jesters. Slaves, bring a cushion! Sit thee down, so, beside me--we be the only two sober ones. Cupbearer, the cup! And bring the snow from holy Himâlya to cleanse it; for see you most Brahman Birbal, Siyah Yamin is fast Mahommedan since she married! *La-illaha-il-ullaho.*"

"Madam," said Birbal interrupting her mocking creed impatiently, "if you would play your part as the wife of a Syed of Bârha----"

Siyah Yamin gave a little shriek of dismay. "My veil! Here! women, my veil! lo! I was forgetting."

"A truce to jesting, madam," said Birbal sternly. "Time will show if what thou sayest be true; meanwhile----" he glanced round, hastily taking in the company. "So! Meean Khodadâd! Hide not thyself behind the Prince as ever! God! if I could kill thee 'twere better for us all!"

Khodadâd, on whose face sate enthroned all the evil which in the younger revellers showed as yet fleetingly, roused himself to laugh insultingly.

"What! Kill a Tarkhân? Lo! Brahman, even thy caste in that case would not save thee from the hangman's noose. None can punish me, fool, I am Khodadâd--'God given.'"

"God given!" echoed Birbal passionately. "That brings *one* balm--no man need shrink calling thee son! And as for thou, Lâlla!--go! accursed by thy father!"

"What'sh all this," murmured Prince Salîm rising unsteadily. "What'sh all this fush?"

"My Prince," said Birbal, restraining his voice to respect, "this is no place for you--no place for the Heir to India--no place for one who will be King when his great father----"

Prince Salîm dashed his cup down with a curse.

"Let be a shay! I tell you I am King here! Am I not King, and the Shadow of God? Am I not a shay?"

He looked round on his company triumphantly; but Birbal, utterly exasperated, bowed.

"No, my Prince," he replied politely, "thou art drunk, boy, and the substance of a fool!"

Siyah Yamin's tinkling laughter led the chorus of mirth in which for the time even Birbal's anger passed.

CHAPTER IV

Beauty is no bond maiden; Lot it holds
The veil which hides it from all earthly lovers
But to holy-hearted noble-souled
Unveils and all its loveliness discovers.

There was another, and very different tinkle of soft laughter, a rustle of silks and satins which in their stirring gave out multi-scented perfumes of orange and rose, musk, and ambergris; for Auntie Rosebody was in full swing of one of her recitals, and all the harem knew that they were as good as cornelian-water for raising the spirits.

Not that spirits required raising on this day of days, on which the accession of the Most Auspicious, the Most Excellent, the King-of-Kings was commemorated! Pleasurable excitement simmered through the whole women's apartments. For weeks past, preparations for the feast had been going on, and to-day would bring full fruition to all their labours. Dressed in their best, the harem waited for the ceremonials to begin.

"Ha! la! la!" went on Aunt Rosebody, enjoying her own tale of past glories. "That was a feasting, for sure A Mystic Palace, and three Houses; one of dominion, one of good fortune, one of pleasure. So my brother Jahânbâni-jinat Ashyâni--on whom be peace--chose pleasure. And he took three plates full of gold coins. 'There is no need to count,' said he, 'let each lady take a fistful.' So we scattered them in the empty tank, and the guests scrambled for them.

"Then the King, my brother, seeing this, said to our Dearest Lady"-- here the little speaker's little hands fluttered faintly as if in blessing--"on whom be God's uttermost peace for ever, 'If you permit, why not let the water in?' At first 'Dearest Lady,' out of the gentleness of her heart said no, but afterward she climbed out and sate on the top steps! Ha! la! la! la! It was like the Day of Resurrection! When the water came, everyone tumbled about and got so excited, but the King called 'No harm done! Come out and eat aniseed candy!' So to end my story everyone came out, everyone ate candy, and none got cold! *Bis-millah!*"

The little lady hitched her veil straight--it had fallen from her abundant gray hair during her vivacious gesticulations--and beamed round on the audience seated about her on cushions.

"*Bis-millah!*" echoed their laughing voices. To look at Aunt Rosebody was enough for laughter. Despite her years, nothing damped the keen enjoyment of life which was hers by right of descent. Her nephew Akbar had it at times also; but the cares of life crept in at others. Not so with Aunt Rosebody. Even her recent pilgrimage to Mekka had not aged her, though Salîma Begum her daughter looked years older, and *her* daughter the little "Mother of Plumpness" had come out of the five years journeying quite thin.

But one thing disturbed Auntie Rosebody's equanimity, and that was the misdeeds of her darling grand-nephew, the Heir Apparent. These she would weep over, scold over, and finally condone.

So the smiles died from her puckered face as Lady Hamida Begum, the boy's grandmother, swept into the arcade her face pale with proud vexation.

"Say not so! sister-in-law!" exclaimed the little lady, tears in her voice already. "Say not he hath been drunk again? Oh! my life! What is to be done?"

Lady Hamida set her lips. "It is true," she replied, "and my son--his father--is deeply angered. And what wonder, though in truth"--she sighed-- "this setting aside of all loose livers in Satanstown----"

"Oh! 'tis a premium on discovery," moaned Aunt Rosebody. "Why cannot my nephew let folk go to the devil discreetly, and none be the wiser save Providence? Oh! my life! what is to be done?"

"Pray for him," suggested Salîma Begum nervously.

"Yes! Pray for him!" assented an older Salîma who, being related in cross-road fashion to half the harem had lost all individuality.

"Prayers!" whimpered the little lady wrathfully. "Have I not already given up my pilgrimage to the scapegrace, and if that avails not, what are prayers? How was it, know you, Hamida?"

"The tale is not for virtuous ears," replied the Lady Hamida icily. "It is sufficient that my grandson has once more been brought home in a state unbecoming the heir to my son."

"Tra-a-a!" said an elderly woman dryly, as she looked up from the *tarikh* or numerical hemstitch she was laboriously composing in a corner. Then she took a pinch of scented snuff and removed her spectacles; for Râkiya Begum, as the political wife of Akbar's boyhood, was titular head of the Mahommedan harem as the mother of the Heir-Apparent was head of the Hindu.

"With due deference," she went on composedly, "it is in the blood. His great-grandfather----"

Aunt Rosebody caught her up fiercely. "But never clown-drunk like this boy! When my father of blessed memory was drunk, he was as the Archangel Gabriel,--of the most entertaining--the most exhilarating--And he gave it up! Does he not say in his blessed book of memoirs: 'Being now thirty-nine and having vowed to abandon wine in my fortieth year, I therefore drank to excess.' What would you more? And his recantation! 'Gentlemen of the army! Those who sit down to the feast of life must end by drinking the cup of death!' It stirs one like the Day of Resurrection! But this boy--'tis all his Hindu mother's fault."

"And his grandfather took opium," continued Râkiya, relentlessly.

Lady Hamida looked up with chill dignity. "Let the earth of the grave cover the dead, daughter-in-law. What my husband did is known to me better than to you."

Râkiya Begum put the spectacles on her pinched nose once more.

"I offer excuse," she replied ceremoniously. "I was but going to remark that both blessed saints, despite these habits, were good enough kings. It is the unprecedented abstemiousness of the present Lord of the Universe, who looks neither at wine nor women, which throws the Prince's indiscretions into relief."

Her words brought solace. After all who could expect a boy of eighteen to be Akbar?--who, in truth, scarcely slept or ate. And this brought the remembrance that if Salîm was sick--as he invariably was after a drinking bout--the pile of good dishes which the Beneficent Ladies had been preparing these many days back against this feast might as well not have been made! The thought was depressing.

"I wonder," sighed Aunt Rosebody, "what 'Dearest Lady' would have advised."

A hush fell over the company. It seemed as though the sweet wise presence of a dead woman filled the room. A dead woman who even in life had earned for herself that title, who lives under it still in the pages of her niece's memoirs.

"She would have counselled patience as ever," answered the Lady Haimda. "Lo! Elder-Sister-Rose! Such tangled skeins can be but disentangled by Time. I remember when my marriage----" She broke off and was silent. Elder-Sister-Rose might know the story, might even remember for her memoirs the very words of the pitiful little tale of girlish refusal overborne; but these others? No! sufficient for them the fact that the unwelcome marriage had made her mother to the King-of-Kings.

"It must not spoil the day anyhow," summed up Aunt Rosebody at last, decisively drying her eyes, "and by and by, perhaps, when his mother hath done giving the boy Hindu medicines--in truth, though I admit my nephew is right in deeming the idolaters fellow mortals, their drugs are detestable-- we may have a chance with a cooling sherbet such as my father--on whom be peace--ever loved after a carouse. Meanwhile is everything ready for the weighing?"

"All things," replied Lady Hamida proudly. "My son shall lack for nothing."

"Then the poor will at least benefit, God be praised!" said Râkiya Begum tartly as she rose. "Though this weighing of the Sacred Personality is a heathenish custom unsanctioned by our Holy Book; but what with his Majesty's divine faith, what with the shaving of beards, the keeping of dogs, and mixed marriages, a pious Musulmâni such as I, had best take off her spectacles lest she see too much."

She took them off with a flourish and a loud *Sobhan-ullah!* which echoed militantly through the wide arcaded room.

Then she prepared to put on her *burka* veil; for trumpets were sounding outside that it was time for the Beneficent Ladies to take up their secluded coign of vantage in order to see the coming show.

"There is no need for all-over-dresses," suggested Lady Hamida gently. "My son hath arranged seclusion in a new fashion."

"I offer excuse!" replied Râkiya with a sniff, "but my honourable veiling is of the old fashion."

With that she led the way in her ghostly goggle-eyed wrapper.

Such tinkling of jewels! Such perfume from stirred scent-sodden silks! Such hurried needless mufflings with diaphanous veilings! Such final eagerness of outlook, when they could peep through the latticing, see the throne almost within touch of them, and--curving from it in a vast semicircle of which it was the centre--see the packed rows on rows of nobles glittering with jewels awaiting the coming of the King. So entrancing was the sight that the due and stately greeting of the rival women who trooped to their places from the Hindu harem, lacked something of lengthy dignity, and there was a general sigh of content as every eye settled down to a peephole.

"Look!" chattered even silent Salîma. "Yonder is Sher Afkân new back from the Deccan war! A goodly man, and betrothed, they say, to Ghiâss Beg, the Treasurer's daughter--a little witch for beauty. They call her Queen of Women--Mihr-un-nissa--and she not twelve years old!"

"See, Amma-jân!" whispered little Umm Kulsum, the "Mother of Plumpness," "that is Budaoni beside the Makhdûm--O God of the Prophet, may the Holy One's blessing rest on me!"

"Yonder is Faiz, the poet--oh fie! He hath his dog with him--the unclean beast," giggled another.

"Aye! Abulfazl, his brother, will likely come with the King; they say his stomach grows bigger every day trying to swallow what his Majesty will not eat."

Râkiya Begum gave a cackling laugh. "Stomach or no stomach, he is the wonder of the age. He hath approved this concealed one's verses."

"Mine also," bridled Aunt Rosebody. "He hath asked and used my memory in his history. But wherefore delays the King? The show is like a peacock's tail without an eye, and he away."

It was an apt simile. The almost inconceivable magnificence of the scene made the eye wander. The acres on acres of gorgeous pavilion flashing with silver-gilt columns, glowing with silken Khorasân carpetings, filled to the roofing with tier on tier of grandees of the empire ablaze with jewels, multi-coloured as a flowerful parterre--all this needed centralising, seemed incoherent without a figure on the throne. The very curve of waiting elephants--a solid wall of gold trappings encrusted with gems which stretched on and on beyond the pavilion on either side like some huge bow--seemed as if it might have gone over the horizon, but for the tight-packed bowstring of the populace blocking the distant view from sight with myriads of eager watching eyes.

Suddenly a great blare of sound!

At last--at last! The Royal *nakarah* at last! And see! sweeping round ahead of a scintillating knot of horsemen, banners, lances--one man!

The King! The King!

A low moaning surge of sound came from the packed humanity for an instant. The next it was lost in the wild shrieking bellow which seemed to crack the skies as two thousand elephants threw up their trunks head-high and let loose their leviathan throats.

An imperial salute indeed! One that never grows stale, and the thrill of it paled Akbar's cheek as, with the shining sun, standard of the Râjpûts on one hand, the glorious green banner of Islâm on the other, he rode forward to take the throne which he had wrung alike from Hindus and Mahommedans.

Of what was he thinking, as grave, courteous, he returned the obeisances of all? He was thinking with a passion of regret in his heart of a lad of eighteen found drunk in Siyah Yamin's Paradise.

And now, seated on the throne, his figure, clad in simple white muslin--with the milky sheen of a rope of pearls, and the dull white gleam of the diamond he always wore in his turban--its only ornament--seemed to centre the magificence in curious contrast.

"The King--may he live for ever!--looks well enough," commented Râkiya Begum, charily concealing her pride, "but why doth he not wear a gold coat like his fathers? These innovations will surely lead him to hell."

"*Sobhan-ullah!*" assented Salîma nervously.

They were such simple, straightforward Beneficent Ladies with their high features, high courage, high sense of duty, of family, of tradition, all swathed and hidden away in scent-sodden silks and satins. They formed as it were a masked battery of pure benevolence behind the throne, unseen, but felt; for Akbar gave a glance round to where he knew his mother must be sitting ere, facing his empire for a second or two in silence, he rose and stepped forward to the great silver-gilt steel-yard which stood in front of the dais.

A blare of *nakarahs* sounded the advance, and Aunt Rosebody from her peephole said in an agonised whisper: "God send everything be ready!"

"Even the Mystic Palace, O Khânzâda Gulbadan Khânum! was not more prepared!" replied Lady Hamida, "Eunuchs! take out the gold!"

Then, as the slaves staggered forth under their burden, she sate clasping little Umm Kulsum's hand murmuring softly, "He did not weigh so heavy--once!"

She was back in memory to the terrified travail of long years ago in the wilderness when, as a queen flying from her enemies, she had first wept at the rough looks of the hastily summoned village midwife, then hugged her for very joy when the boy-baby was put into her young arms.

The "Mother of Plumpness" nestled closer to her in the sheer sympathy which she had, and to spare, for all comers. Her round bright eyes, indeed, had already sought and found the posy of violets which the King wore half-hidden by the rope of pearls around his neck. She grew them in her garden, so that the Most Excellent might ever wear the flower he loved so well; that his grandfather Babar had loved so well also.

Akbar, meanwhile, seated in the scales awaited the great platter of gold, and a sigh of relief rose from behind the lattice as the steel-yard, recovering from the impact, oscillated, then settled to fair equipoise.

The gold, anyhow, was of the right weight!

"Give it to the poor!" said the King and the taut bowstring of the populace gave out a surging thrill.

"The ornaments next!" whispered Aunt Rosebody feverishly, and held her breath as with due decorum the second huge tray was hefted to the scale.

What had happened? Was there a faint unevenness in the swing? Would there be the least deficiency?

Ere the question, rising in ten thousand minds, could be formulated fairly, it was settled by one small hand which flashed through the latticing, and a scarce-heard chink told that a little gold bracelet had fallen just where it should fall.

Akbar holding to the gilded chains as the balance steadied to level rest, did not smile. He only threw back at the lattice one all-comprehending remark of superhuman gravity.

"Thanks! most reverend aunt!"

Gulbadan Begum fell from her peephole with a little shriek of outrage, and the remaining ten weighings, and the distribution of chicken, and sheep, and goats, one of each for each year of the Most Auspicious reign, had all been set aside for the poor ere she had recovered her composure.

"Now is there peace, as the squirrel said when he had pulled the sting out of the wasp," she remarked, hurriedly fanning herself with the plaited edge of her tinsel-set veil, "but 'twas like the Day of Resurrection!" This being her favourite standard for a disconcerting event.

"Who flings, finds as he flings!" remarked Râkiya Begum with much acerbity, "and if women learn men's tricks they must expect scandal. 'Tis the fault of ill-regulated youth!"

"Ill-regulated?" burst out Aunt Rosebody in instant wrath. "My father-- on whom be peace--loved to see his girls--but there! No quarreling on this great day! Here come the elephants!"

They came, heading the review. Close on two thousand of them, three abreast, moving like a wall, only their slow shifting pads showing beneath their fringed war-armour. And as each trio passed, up went the snaky trunks, and from between curved tusks a bellowing trumpet shrieked out.

"Not to-day, Guj-muktar!" called the King appeasingly as one mighty beast paused; and the wise monster passed on shaking its huge head as if to rid himself of an unwelcome burden; for Guj-muktar was Akbar's favourite mount, and objected strongly to a strange driver.

Then came the camels all scarlet and gold, with swinging tassels, their riders bent almost double in sitting the long stilted stride. Then the horses neighing, prancing, curvetting, led by gorgeous grooms waving long yak's-tails. Next the hounds, lean, hungry-looking, pacing beside their keepers, followed by the hawks quaintly hooded and leashed, their bells jingling, looking like stuffed birds, so still were they upon the falconers' wrists.

Finally--quaintest sight of all to the three Englishmen who seated beside Pâdré Rudolfo the Jesuit, watched the scene with wide eyes--the hunting leopards, their cat-like faces shifting and peering, their dog-like limbs sinewy and sinuous, their long slender tails swaying at the tip with rhythmical feline regularity.

"Samand!"

The King's voice echoed softly through the hot air. There was a spotted, painted flash in the sunlight as a leash was slipped, and a great creature was purring at Akbar's feet like a huge cat and rubbing its back against the throne. The King's hand went down to it, and its head continued the rubbing with still louder purrs.

"Lo! It is not meet," remarked Râkiya Begum with dissatisfaction. "The Most Auspicious is no better than a *mahout* or a hunter."

"He cannot help the beasts loving him," spoke up little Umm Kulsum hotly.

"I offer excuse," snapped the head of the harem. "He need not love them in return. Come, ladies! All is over save the soldiery, and they are of no interest to virtuous women."

She gathered up her flock austerely, the Lady Hamida and Auntie Rosebody lingering to discuss Prince Salîm's absence from the assemblage.

"He was not there! I looked even in the backmost row," declared the little lady in a flutter. "What thinkest thou, Hamida? Can he be in prison!"

"More likely sick in his mother's hands," replied Hamida coldly. "She was not with us either, and, didst see? They were feeding Prince Danyâl with sweeties all the time!"

"Trash!" ejaculated Aunt Rosebody vehemently. "What can they do but drink with sugar in their mouth from morn till eve? If they would but give the lad over to me----"

Here she gave a little shriek of relief, for there, as she entered the arcaded reception room, was the scapegrace seated sulkily among cushions.

"Thou--thou evil one!" she began in shrill tones which yet suggested endless excuses. "So thou hast been overtaken *again*, and in a public place! Why canst thou not be as thy great-grandfather was in his cups--but that is not edifying for the young. Ah! Salîm! Salîm! How came it about, sweetheart?"

"'Twas the meddler Birbal--may God scorch him," growled Salîm sulkily. "He came after his cub--else Khodadâd had stuffed the guards full of gold."

"Khodadâd! Lo! Tarkhân though he be, he should die for high treason. And where was it?--What? thou wilt not say. Go! Umm Kulsum and thou also Khadîja--go to the threading the beads. Thou *shalt* tell me, boy. Whisper it--What! Siyah Yamin's! And thou new-betrothed! Oh! had but thy father settled thee with a true bride of my race she would have kept--or killed thee!" She gave a little shriek. "What! Jamâl-ud-din--the scorpion! saith he hath married her--the piece! Shame! Shame!"

Then she suddenly put her head on one side and regarded her grand-nephew distastefully. "Lo! Salîm thou growest too fat. Wine and women will kill thee, and 'tis well that Birbal--mind you I say naught for him or against him, though he hath made me laugh often enough."

"He shall laugh on the wrong side ere long," cried Salîm savagely. "Aye! he shall learn not to jest at me."

The lively little face grew keen. "At thee? What said he? Come, sweetheart, let me hear. I will decide if there be wit in it."

"Wit!" echoed the Prince angrily. "No wit, but insult for which he shall pay. Look you, when the Hindu infidel interfered with sermons I bid him silence. 'Am I not King?' said I (as I shall be), 'and the Shadow-of-God?' 'No,' says he with that cursed bow of his, 'thou art drunk, boy, and the substance of a fool.'"

Aunt Rosebody attempted gravity; then her laughter brimmed over, and the whole room giggled in response, including the bead-threading girls.

"Oh! my life," the little lady was beginning when one of the women guards entered hurriedly, crying, "The King! honourable ladies, the King!"

He was amongst them almost before the circle of fond relatives about the young Prince had time to rise, so hiding him from view. For an instant Akbar stood to make his courtly greeting, then, seeing his mother's pale face light up, he flung his turban with its royal heron's plume aside--his shoes he had already left at the door--and so passing quickly to Hamida's side took both her hands and raised them to his head.

"Mother! I thank thee--for all!"

Her fingers even in his strong grip lingered there lovingly as if she felt the child's curls still; then she said with a quiver in her voice:

"It was nothing, son--the good wishes were more weighty than the gold."

He gave her hands a little squeeze ere he released them.

"Than the jewels, mayhap!"--here he turned with a mischievous smile to Aunt Rosebody who stood divided between joy at seeing him, and dread lest he should see Salîm. "For *them* I have to thank my aunt----"

"How dost know it was I?" she challenged furiously.

He looked at her with immense gravity.

"First," he said, "'twas the smallest hand in India! Next, no other woman could shy so straight. When one has played ball, polo, God knows what, in one's youth----"

"Calumnies! Calumnies!" interrupted Aunt Rosebody, her face puckering with amusement. "The Most Excellent's remark was truly scandalous!"

The word was unfortunate; it roused memories.

"There be worse scandals than that to the King's honour this day," he said, his face clouding. "Know then, Beneficent Ladies, that the son I have forgiven--how many times? sure it comes nigh to the Pâdré's seventy times seven--has been found drunk again in a common stew. And he is coward too; he hath not dared to face his father----"

He paused, his anger turning to ice, for Prince Salîm--to do him justice no coward--took heart of grace, and rose above the shelter of the women-folk, who seeing themselves no longer needed stood back, leaving the father and son face to face.

They were a great contrast. Both tall and strong; but the one all curves and softness, the other lean, sinewy.

"I was ill," began the Prince sullenly, when Akbar interrupted him with a contemptuous laugh.

"Ill? Hast not even a body for drunkenness? Go thy way, boy, if thou wilt. I have other strings to my bow."

"My son!" appealed Lady Hamida who, knowing the King's temper, knew that once lost it might carry much with it, "the boy has come to us----"

"And what does he here amongst virtuous women, madam, and how came they to admit him?" asked Akbar sternly. "Did I, son and nephew, even in the hottest hours of youth inure them to such insult? Go, boy! Go with Jamâl-ud-din, the exile, and his paramour. I have other sons!"

A blank horror settled down on the Beneficent Ladies. Never had things come to such a pitch before, and some of the younger women sobbed audibly. Only little Auntie Rosebody, with the courage of despair stood looking first at the father then at the son, regret, anger, irritation, showing in her small puckered face.

"Oh! my life! Oh! nephew Jalâl-ud-din Mahomed Akbar," she cried at last. "Look at him--oh! look at him! He is a fat-tailed sheep and thou art a hunting leopard! How can he race with thee? Give him time, nephew, give him time!"

Something in Salîm's sheepish attitude appealed to the King's sense of humour, a suspicion of a smile showed about his mouth.

"At his age, madam," he began sternly, the memory of his strenuous youth rushing in upon him. Why! at eighteen, dissatisfied with his agents of Empire he had dismissed them, and taken the whole conduct of affairs upon his own shoulders. At eighteen he had begun to dream. At eighteen his mind was busy with the problem of how to unite a conquered India; how to efface from it all memory of coercion, and make it look to him and his, not as to ephemeral conquerors but as God's viceregents, the upholders of justice, mercy, toleration, and freedom. At eighteen----

Suddenly he flung his right hand out in a hopeless gesture of finality. What use were dreams, even the dreaming of a King, if they were only to last for one poor mortal life?

"There is no end to the dreaming of Kings." Bah! The woman had lied. There was an end! An end to all things.

But the worst of his passion was over. He turned yet once more to his son and forgave him yet once again.

CHAPTER V

The world-revealing cup of the King Jamsheed
Counselled the King in his pleasures and in his need.

--FIRDUSI.

The Prince Salîm, despite all efforts of his friends, accepted his father's reprimand in dutiful fashion. Truly Akbar--may he be accursed!--hath a very devil of persuasion in him for those he loves."--The scribe's hand paused in its swift swooping over the Persian curves, and he looked up for an instant with all the evil of his handsome face concentrated into an expression of bitterest antagonism. Then he turned his head, listening ere he went on with his news-letter.

"So far little has been gained. Yet the poison works. The prince, grown older, than his brothers--who are themselves coming on for rebellion--resents this leading, as of a young colt, and will ere long assert himself. Already he is fit for intrigue; by and by it may be for murder. And Akbar once gone--by what means God knows!--Salîm will be our tool. Thus the dead to-day brings forth another to-day, and so we (more especially this Mote-speck-in-the-Light, Dalîl, of the Kingly House, Tarkhân, who waits in unmerited exile for his Lord's service expectant of his Lord's recall) hope, knowing that all God's strength dwells not in one man's body. Meanwhile the King's action in this matter hath stirred up the whole city. Ere noon Jamâl-ud-din left, accompanied by a goodly gathering of his clan all incensed at the sentence of exile passed on their captain. He hath gone to his relatives of Bârha and will doubtless rouse them to resistance. But the jade Siyah Yamin hath done more for our cause than any, since I have but now returned from seeing her leave-taking; for the baggage hath elected to follow her lawful spouse. Truly 'tis said 'A torn ear clamours for more earring!' Half the town were at the heels of her palanquin wherein she sate veiled like any cupola of chastity, but full of an evil tongue. Truly it was a sight to set pumpkins a-sinking and mill-stones a-floating, since none knew what to make of it, with the light men gathering up the flowers she flung, and the light women praising her in jest for her fidelity. But it hath done our cause good service, and the King may repent him of his virtue ere long. Thus remaineth matters at this present. Whilst I, Dalîl, knowing that straight fingers hold naught, crook mine in the service of the Head of my

House, Mirza Jâni Beg, *looking for reward*. This goes by the hand of Sufardâr, envoy, whom I await this day past, but----"

In the act of writing the words "who comes not" the scribe paused again. This time there was no doubt of a sound presaging interruption, and the writer, thrusting the papers under a fold of his embroidered shawl took up a lute which lay beside him, and leaning back amongst the scented cushions began to strum a love song and sing in a high tenor voice:

Oh! Love! I am caught in the snare
Of the scented net of her hair
Oh! Love! I am stricken dead

    With hunger for her, and with drouth

Her foot is upon my head

    Would my kisses were on her mouth.

"A merchant selling essence of rose by my Lord's orders," said an obsequious dwarf extravagantly dressed; one of the smartest deformities in fact to be found in the service of the young nobility of the court. His cunning face, full of almost malignant comprehension, had been overlaid with servile admiration as he had waited for the song to end.

"Let him enter," came the yawning reply, "and, Yahéd, close the doors on us. The lamp flickers in the evening wind!"

The song went on lazily--

Oh! Love! I am held by the power
Of her bare brown bosom-flower
Oh! Lo/ve! I am lost in the mesh!

    In the very thought of a sip

At the nectar of soft warm flesh

    And the touch of her lip.

Then the door closed, and he turned swiftly on the figure which had entered.

"So, at last! I have been awaiting thee these four-and-twenty hours. And wherefore was there no due notice of arrival? Lo! my liver dissolved when the arch-heretic, Abul, spoke at the King's audience of an envoy from Sinde. For aught I knew Jâni Beg might have failed to secure the crown. It was a relief to see thy face--but how came all this Sufardâr?"

He spoke as one having authority, but the supposed merchant answered sulkily as he unwound his close-draped shawl, so disclosing, in truth, the slender spareness and the high pallid features of the envoy from Sinde.

"If thou canst tell me how it came about, Oh! Dalîl Tarkhân of the House of Kings," he said, "thou knowest more than I, the companion of thy youth; since I know naught. A blank as of death lies behind me from the time we encamped at noon yesterday, five miles beyond the city."

The whilom scribe looked cynically at the dull opium-drugged eyes.

"A blank!" he echoed. "How much of the Dream-compeller goes to make that for thee now a days, Oh! Sufar?"

Those dulled eyes lit up with sudden fire. "No more, I swear to God, than the noon-day pellet of twelve years agone. Thou knowest the old Tuglak tombs about Biggâya's Serai? The tents were late and it was hot, so I slept in one of them----"

"Curse thee! Sleep where thou willst," interrupted his companion impatiently, "but give me the packet. I must answer it, if answer be required." He held out his hand, scented, manicured, be-ringed like any modern lady's.

The envoy's face showed uneasiness. "If thou wouldst listen, thou wouldst learn," he said vexedly. "I slept and dreamed. Then I woke; but it was to to-day, not to yesterday."

"But thou wast at the Audience--for I saw thee! Aye! and I wondered what Birbal, the heretic pig, had to say to thee as he kept the King waiting."

The envoy shook his head slowly. "It is a blank; and hearken, *Mirza sahib*, the packet hath gone!"

"Gone!" echoed the other again, his face paling at the thought of Akbar's ever-swift punishment for treason. "Thou hast lost the letter; and this tale of forgetfulness----"

The envoy from Sinde leant forward and laid one warning finger, slender, almost emaciated, on his companion's well-kept hand. "'Tis no tale, but a mystery. The packet was ever in my girdle cloth, and left not my side day nor night. None knew of it. And I remember nothing of my sleep, except my dream." He shivered and looked round apprehensively. "It was a dream of nigh thirteen years ago--of--of a rose-garden, *Mirza Dalîl!* Oh!

thou mayst laugh, but I curse the day that ever I took a part in that damned work of thine. It comes between me and my prayers."

Mirza Dalîl laughed airily. "It comes not between me and mine; but then I am Tarkhân. There must be nine deadly sins ere even earthly punishment be thought of, and I am but at my seventh; or stay, is it eighth? Truly I know not and it matters not. But this tale of thine--What says thy retinue?"

The envoy's face fell.

"They say I woke as ever, and gave the orders for the audience but I remember naught, save----"

"Turn thy forgetfulness toward rose-gardens, opium-eater!" interrupted the man he called Dalîl sternly. "Have I not ever told thee thou wert but as a beast to give up the heavenly dreams of hemp for the clogging sleep of the poppy. Thou wert drunk, that is all--or hast been since. So remembrance is left with the drug. As for the packet--thou hast lost--or sold it. Lucky for me, no names come from Sinde, and none here know me save as Khodadâd--Khodadâd, the gift of God, the companion of princes, the chamberlain of pleasures to the Heir-Apparent! Khodadâd adventurer, made Tarkhân on the battlefield by the King's brother, the rebel of Kabul, because, being above myself with hemp, I saved his life! *Made* Tarkhân, thou prophet of God! and I a Tarkhân by birth. Still," he continued, checking himself in his reckless mirth, "thou art in luck. But mark me, if by this loss suspicion comes--aye! even a suspicion that Khodadâd is of the Kingly House (younger brother, aye! even though he be a bastard, of the fool Payandâr who went mad over the rose-garden) thy life is not worth much. Go therefore. Here is thy packet." He drew out the paper he had written, set the seal he wore on his first finger to it, folded it neatly, then continued with an evil smile, "Mind I say naught in it against thee. Thou mightest *lose* the letter if I did. But I will see thou comest not with messages again."

"Lo! that will I not," muttered the envoy, wrapping his shawl round him as before. "This very sight of thee recalls the rose-garden--I seem to hear her piteous cries----"

Khodadâd lay back amongst his cushions and laughed.

"Thou art far gone in opium, Sufardâr!" he said chuckling. "Ere long thou wilt see the devil clutching thee, for sure! God's prophet, man, hadst heard as many maidens' screechings as I!" He was silent but smiling, evidently in pursuit of memory, and when the envoy had gone he lay back among those scented cushions and allowed himself a certain latitude of remembrance. At five-and-thirty there were few experiences of which he had no cognizance; but it needed many experiences to leave a mark on a Tarkhân! As he lounged lazily the soft night air fanning his perfumed hair, his smooth yellow skin oily with unguents, every atom of his body and soul surcharged with sensuality, there yet came to him an uprush of almost wild pride in his race, in the honours, the privileges which distinguished it even from the common herd of princedom. A Bârlâs Tarkhân! Bârlâs the brave! Master of seven distinctions in procession or audience. Free of every part of a king's palace by night and day! Aye and more! Having the right to drink with the King! So that when the Royal cup was handed from the right, the Tarkhân's cup was handed from the left. And still more. With the right to set his seal to all royal orders, above the King's seal! Unpunishable too-- until the uttermost. And then? If Mirza Dalîl's face grew gray as he thought of that uttermost assize, it was not altogether in fear, since there are some things pertaining to race which bring with them an almost passionate acquiescence even in terror; and this thought of the final verdict of his peers, to be carried out by those peers with many ceremonials, had in it an element of pride.

Besides, here, in a far country away from those peers, there was small danger of the Silent Session being held.

So he looked out over the vast shadows of the town, wondering vaguely how he should fill up the night with iniquities. He would have an excellent companion--which was half the battle--since he had been asked to sup with Mirza Ibrahîm, the Lord Chamberlain. There would be business first, no doubt, due to the Heir-Apparent's childish knuckling under, since some new intrigue must be set on foot to weaken Akbar's authority; but once that was over Ibrahîm might be counted on to make the hours hum. So he clapped his hands for the tiremen and fresh dressing, and shaving, and scenting; then, after due dallying with cosmetics and dyes, set off--the very pink of fashion--in his gilded litter in which he lay lazily fanned with a peacock's feather fan by a tiny boy who sate at his feet dressed in a girl's tinsel-set garments, his hair braided on his forehead in the virginal plaits.

As he was borne through the silent streets with running torches beside the ambling porters, a host of pipe-bearers, toothpick holders, keepers of aphrodisaical pills, and general panderers trotting behind him, he was Eastern vice personified; soft, perfumed, relentless.

So he disappeared into the Palace and the star-lit world was quit of him for a time; for the night was spangled beyond belief. Spangled with myriads of stars, not white as in northern climes, but holding in their shine faint hints of rose, and green, and blue, and amber.

Against the clear obscure, the terraced town showed like some vast fort, turreted, battlemented, from which one by one the twinkling lights disappeared as the hours of the night wore on; until at last only a few lay sparsely about its feet circling the outcast colony of Satanstown where, by Akbar's orders, vice dwelt and turned darkness into day. Above, all was shadow, save for one light high up on the palace whose outline struck firm against the velvet of the sky. It shone from Akbar's balcony; Akbar who after his usual habit watched while his subjects slept. To-night, however, something more than mere meditation absorbed him, as he sate, girt about the middle of his loose, white, woollen garment like some Franciscan monk. His face dark, aquiline, not so much ascetic as strenuous, was bent on William Leedes, the English jeweller, as he weighed in his balance the great uncut diamond from the King's turban.

The gold and gemmed setting from which it had been removed lay on the floor, and the irregularly ovoid stone itself gave out flickering brightnesses as it oscillated gently under the light of the seven branched golden cresset-stand in the alcove. Beneath this stand, backed partly by the tendril-inlaid curves of agate and chalcedony, lapis-lazuli and cornelian upon the marble wall, and partly by the pearl embroidered yellow satin cushions amongst which the King reclined, was a beautifully embossed silver clepsydre, or water clock, in which the floating bowl was fashioned in enamel like a sacred lotus; and beside this stood the marvellous censer, a triumph of goldsmith's and jeweller's art from which day and night arose the scented smoke which Akbar loved. Beyond, through the arches of the balcony, lay the night, velvety dark.

"Five hundred and sixty carats," murmured William Leedes to himself, "the largest known diamond in this world!--and of a most elegant water; but----" He looked up, his face full of denial. "It would mayhap lose half its weight in the cutting, great King," he said sharply, "and--God knows in His grace but we might cut out the King's Luck thereby."

He looked as if for support to the two men who stood behind him. They were Râjah Birbal and Shaik Abulfazl. The latter, seeing his master frown, interrupted the jeweller in hasty excuse.

"I but told him, Most Exalted, that the populace hold the stone a talisman; and sure at all times the luck of the Most Excellent has been stupendous. Still, we of the enlightened give praise where praise is due and not to stocks and stones."

Birbal shrugged his shoulders. "Say, rather, Shaikjee," he remarked urbanely, "that the wise see an Eternal cause even in stocks and stones."

The eyes of those two counsellors of the King were on each other in rivalry; but the King himself bent forward to touch the diamond with one pliant finger, and a faint fear showed in his face. Then he leant back once more.

"Luck is of God," he said, "and this stone----" he paused beset by recollections of the years he had worn it--ever since as a boy of three he had made his way safely through the great Snow-land.

"The stone, sire," put in William Leedes, firmly, "is as God made it. 'Tis well to remember that----"

He was looking at the King and the King's eyes were on his; for the time the whole of the rest of the world was empty for them both.

"Aye! But what of that He wishes it to be? What of that, sir jeweller?" came the swift answer, "therein lies kingcraft, to see what His will needs--and give it."

William Leedes bowed silently and there was a pause; then bluntly, suddenly, he said, "Yet, Great King, would I rather have naught to do with the cutting thereof."

In an instant Akbar's eyes flashed fire.

"Thou hast not, slave! 'Tis I who order it. Birbal! to thy charge the arrangements. The room next Diswunt the painter's, in the Court of Labour, is vacant. See it prepared. Double the guards if necessary--to thee I leave--the King's Luck."

A faint smile came to his face, but Birbal and Abulfazl looked at each other, and finally the latter spoke.

"This dust-like one," he said tentatively and yet with firmness, "presumes not to offer wisdom to its fount; but to the minds of the Most Exalted's devoted slaves it seems as if to the populace, there might be danger in Royalty appearing without the talisman to which all have looked as security for the King's success in all ways. Therefore if Majesty *will* ordain the cutting of the Eastern gem in Western fashion, let it at least condescend to wear in its place--until the gem return--a veritable Mountain of Light doubtless a substitute. Pooroo, the false jewel maker, who can deceive all but a diamond itself, hath the cast of the King's Luck, made when the Most Exalted changed the setting thereof. Let him fashion a double to deceive----"

"Deceive?" came Akbar's voice with a note of affectionate reproach in it, "deceive whom? Fate or the people? Lo! Abulfazl! to what end? Since if the tale *be not true* that luck lies in the stone, what need to regard it? And if it *be true*, how shall the false gem hoodwink God?"

He raised himself as he spoke, holding the diamond in his palm as an orb.

"Luck!" he said dreamily, "thou art mine to-night; and to-morrow is Fate's! Go!"

He gave the Eastern wave of dismissal and sank back amongst his cushions; sank back with more than usual lassitude, for the day had left him weary. It was no small thing to one of his temperament to quarrel with his son, his heir. It was a still greater thing to forgive him causelessly.

Therein lay the sting. The causelessness of the forgiveness, the lack of any security against a recurrence of the offence. So, as he thought of this, with a rush came back the memory of many a similar scene, and his fingers clasped in upon themselves as the disappointment ate into his very soul. Surely he had a right to expect more of Fate?--he who had waited so long, so patiently for an heir--since in those long years of waiting the very thought of mere sonship had been forgotten in the heirship. Yes, even now, Love seemed too trivial to count against Empire! Yet it was Love which had prompted forgiveness. Love of what?--what? Of himself surely-- the love which claimed to live in his son--to live on....

"Shall I bid the Reader of Wisdom to the Wise resume his task," came Birbal's voice. Noting the King's weariness he had lingered behind the others.

The King started, then looked round cheerfully. "Not to-night, friend; I have food for thought, and if I lack more--it waits below," he said, and leaning forward, rested his arm on the marble balustrade of the balcony, so pointed downward into the void darkness of the night. Through it like a little line of light fading into nothingness, ran the signal string attached to the quaint contrivance by which the King could secure, when the mood seized him, the presence of an opponent for some midnight argument. One touch at the cord and through the darkness the disputant waiting below, would by an ingenious system of counterpoise rise in a domed dhooli to the level of the balcony. Akbar laid his finger on the tense string, then once more looked back suddenly into Birbal's face.

"Ah! friend!" he said bitterly. "Could we but sound the Great Darkness as I can sound this little night, certain that my need will bring some sage, or fool, or knave, to keep Jalâl-ud-din Mahomed Akbar, Defender of the Faith, from wearying for sleep! But from the great Depths there comes no answer. The mystery is unfathomable--man's reason wanders bewildered in the streets of the City of God."

His voice sank in silence; then yet once again, he roused himself.

"Farewell, friend, for the night--the night that will bring to-morrow--Ye Gods! How will it be when the Night of Death closes in--on one of us?"

Birbal sank to his knees and touched his master's feet with his forehead. He had no other answer; so silently he passed through the great wadded curtains of gold tissue which separated the alcove from the rest of the room, leaving the King alone, lost in thought.

The problem of a future life had pressed on him all his days, and yet, he told himself as he sate thinking, the fact had not interfered with his enjoyment of the present one. Verily he had drunk of the cup of life to the dregs. His vitality had spared neither himself nor his world.

The memory of man is curiously creative. Out of the welter of remembrance it chooses this and that in obedience to no law, but arbitrarily, whimsically. It passes by unseen the peaks of past passion, and makes mountains of the merest mole-hill of caprice.

So, as Akbar looked back over his life, he found many a triviality standing out as clear, as untouched by Time, as many a tragedy, many a palpable turning point in his career.

The first snow he ever saw? The sight came back to him as if he had seen it yesterday, though five-and-forty years had passed since that perilous journey from Kandahar to Kabul in charge of his foster-nurse Anagâh. Dear Anagâh! How he had loved her! More, in a way, than he had loved his absent, stately mother; but he had vague recollections of that quaint meeting with the latter after three long years of separation, when his father, as a joke, had brought him--a little lad-ling of six--into a great circle of unveiled women and bidden him to choose a mother for himself.

He had chosen right, but the very recollection of his choice had gone. All he remembered was quick clasping arms and a kiss--surely the sweetest kiss of his life.

The sweetest? No!

That (even after five-and-twenty years the horror, the despair of it seemed to overwhelm him again) had been the last passion-fraught kiss he had given to--to a murderer--to Adham! Adham his foster brother--his playmate Adham, whom he loved, whom he trusted.

Oh! God! the tragedy of it! Why did such things come into this little trivial life?

Yet it was inevitable. If Adham were to come to him now as he had done that day; reckless, defiant, presuming on his position, boasting of the foul murder of an old man whom he conceived to be his enemy, the same swift justice must follow.

The beads of sweat started to Akbar's brow as he remembered the sudden grip of his own strong young arms, the relentless forcing backward to the parapet's edge, and then--before the final fling--that kiss!

And thereinafter silence. No! not silence--tears! Anagâh--dear Anagâh's tears. She had died of a broken heart because of her son's death--died without one word of forgiveness for the doer of justice.

Yet he did not regret the deed, though he had always, even as a boy, been tender of life.

"I will fight a whole enemy, I will not slay a wounded one."

The very words of his refusal when his tutor had bidden him whet his maiden sword on the rebel Hemu came back to him, and led him on to remembrance of the day when this feeling for the sanctity of life had risen in him not toward man only but toward all creatures. That was a later memory, and the scene reproduced itself before his mind's eye complete in every detail.

The long laborious encircling of game drawing to its close--the opposing ends of the great arc of thousands upon thousands of men who for two days had been sweeping across the country driving all wild things before them, were narrowing, closing in--and he, the man called King, was watching, luxuriously posted, his court about him, for his first shot.

And then? Then close beside him a *chinkara* fawn, looking at him with great soft dim eyes, startled, but not afraid!

"His Majesty was seized suddenly with an extraordinary access of rage such as none had ever seen the like in him before, and the *battue* was given up; nor has he since, so pursued game, but prefers to go out alone and spend hours in arduous chase."

That is how his quick, almost despairing remorse, regret, pity, anger with himself had appeared to the outside multitude. To him it had been a crisis in his life; one of the few things which had left an indelible mark on his mind.

Aye! few things. For love had not touched him as, for instance, it had touched his grandfather.

"To-night at midnight after three long years, I met Mâham again."

Babar had set that down in his memoirs, after--according to Aunt Rosebody's tale--he had run out on foot from the palace on hearing of the near approach of the long expected caravan from Kabul and met his dearest dear six miles out along the road. Even his father's more passionate love for the fourteen year old Hamida, seen when Humâyon was five and thirty, had not been his. If it had been, perhaps his sons might have been different!

And so in an instant, overwhelmingly, Akbar was back in the old dreary disappointment; the old defiance of fate following fast on its heels.

The boy would do well enough! Even if some things passed, even if ideals had to go, what then? The dynasty would remain. He and his and the City of Victory he had built with such high hopes should endure for ever, even if churlish Nature denied them a cup of cold water.

For ever! For ever! With the words came back the old puzzle. Oh! If he could only see, only know!

He sate staring fixedly, abstractedly, at the clear translucence of the diamond which he still held in the palm of his left hand, while his right rested on the marble balustrade close to the summoning string which dived into the depths below.

So after a while he seemed to sleep, for his muscles relaxed and the right hand slipped, to hang over into the darkness, whence a faint sound as of metal on metal rose waveringly, followed almost immediately by the monotonous burr of a rope passing over pulleys.

It did not rouse the King, though it sent Birbal, who was lingering beyond the wadded curtain, to peer through it stealthily, curious to see what antagonist in argument the King had summoned.

Beyond the arched openings of the balcony, the domed roof of the swinging dhooli rose into sight, and a moment afterward its occupant laid a thin hand on the balustrade steadying himself to arrest.

Despite the high-peaked, white, woollen cap, the white, woollen robe of a Sufi ecstatic which the figure wore, Birbal's recognition of the face was instant, complete.

"Smagdarite!" he exclaimed.

The newcomer held his finger to his lip, but his eyes were on the King. "Hush!" he whispered, "See, he dreams. The diamond hath found him, and he knows himself."

Something in the man's tone sent a thrill through his hearer, and his eyes followed the lead given them swiftly.

Akbar did not move. He leant amongst the cushions, gazing at the diamond, but seeing it not; for the veil had fallen from the Unknown and lay hiding the Known.

"What doest thou mean--mountebank!" whispered Birbal in return, his own voice sounding strange to his ears as he stepped closer, bending over the King. "He doth but doze. Wake, my liege, wake!"

The other's fine fingers were on his wrist, gripping it hard.

"At thy peril! though, mayhap, thou couldst not wake him if thou wouldst. Lo! Birbal! Philosopher! learned beyond most! seest thou not that the man sleeps indeed! Hast thou not heard, hast thou not read of the death in life whereby the soul, set free, wanders at will, not in Time, but in Eternity? So wanders Akbar now! He is not here--he is in the future."

Birbal paled despite his disbelief.

"Who art thou, man of many faces," he gasped, "and how earnest thou here?"

"He summoned me," replied the Sufi solemnly. "Wherefore God knows. As for me, I am the Wayfarer of Life. What I have learned I have learned. And this"--he pointed to the dreaming figure--"I know, that if my lord desires to hear the future he has but to ask this sleeping soul. The Self which lurks ever behind these trivial selves of ours will tell him."

For an instant Birbal hesitated. Beset by curiosity as he was, something in him cried aloud not to know; for, agnostic at heart, doubter to the very core, he knew already. Knew that all his master's dreams were but dreams; that like all other things in heaven and earth they must pass. Then came the thought that the forewarned are forearmed, and he knelt at that master's feet.

"Great King," he whispered, "tell us what is seen?"

There was no answer, and on the silence the Sufi's voice rose quiet, but compelling.

"Oh! Self-behind-the-Self, speak! What of the future? Is Jalâl-ud-din Mahomed Akbar there, as King?"

There was no pause; the reply rang immediate, resonant.

"He is not there and yet his work remains, to run, a glittering warp among the woof. See! how the westering sun turns all to gold--gilt that is pinchbeck of all baser metals.

"The land is thick with little crooked lines, but Akbar's roads were measured straight to give an evening rest to tired travellers. He is not there, but I--who lived in him--I linger still in Justice, Mercy, Truth. Sons of his soul are these, sons of his love, not of his mortal body--Oh! Salîm! Salîm----!"

The pause was eloquent of sudden personal distress, the clear dreaming eyes clouded and there was silence. Then hurriedly, disconnectedly, the voice took up its tale.

"What was the thought which racked me to the soul? Something I have forgotten utterly."

So once more came silence while those two watchers waited.

"Hush!" whispered the Wayfarer, signing back the fresh questioning which trembled on Birbal's lips, "he speaks again!"

The King's head had drooped as if to deeper sleep, for his voice lost its resonance and seemed to come from very far away.

"And they too--in the years they shall forget. Their dream of empire shall die as mine; and so we Twain, soul-welded into soul, shall pass, shall live forgetting, unforgotten ('the dreaming of a King can never die'). And all their faults shall fall from them. Ah God! The cry of little children, the wail of murdered women in my palace walls--do ye not hear them, aliens! Lo! I swear, such were not raised while Akbar reigned as King. Yet even this shall pass to peace, to rest--to greater ease--more gold--more luxury.

"Oh! subjects of Akbar! arouse ye! Wake! Life is not comfort! there is that beyond which India always sought, for which she seeks. This is no land of golden sunsetting--it is the land of coming dawn, of light in which to search for Truth unceasingly.

"What do they say arousing me from sleep? 'They wait me in the House of Argument?'

"Ah! well! I go, though it avails us not! India is Akbar's to the end of Time--like him it knows not and it fain would know, the secret of its birth and of its death. What are the words thou soughtest for in the years--Akbar? His son? I see them not! I only see the Self that knows, that sees, that hears, the everlasting Truth behind Life's lie.

"The rest I have forgotten."

The voice sank in silence, the head to deeper sleep, and the left hand slacking its grip dropped nerveless on the knee, so that the shining orb it had held rolled from it like a giant dewdrop until it found a resting place at Akbar's feet.

Birbal with a little cry caught at the King's Luck.

"Take it back! Oh, Master, take it back!" he whispered, laying it once more softly in the King's empty palm. "Hold fast to thyself. Lo! the whole world equals not Jalâl-ud-din Mahomed Akbar."

Then in a perfect passion of resentment he turned to the Wayfarer. But in those few seconds the latter's hold upon the balustrade had been withdrawn, the counterpoise had reasserted itself, and Birbal peering out over the balcony could see the dome of the dhooli disappearing in its downward course of darkness.

To slip through the wadded curtain and make his way to the swinging station at the foot of the wall was but the work of a minute or so. Yet he was too late. The newly arrived Sufi from Ispahân, the yawning attendants declared, had had his interview and gone--none knew whither.

The east was all flushed with rose-leaf clouds when Akbar awoke and smiled to find Birbal wrapped in his shawl watching him with curious, doubtful eyes.

Would the King remember? That was the question.

"Lo! friend," he said affectionately. "So may I wake in Paradise after a dreamless sleep and find thee there."

CHAPTER VI

The current of a deed will work its way
Through the wide world and cannot be resisted,
'Twas seasonably done--the seed is sown
And in due time will bear the fruit of discord.

--KALIDASA.

The wide mosque lay empty save for a group of long-bearded doctors of the law, who, lingering after service was over, discussed as ever the unfailing topic of the King's innovations. Such purposeless innovations too! Leading to nothing, to absolute nescience; for what else was all this talk of freedom, of equality, of universal brotherhood? Were not kings, kings, and nobles, nobles, since the very beginning?

These reverend seigneurs surcharged with pride of race, the pride of the conqueror, fiercely fanatical in faith, felt resentfully that in religion, in manners, in morals, Akbar, their King, stood absolutely aloof from them.

Yet they, in their turn, stood as absolutely aloof from the real heart of India which beat placidly in the simple lives of the husbandmen toiling in the ample fields which, seen through the great Arch of Victory receded into a dim blue distance that lost itself in a dim blue sky. So each, the conqueror, the conquered, went on his way, while a man dreamt of blending the two into one.

"Yes! it is true," murmured Budaoni the historian regretfully; "from his earliest childhood his Majesty hath collected everything in all religions that is worth remembering, with a talent of selection peculiar to him, and a spirit of inquiry opposed to every principle of our Faith."

"*Sobhan-ullah!*" assented the Makhdûm-ul'-mulk, who had been the highest religious authority in the land until the King, with one sweep of his pen, had made himself the Head of the Church. A direful offence to the orthodox who refused assent to Akbar's reasoning that since there was but one law, the law of God, there could be but one authority; therefore the intervention of a priesthood between the people and God's vice-regent on earth was unnecessary, impolitic.

An old man, white-bearded, high-featured, murmured to himself, "Yet is he King indeed," then fell hurriedly to the telling of his beads; but Ghiâss Beg, the Lord High Treasurer--a stout, good-humoured looking man, whose fat paunch stood evidence for his love of good living--shook his head and sighed.

"It cometh of abstinence, see you," he mourned. "When the stomach is empty wind rises to the head. And, were it not for that damned sense of duty which leaveth the King neither by day nor by night, Akbar would give up food and sleep altogether. So far hath he wandered from the Sure Pivot of Life that the very question of dinner ariseth not in his mind; he eats but once a day, and leaveth off unsatisfied, nor is there even any fixed hour for this food. Sure! 'tis the life of a very dog."

"So he keep it, and his dogs, and his uncircumcised friends to himself," muttered a sour-visaged elder, "I quarrel not with his starvations. Belike they may bring the Heir-Apparent to his rights sooner, and that would be a glad day for Islâm."

The old man with the white beard who was telling his beads murmured once more under his breath: "Yet is he King indeed," and went on with his prayers still more hurriedly.

"Lo! mullah jee!" yawned another sour-visaged one, "Prince Salîm will be in the idolaters' toils ere then. With a Râjpût to wife there is small hope for a Ruler of the Faith."

In the hot sunshine where they sate whispering like sleepy snakes, ready, yet too lazy, to strike, a leisurely groan ran round the whole assembly. That the first wife--practically the only real wife--of the Heir-Apparent should be a Hindu was simply an outrage. It was bad enough that the King himself should have taken the Râjpût daughters and sisters of his conquered foes into his harem, in order--heaven save the mark!--to cement friendship between the races; but he, at least, had been first married in orthodox fashion to a daughter of Islâm. Could he not do even so much for his son?

Ghiâss Beg heaved another fat sigh and his face took on obstinacy.

"True," he assented, "and 'tis not that as fair a bride could not be found----"

"In the House of the Lord High Treasurer," interrupted a sneering voice. It came from Mirza Ibrahîm, who, at that moment, followed at a little distance by a posse of courtiers and others, came from the cloisters full upon the half-drowsy group of malcontents.

"God forbid!" gasped the horrified High Treasurer weakly. In his heart of hearts he had been thinking--and not for the first time--of his little daughter Mihrun-nissa, as a future Empress of India. But this was an outrage on decorum, an indignity! He began to splutter remonstrance.

"Prayers are over! Up with the carpet!" interrupted the Mirza irreverently. Whereupon the Makhdûm interfered with pompous frowns and craved to know what my Lord High Chamberlain meant by the unseemly remark.

"Nothing, Most Holy," replied the latter cheerfully, "save that if the pious deliberations of the wise are ended the ignorant have a point of law which they would fain lay before authority. Is it not so, oh, sahibân?"

He turned as he spoke to a little knot of curiously distinctive-looking men who, having separated themselves from the remainder of his following, stood together in the full blaze of sunlight. They were singularly alike. Small, fine-drawn, with watchful eyes, and a little stoop forward of the head, reminding one irresistibly of a bird of prey. In truth the Syeds of Bârha were wild hawks indeed; and to-day, still travel-stained with their quick march from their eyrie of a fortress far in the distant plains, they were ready to swoop fiercely on any cause of offence. For they were red-hot with anger at the exile of that ill-doing scion of their house Jamâl-ud-din. Not that they defended his choice of a wife--it was one which sooner or later might necessitate a sack, and the nearest river--but, if Siyah Yamin was the lad's wife, what right had even the Great Mogul to interfere?

They assented with a scowl; but Khodadâd (he who called himself by another name when he wrote to Sinde) smiled urbanely. He was evidently prepared to play the indispensable Eastern part of applauder and general backer-up.

"Even so, Most Holy!" he replied effusively, "a point of law which can only be settled by God's most chosen Judge, before whom even these lineal descendants of our Great Prophet bow humbly."[10]

The speech was full of malicious intent, purposely provocative, and succeeded in its purpose.

"Then let them go to the King," began the Makhdûm acrimoniously, when Ibrahîm cut him short, concealing a yawn as he sought a comfortable place for himself where his feet could be in sunshine, his head in shadow.

"Who hath usurped the Judge's seat? Nay! Most Holy! It is only time-servers and idolaters who yield such function to Akbar. We faithful ones and true----"

"Had best keep silence in a public place," put in Budaoni eyeing the other with a glassy stare. He himself might take his own part in discontent, but being, by virtue of his voice, precentor in the Court Mosque, he did not choose to encourage Ibrahîm, whose evil life was notorious. The latter smiled and skilfully drew another red-herring of provocation across the path.

"Public?" he echoed with a leer of malice. "Sure there is no more private place than the Court Mosque since the King started his Divine Faith! Hast heard, Most Holy, what the idolatrous pig Birbal jested last Friday when the King, for a marvel, put in an appearance at prayers--that he came not in order to listen to what you preached as of God, but to hush the slanders you borrowed of the Devil."

The Makhdûm spat solemnly, the senior canon let loose a thundering "God roast him," which echoed and re-echoed through the wide arches.

"Except," remarked Budaoni with a sneer, "when his Majesty reads prayers himself; then he comes to stutter!"

This allusion to the day not so far past when Akbar, assuming the Headship had--whether from nervousness or emotion history sayeth not--broken down in repeating the *kutba* composed for the occasion by Faiz, the poet-laureate, produced snorts and smiles of assent.

"Yes! yea!" assented the sour-visaged elder fiercely "he stuttered indeed--mayhap because the words were by Faiz, the dog poet--may God rot him for defiling His Holy Place."

The old man with the white beard looked up suddenly.

"Yet, sirs, was there ought wrong with the words?" he asked; so stretched out his lean old hand, and his wavering old voice rang out through the sunshine:

Lo! from Almighty God I take my Kingship
Before His Throne I bow and take my Judgeship
Take Strength from Strength and Wisdom from His Wiseness
Right from the Right, and Justice from His Justice
Praising the King I praise God near and far
Great is His Power, Al-la-hu Akbar.

The echoes died away and there was silence. Then Ibrahîm indulging in a yawn of contempt for the digression his words had caused, said patronisingly, "The question we ask is not of *kutbas*; it is of a marriage, most Enlightened-One."

But Budaoni's virulence was incorrigible. "His Majesty hath propounded not a few such problems to this poor court already," he remarked caustically; "doth he perchance propound another?"

This further allusion to the hot dispute between the King and the doctors concerning the legality of the former's political marriages with Râjpût princesses, would have met with equal favour, but for Ibrahîm's quick frown. To him, as chamberlain, the King's present austerities and general asceticism were a continual grievance.

"Thy wits must wander, Budaoni," he interrupted sharply, "or thou wouldst know the very name woman is at a discount at court! Mayhap the translation into civilised language of the Hindu Scriptures proves too much for thee!"

The historian scowled, for his task of translating religious books from the Sanskrit into Persian for the King's benefit was utterly abhorrent to his orthodoxy.

"And small wonder," he replied hotly. "These useless absurdities confound the eighteen worlds! Such injunctions! Such prohibitions! A whole page against the eating of turnips! May God forgive the enforced spoiling of orthodox pen, ink, and paper over such puerilities!"

It was the Syeds' turn to shift impatiently. "Good sir historian," said one, handling his sword as it lay on his knee, "we come not hither to discuss literature, but to ask an opinion. Hath the King right to exile a man for the marrying of a woman?"

"What man, and what woman?" asked the Makhdûm portentously. "On that hangs law. Hath the man already four wives?"

"The King hath nigher to forty," interrupted the incorrigible Budaoni.

"Peace, preacher!" reproved the great man, wagging his head. "Cloud not perspicacity with allusions. And the woman? Is she virgin, widow, or duly divorced?"

There was a general sort of chuckle from the hawks-brood.

"None of them i' faith," said the head of the clan at last, "'tis Siyah Yamin whom all know; but she hath said the Creed and the lad hath married her."

"By legal marriage?"

"How else?" asked the spokesman hotly. "We of Bârha, descended of the true Prophet--may His name be exalted--deal not with customs borrowed of the idolater."

"Then are they true wed, and none can dissolve the tie save the husband himself by----"

"Traa!" interrupted Ibrahîm impatiently, "that is for them to settle between them! These gentlemen desire to know by what right the King forbids this virtuous young man to bring his screened and lawful woman into the town? Such cupolas of chastity are beyond the power even of majesty; is it not so, most learned doctors?"

A little stir shifted through the assemblage; it sate up literally, metaphorically, keen for ground of offence against any of the King's decisions.

"Of a truth," pronounced the Makhdûm pompously, "he hath no right. By all the laws of Islâm a screened and lawful woman belongs only to her owner."

So in the sunshine the enmity of the Old against the New rose hot as the sunshine itself, and conspiracy sprang into being.

It was a good half-hour ere Mirza Ibrahîm summed up the situation in these words:

"We meet again then, in the Hall of Public Audience to-day, and demand revision of the sentence as being contrary to the Revealed Word; and if the King----"

Khodadâd broke in on him with a sudden laugh--"Nay! my idolatrous quarry will be Birbal! God and His Prophet! how I loathe the dog!" He paused, seeing the unwisdom of his confidences, for the Syeds of Bârha rose, to stand packed, fingering their swords.

"God's truth," said their leader, turning insolently to the speaker, "keep thy carrion to thyself, Tarkhân! We of Bârha mix not in court cabals--we be not buzzard-cocks to whom the smell of death brings but gluttony. No! if the King rescind not his order we fling our allegiance at his feet, we and our goodly following; so, escaping free of false law to our strongholds, there to defend ourselves against tyranny. But for quarry! Stab whom thou willst, Tarkhân, but reckon not on our knives."

Khodadâd, deprecating a scowl at his indiscretion from Mirza Ibrahîm, smiled lightly:

"Quarry for my craft is all I ask, though God knows His world would be better without the Hindu pig who, see you, comes yonder defiling the sanctuary and hatching new plots against our pockets, with the accurst Khattri, Tôdar Mull, the Finance Minister."

It was a deft distraction, for the constant cutting-down of perquisites and fees in Akbar's efforts to ameliorate the condition of the poor, was a continual source of irritation to the upper classes. But the Syeds of Bârha were large landowners, and they knew on which side their bread was buttered. So they salaamed respectfully to the two statesmen as they passed at a distance arm in arm, and the oldest of the little group said sharply, "Hindu or no, he hath his grip on the collector of taxes. So good luck go with him--aye! And with the King, too, in such matters. Save for this about Jamâl-ud-din we find no fault in him."

"Neither see I fault in him," came a sudden voice loud yet wavering. It came from the white-haired old man who had been telling his beads, and who now stood, his thin bent figure outlined against the distant blue of India that showed through the Arch of Victory.

"Neither see I fault," he repeated, his tone breaking in his vehemence. "God give him ever what he prays for--'a tranquil mind, an open brow, a just intent, a right principle, a wide capacity, a firm foot, a high spirit, a lofty soul, a right place, a shining countenance, and a smiling lip.' Of such are kings indeed!"

They looked at the old man in haughty scorn, as stumblingly, his old eyes half-blind with tears, he passed through the archway, so down the steps to disappear as it were in the heart of India widespread, remote, indefinite. But Budaoni murmured under his breath, "Lo! the glamour of the King is upon him. God knows one can scarce live in sight of him and not feel the very soul of one go out toward what lies beyond. Even I myself----" he paused and was silent, knowing that through all his diatribes, all his wanton misreadings of Akbar's character, ran admiration.

Meanwhile Tôdar Mull had in passing given a quick glance in return for the salutation which had come from the Syeds of Bârha.

"That bodes--what?" he had asked of Birbal, who had shrugged his shoulders and given a still keener glance at the group in the sunshine.

"Since Khodadâd is in it--mischief! Mirza Ibrahîm ever equals immorality, and the Syedân--I wist not they were here--bode--with Jamâl-ud-din and his chaste spouse in exile--marriage! As for the Learned of the Law, they contribute 'Mahommed is His Prophet.' The whole doubtless forming conspiracy--what else is there in the court with this accursed peace of Akbar's giving time for the cooking of cabals? Would to God----" He broke off, his mind besieged in a rush with the fierce regret which had been his ever since, but a few hours before he had heard the words of self-renunciation fall unconsciously from his master's lips. But--fate willing--there should be no more such talk! He, Birbal, would force on war; he would make Akbar, as unconsciously, play his part in common-sense, grasping Kingship. "Yea," he continued urbanely, "were it not that the poor, thriving, are content, thanks to Tôdar Mull's wise ruling----"

The Kattri's face, yellow of tint, fleshy of contour, seemed to take on bone and muscle, and his oiliness of manner roughened into swift decision. "Aye!" he returned, "they grow more content, poor souls, but, 'tis the King who starts me on the trail. I go even now to discuss a new idea of his with Abulfazl, whose head truly hath no peer for detail."

"Yea!" put in Birbal, "but the King's Diwan is even now using it in showing the details of the King's work to the Englishmen, while the Portuguese priests scowl at the intrusion of new claimants to commerce. Lo! I grow weary of these strangers. Why should Akbar make their way smooth?"

Tôdar Mull, his inherited aptitude for the problems of money showing in the eyes which were keen even for fractions in a man's character, looked at Birbal doubtfully.

"Wherefore not?" he asked. "Lo! I have had speech with these new men, and there is that of free-trading, unfettered by aught save gold or the lack of it, in them which compels approval. For see you, in the end gold is the essence of all things. I tell thee were it not for piety I myself would bow down to it and worship with a 'Hallowed be thy name.'"

Birbal's mimetic face became preternaturally grave, but there was a twinkle in his eye: "'Twould not"--he bowed courteously--"be so bulky a divinity as Tôdar Mull's present pantheon, which, if rumour says sooth, already runs to cart-loads."

The financier flushed. This allusion to his habit of carrying waggons-full of household gods about with him when on tour brought a quick reproach: "Jest not at the Gods, O! Brahmin-born," he said.

Birbal's whole expression changed. "Not at the All-Embracing One, for sure; but for the little brass god-lings."

Tôdar Mull edged away nervously. "Let be--let be! Râjah Sahib. Each for his own belief, and the Almighty's curse lodge on the hindmost, so it be not me! Now go I to the statistic makers; for see you, without figures man is lost in this world."

They parted company, and Birbal looked after the retreating Finance Minister with a frown.

What was the use of it all! Was it not better far to eat, to drink, knowing that to-morrow one must die? So his thoughts turned, as they always did, to the present; to the one portion of time which even Fate could not filch from a living man. The advent of the Syedân of Bârha meant, doubtless, appeal to the King. An appeal to which the King must not, of course, listen. As to that, Abulfazl must be seen, and at once.

He found him in the royal storehouses, his yellow-brown eyes clear with pride as he pointed out the system on which they were worked to the three Englishmen who stood, centring, with the curious half-contemptuous gaze of another world, the leisured bustle in the wide courtyards.

"His Majesty," explained Abulfazl grandiloquently, "having acquainted himself with the theory and practice of every manufacture, is thus able to distinguish between good and bad work. So, the intrinsic value of each article being settled by the State in reference to a certain fixed standard, neither worthy labour nor true art can fall into discredit."

Ralph Fitch looked queerly at the carts unlading and lading, at the groups of experts settling true values, at the artificers waiting patiently for the verdict; certain, if their work were up to the standard, of immediate sale.

"And what of the merchants?" he asked sharply. "Where does their profit----?"

"Their profit is settled also," interrupted the Diwan with simple pride, "and they are content." His voice took on sternness as he added, "They have, indeed, no choice; since all articles unstamped by the testing houses are liable to confiscation, and the possessors thereof to fine."

"Cheer thee up, Ralph," laughed John Newbery into his companion's appalled face as they moved on to a new court, "and thank heaven we be not thus tied by the apron strings! Though, by our Lady, this King Echebar has a trick o' keeping cables taut which would make me almost wish to enter his service would he but command some adventure to the Poles."

William Leedes looked up quickly. "Nay," he said, "before God I would rather quit this land and leave it--as it is."

He paused, for John Newbery's attention had passed as his roving eyes settled themselves surprised, yet approvingly, on the long lines of light which followed the rows on rows of steel lance heads, swords, and matchlocks lining the walls of the vast armoury into which they entered. It was full to the brim with every conceivable instrument of war, many of them strange to Western eyes. But Abulfazl gave no time for inspection. With the brief explanation, "The Most-Excellent is yonder at work," he passed through one of the wide arches fitted with massive doors which were now set open to the sunlight, and joined a group of men who stood in the courtyard beyond.

A sharp report, followed by the whistling ping of a bullet as it struck a target outlined on the farther wall, cut the hot air keenly, and Akbar, who had been kneeling for better aim, stood up rubbing his shoulder. He was dressed in a white overall, not unsmirched with grease, and his grizzled hair showed free of covering.

"It hits hard enough behind anyhow, sir smith," he said good-humouredly to a swarthy half-naked workman who looked down the still smoking barrel of the newly tried gun with a doubtful air. "Nay! 'tis not the grooving. That idea holds good. It is something in the chamber. Bring it this evening to the Palace, and we will see to it. Hast aught else for trial?"

The next instant, after one careless salute to the newcomers he was deep in the mechanism of a complicated gun, and his face lit up as he looked. "See you," he went on--apparently as much for himself as for those others who, left behind by his imaginings, stood patient, half-comprehending--"if this moving wheel duly loaded, could fit the one barrel what need for more? The twin cannon fired by one match which we made last year works well, but this will be better--if it can be compassed." And then suddenly as his hands fingered ratchet wheel and eccentric, bolt and socket with sure practical touch, his eyes grew full of dreams.

"Lo! we work in the dark," he murmured, "since none know why the bullet curves, and so the worst may do as well, nay better than the best. 'Twas an old matchlock snatched from a sleepy sentry which gave me empire."

He paused, back in thought to that false dawn before the trenches at Chitore when, going his rounds after his wont, alone and in darkness, he had seen upon the ramparts of the besieged town the figure of his foe also going his rounds, but by the light of lanterns.

It had been a long shot, but in the dawn Chitore was his, and he was Emperor of India. Yet, once again, almost overmastering regret came over him for the past horrors of that sun-bright dawn. The awful onslaught of saffron-robed heroes, doomed to desperate death, which he had seen against the rolling clouds of dense white smoke that rose from the very bowels of the earth, where, in dark caves, the Râjpût women were burning--self-immolated!

Then as he stood there fingering the outcome of his uncontrollable desire for success, all his victories seemed to slip from him for the moment; he remembered--as, nearly two thousand years before him another great King of India had remembered--nothing but his regret. At the moment he, also, could have inscribed an edict for all time setting forth his sorrow for "the hundreds of thousands of God's creatures needlessly slain." But the next instant the mood passed and he turned with almost insolent regality to the English adventurers.

"Yet tell your queen, sir travellers," he said, "that Akbar holds the best gun to be the best key to empire."

John Newbery looked at Ralph Fitch, who bowed his answer:

"Most Excellent, we will give the message without fail."

As they passed on, Birbal paused a moment beside Abulfazl to whisper in his ear:

"The Bârha hawks are in. Hast news of them?"

The Diwan nodded: "The King sees them at audience to-day to consider----"

Birbal interrupted with a bitter laugh: "Before God, Abul," he said, with his habitual shrug of the shoulders, "when the Most-Excellent thinks of himself as Head of the Church and Defender of the Faith, he is too excellent for this world. Better sure a little injustice than that the King should back on himself. It is not time for weakness. What does he say?"

"'The Law-maker cannot break the law,'" replied the Diwan softly, and in his voice there was a touch both of irritation and of pride.

So in the sunshine the eyes of those two followed the King who dreamt such strange new dreams of duty and responsibility toward his subjects.

CHAPTER VII

What makes a monarch? Not his throne, his crown,
But man to work his will, to tremble at his frown.

--SA'ADI.

The city was astir, sleepily astir. In the blind tortuous alleys where the hot May sun struggled in vain to shine, shut out on every side by the high tenement houses hiving swarms of men, women and children, rumour spread like mushroom spawn in the dark; spread aimlessly, idly, sending its filaments at random, here, there, everywhere, ready at a moment's notice to shoot up into some fantastic mushroom growth. Even in Agra itself, connected with Fatehpur Sikri by that twenty-mile-long ribbon of shop-edged road, the talk was all of what was about to happen in Akbar's City of Victory. The King had accepted the appeal of Jamâl-ud-din Syed concerning his marriage, and had appointed the next Friday audience for the hearing of proof concerning the same; so much was certain. But would he really go back on his own order? Could a King possibly own himself in the wrong? If he did, what became of his claim to divine guidance, and how could folk in the future live content on his judgment? Had a body ever heard of the Learned-in-the-Law eating their own words? No! they stuck to them; in that way lay safety, confidence, authority.

And what was this still more vague rumour concerning the King's Luck, the diamond which had of a surety been his talisman these many years? Was it really to be given to the foreigner to hack and hew?

This was a question which disturbed more than the populace, which brought anxiety to the most highly cultured mind in Fatehpur Sikri.

"If it be true," said the Right Reverend Vicar of Christ, Father Ricci, head of the Portuguese Mission in Goa, who had come up to Agra on one of his periodical visits to the little colony of Christians to whom Akbar gave patronage and protection, "if indeed this diamond, whose worth is the ransom of a world, be given into these Englishmen's hands, it is time we bestirred ourselves, son Rudolfo; and thou must press the King yet once again for some speedy answer on his politics."

Pâdré Rudolfo, the Jesuit who for long years had lived at court, hoping against hope for the King's definite conversion to Christianity, spending himself body and soul in good works, good example, sighed uneasily.

"Sure, my father, the grace of God must work in the end--and Akbar is so close to the Kingdom! In tolerance alone----"

Father Ricci interrupted him sharply:

"It is anathema! He tolerates all faiths, all things, even these new Englishmen who at best are heretics."

"One at least is good Catholic," interrupted Pâdré Rudolfo mildly. "He was at the Mass in the Palace Chapel this morning."

The Superior of his order frowned. "See you, then, that he remains within the influence of Holy Church. These Englishmen must gain no foothold here. As for the King, I will write from Goa threatening your removal--for surely he hath great regard for you, as you for him. Yet I say to you that despite his good qualities, his justice, his forgiveness until seventy times seven, Akbar is a stumbling block in our way. Prince Salîm might serve our purpose better--our purpose, which is Christ's," he added hastily as if to rectify any possible confusion of meaning. Yet the meaning *was* confused, for the world holds few stories more strangely complex than the tale of the Jesuits' struggle between greed of gold and greed of souls, which for close on a century found arena in the court of the Great Moguls. Tragic it is at times, at others comic, yet pathetic throughout in the certainty that greed of gold must eventually prevail against the greed of souls.

Pâdré Rudolfo sighed again. Long living within reach of Akbar's atmosphere had made him in his turn tolerant and there was always hope; hope that his prayers, his penances, his sleepless nights might at last count for righteousness in the King's long record of hesitation. And yet in his heart of hearts Rudolfo Acquaviva knew that there was no hope, was conscious even of a vague content that there was none; for in the Father's house were there not many mansions, and what was man that he should dictate to God what gave the right of entry to them?

So from the highest to the lowest the passing days brought a sense of strain. To Âtma Devi, however, in her secluded sun-saturated roof, the general unrest did not penetrate to add to the dull distress of her own disturbed mind.

For the joy which had come to her from even the half-jesting recognition of her hereditary claim, had passed before the slow assurance that, as woman, she was helpless to support her rôle of champion, before the certainty which grew with the passing days, that the King had no need of her.

She had discarded her poppy-petal red petticoat for the white robe of the Châran, and with the silver hauberk fitting loosely to her tall slenderness, her long hair unbound circled with a silver fillet, would stand for hours, her hands clasped over the silver-hilted sword, looking out over the low parapet wall across the blue distance. That limited vision of hers held all her world; for the years had obliterated memory of the far-off Central Indian home whence she had been brought while still almost an infant by her father. But one or two scenes of that childish life which had been passed beyond her present outlook remained with her, clear yet dreamlike. The most distinct of these being her surpassing affection for Siyâla, who was now Siyah Yamin. As she thought of this a dull vague wonder possessed her as to what purpose Fate could have had in making their two lives so dissimilar--the one sexless by virtue of her widowhood, the other sexual beyond even womanhood.

Âtma's was a limited mind: her soul groped blindly in the dark, yet found what it sought and held fast to it.

So she waited as patiently as she could, hoping for some means of vindicating her claim to the Châran's place, forgetting not one jot or tittle of the many ceremonials of her race. Even if nothing else came of the King's grace save the permission to challenge the world on his behalf from her secluded silence, that in itself was gain. In one heart, surely, his honour would be held sacred utterly.

She had a quaint companion in her solitude, the *rebeck* player's child Zarîfa. For on the morning after Âtma had taken Birbal to see the musician asleep, with the young girl's flower-face upon his bosom, he had appeared in Âtma Devi's roof, bearing the light burden of the crippled child in his arms, and begged asylum for her during the space of an hour while he went on an errand. But days had passed without his return; so the child had stayed on. Helpless utterly, sustaining life apparently by a mere sup of milk, a mouthful or two of fruit, and sleeping away all the hours of fierce daylight, at dawn and at dusk the soul hidden in the racked, deformed body seemed to be set free from its bonds, and the child would lie with wide-open soft lustrous eyes, smiling and singing to herself. And Âtma Devi as she sate listening would feel peace and content steal over her restlessness, so that as often as not, as the shadows crept over the roof, and the daylight died, the rising moon would find both the child and the woman asleep; Zarîfa in the dark shelter of the slip of a room--whence she seldom stirred since the light seemed to scourge her--Âtma crouching in the corner beside the little lamp which burned ever before the death-dagger of her race.

Birbal, coming at dawn in search, once more, of the *rebeck* player, roused Âtma from such a sleep, and entering while--after unbarring the door at his password "From the King"--she stood rubbing her eyes, was met by such a strong perfume of roses that he turned quickly on her:

"So he is here!" he cried; then looked curiously at her, at the little slip of room. "Within, I suppose," he added, passing to its entrance. But Âtma barred the way.

"It is the child, my lord," she said quickly, "the musician left her with me when he went away. And she is so timid, the very face of a strange man is like a strong light upon her--it scorches and shrivels."

Birbal laughed shortly. He was of the world and knew its evil ways. "So does love," he replied mockingly. "Nay! I find no fault with thee, widow, but call him out--I would see him."

Âtma flushed darkly. "My lord cannot see him; he is not here."

"Nor the child neither? Am I not even to have sight of her pretty face to attest truth?" asked Birbal.

The woman met his jeering smile with a peremptory gesture. "Let my lord sit silent yonder on the parapet," she said, in a voice of command, "and from the darkness he shall hear."

So, closing the door behind her, she called softly, "Sing to me, my bird," and stood listening.

Birbal, idly kicking his heels as he sate, looked over the wall down the sheer drop of a hundred feet or more which ended in the red rock. Just below him, brimming up to the very wall lay the tank which Akbar had lately made as a reservoir for the lower part of the town. Half-hidden in morning mist it reflected the morning sky here and there as the vapour, parting, left its surface clear. And behind the rising mist? Did it reflect nothing but the shifting gray curves above it, or did the cool depths of rock below have their chance to shine mirrored on the water?

Bah! who could tell!

The little roof lay still in the first sunlight. A few pigeons wheeling about overhead sent shifting shadows to chase each other on the purple bricks of wall and floor, and in the topmost branch of the peepul tree whose roots throve beside the tank below, a white-throat was singing its little limited song. So, suddenly, there rose on the cool air of dawn another limited little voice.

Rose leaves wither away so fast?
Is the sun's kiss cold? Is the summer past?
Whither away like shallops at sea
With torn pink sails and never a mast
Whither away so fast?

Sun kisses are warm, and the summers last
But the shadows are calling us dim and vast
So we set our sails like shallops at sea
And drift away without rudder or mast

To the dark that will last
For eternity!

Birbal, artist to his finger tips shivered slightly; Âtma, standing, her hands clasped over the old silver-hilted sword, gave a soft sigh. To both of them the creeping step of the Dark that will last for Eternity, seemed to invade the present, claiming all things.

All things save Love, that essence of the Rose of Life.

"Only the dust of the rose-leaf remains to the heart of the seller of perfumes."

The mystical meaning of the Sufi saying came home for once to Birbal. As usual, he resented the intrusion and stood up ready to go, prepared to jest.

"Farewell, then, widow! God send thee a lover if thou hast not one, since even Châranship to Kings is not sufficient for a woman! Now, wert thou but man thou mightst be true.----"

It was as if the dam of the lake below had suddenly given way, letting loose a flood over the land, and he raised his arm in unconscious self-defence as, like a tornado, Âtma swept upon him, flourishing the sword.

"Lo! Maheshwar Rao, Brahmin, Bhât-bandi!" she cried, giving him all his racial titles, "have a care what thou sayest! Yea! since the long-dead day when Shiv-jee created us from the sweat-drops of his godly brow, and jealous Parvati his wife--womanhood incarnate--exiled us from Paradise because we sang his praises overloud--ever since then we Chârans have been true, whether God makes us man or woman! Dost deny it? Then by the long discipleship of thy upstart race--formed by Parvati to sing her trivial worth--to mine, I do command thee to remember that I am champion to the King. Dost hear, Maheshwar Rao? Does Akbar need aught? Stands his honour firm? Lo! if thou speakest not, I die!"

The sword's point clattered on the brick roof, she snatched the death dagger of her race from its altar and stood ready to strike.

"Nay! sister," replied Birbal coolly, for the very heat of her harangue had given him time for calm. "There is no need to die--yet." Here, in a flash, a sudden thought came to him and he settled himself back on the parapet with a faint laugh. Set a thief to catch a thief, a woman to catch a woman! The intensity on this one's face might be useful to him. Having long since constituted himself the eyes and ears, as it were, of Akbar's empire, he had countless emissaries, endless spies, everywhere; but he had not yet employed a woman. It could do no harm to try one where all the cunning of man had failed.

"Sit thee down, sister," he said, after a moment's thought, "and I will tell thee wherein thou canst serve the King's need. Thou knowest Siyah Yamin----"

"What! hath the King need of *her?*" asked Âtma incredulously.

Birbal laughed shortly. "Nay, no one hath need of her; so she must die."

The face opposite his paled. "Wherefore?" she asked briefly.

"Because she may be the undoing of empire," he replied. "Hearken, so thou mayest understand."

"Siyah Yamin," she echoed in a puzzled voice when he had told her of the Syed's appeal and the certainty that the courtesan would swear to having read the Kalma and thus prove the legality of her marriage. "Nay! she cannot swear!"

"Not if a bowstring find her throat first," retorted Birbal viciously; "naught else will stop a woman's tongue, especially if marriage be the subject. Therefore she must be found and--and--lost again! She is in the city; that we know. Where, no one can compass. If thou couldst find out----"

"There is no need," said Âtma slowly; "she--she will not swear!"

Birbal was on his feet with a laugh. "A woman will swear anything for one she loves or hates, and Siyah Yamin hates the King. Whether she love Jamâl-ud-din is another matter. So fare thee well, Âtma Devi championess of Kings. Lo! I have given thee thy Châran chance. As for the *rebeck* player--I shall find him yet!"

After Birbal left, Âtma sate thinking. There was something which she remembered about Siyâla, which little Siyâla, the darling of the Gods, must remember also.

Or would she pretend to forget it? If she did, then she, Âtma, must speak, must protest, if needs be die to witness to it.

Then, if she died it would be death to Siyah Yamin who was Siyâla, sister of the veil.

Âtma roused herself and stood listening. A faint sound of slumbering breath drawn evenly met her ear as she paused at the door of the slip of a room where Zarîfa lay hidden. The child was asleep and could be left for an hour or two at any rate.

Hastily discarding her Châran's dress she put on the poppy-petalled red skirt and veil of the mad singer, so catching up her hourglass drum passed into the street. Her cry,

"*May the Gods pity us, dreamers who dream of their Godhead*"

echoing out into the closed courtyards as she hurried down the narrow alley.

"List! that is Âtma back again," yawned a woman sleepily sitting down to the mill-wheel beside the piled basket of wheat which was to serve for the family breakfast. "I deemed she had been dead these days past. But I will get her to tell me my fortune. What she told Gobind Sâhâi's wife hath come true. She hath twin sons, and praise be to the gods! her husband is not suspicious."

The last item of information was evidently more racy than the first, and the women's voices gossiped over it rising above the hum of the mill wheel.

Âtma meanwhile had made her way straight to the bazaar. Here and there a figure huddled in a white shawl showed wandering outward, water-pot in hand, a seller of milk or two, a woman bearing a heaped basket of green-stuff passed inward, but for the most part the cavernous shops stood closed or empty, for it was yet early hours. A woman blew loudly at a pile of dried leaves under a toasting pan. The little spark left in the charcoal below showed red, then white, amid the gray ashes, and with a roaring crackle the flame leapt upward. A man guiltless of all clothing save a rag, pared his nails solemnly into the gutter. But in the house where Âtma entered all was silent. A medley of musical instruments lay piled on the floor, and in a corner, his head resting on his drum, snored Deena the drum-banger. Âtma passed over to him swiftly and woke him by a touch. The old man started to his feet with commendable activity; then was on the ground again in profuse salaam.

"Now am I saved from sin, mistress most chaste," he began vociferously. "Lo! since I ceased drumming to the deeds of dead kings, I have been a lost soul utterly. I have damned myself by giving time to profligate steps. I have sung lewd songs. But what will ye? A drum ever keeps bad company; being in sooth naught but the devil of a noise that groweth worse instead of better by being whacked----"

"Peace, fool!" said Âtma sternly, "I have need of thee. Where hast been of late?"

Deena sate down and began drumming softly with one finger, an insistent, devilish sort of drumming that seemed created to conceal something. Then he winked a wicked old eye.

"Hal-lal-lal-la-la!" he said gaily. "So old Deena is best gossip-maker to the town. Truly he hears much; for, see you, there is something that brings confidence to scandal in the continuous burring of a drum. It seems to cover all, so folk speak free; and an old ear listens. What dost desire to know, mistress most chaste?"

"Hast heard ought of Siyah Yamin?" asked Âtma readily.

Deena chuckled. "Other folks ask that, my lord Birbal to wit. Hol-lah! The whole town is agog to know news of God knows what--Siyah Yamin, the King's Luck----"

"What of the King's Luck?" interrupted Âtma Devi with a frown.

"Only that he hath given it away as a present to the Queen from over the Black Water of whom the new infidels talk," replied Deena with a yawn, for he had had a night of it at the Lord High Chamberlain's.

The frown deepened. "It is a lie!" she said peremptorily. "The King is no fool; his luck is with him ever. But see--take up thy drum and follow. To-day I will sing of dead kings and listen for the sake of a living one; so I need thy banging."

Deena rose with alacrity. "And my drum needs thee, mistress. 'Tis an evil instrument. But for its hindrance I could sing hymns"--he began one dolorously, then paused shaking his head. "Lo! it hath no discrimination--a holy psalm is even the same to it as a ribald rhyme. Yea! yea! I follow. I will drum to the herald of a live king and forget my sins."

So that day Âtma Devi, the mad singer, reappeared in the city, flitting hither and thither, chanting of dead kings, listening for the sake of a live one.

But she heard nothing; yet as the day drew down she realised that the need of news was urgent; for the whole town talked of Siyah Yamin and the King's Luck.

As she sate in the moonlight on her roof that night she told herself yet once again that if the worst came to the worst she could but die to attest the truth of what she remembered. But then the burden of disproof would be laid on the courtesan, and if she failed she too must die.

Poor little Siyâla! Better far if she could be warned; be persuaded not to affirm this marriage.

"At the tank steps at dawn to-morrow," said Âtma briefly, as late in the evening she parted with Deena at the foot of the stairs. She would do her utmost. Zarîfa could be put to sleep with a pellet of the Dream-compeller; so she would be free to spend every hour in search of Siyah Yamin.

CHAPTER VIII

Dear, the Sun that shines above thee
Spends his gold to see thee, sweet
Let me like those rays that love thee
Kiss the dust about thy feet.

--NIZÂMI.

There was a faint half-kissing sound as of bare feet on a wet marble floor, and a running tinkle of light voices behind the heavy curtain which barred the archway to the inner bathroom; but in the little balconied alcove at the end of the vestibule, where Aunt Rosebody, attired in a vivid rose-coloured wadded silk dressing-gown, sate drying her gray hair in the wind, there was silence, almost sleep.

For the active little old lady still preferred a swim to paddling in scented waters, so she and Umm Kulsum the "Mother of Plumpness," both being of small size, were used to start earlier, in one dhooli, for their morning bathe in the women's screen at the big tank beneath Âtma Devi's house. Being of the frank old Chughtâi type, they were hail-fellow-well-met with the all and sundry who came down to fill their pots or wash on the steps; so nearly every day a gray head and a black one, both sleek from a dive under the screen arches, might be seen slipping sideways in the overhead stroke far beyond the women's limited range.

Now such exercise is fatiguing even when age is set aside so lightly as it was by Aunt Rosebody. Therefore the time of hair-drying was for her a time of repose also; the more so because Umm Kulsum always dried hers whilst picking her daily violet posy for the King. And the other ladies--heaven rest their souls and bodies!--always spent such an unconscionable time over their scented paddlings; while as for the dressings to come, when, fresh from their baths, they all sate in the balconied vestibule to be perfumed, and manicured and massaged--Why! what with the drinking of cool sherbets or hot tea, scented, almost colourless, tasteless, save for the cinnamon flavouring it, these *séances* seemed unending. They were, however, amusing enough, since this was a recognised time for morning callers; primed, of course, with the latest and most vivacious gossip. Nor were the visitors necessarily of the class which nowadays the East--without thereby in the least impugning their respectability--stigmatises as "street walkers";

since the laws governing seclusion are now far more strict than they were in Mogul times.

Besides, there were always the court ladies, and the wives of the Palace officials.

Always indeed! Aunt Rosebody broke off in the faintest of deep breathings, which even by discourtesy would hardly be called a snore, and remarked with drowsy captiousness, "What? again!" when the African slave girl--whom the dear old lady had imported from Mekka as part of her piety--ingeniously roused her slumbering mistress by actually touching her feet in the deep salaam which accompanied the announcement, "Bibi Azîzan, noble wife of my lord Ghiâss Beg, Treasurer, and her daughter Mihr-un-nissa crave audience."

Aunt Rosebody's beautiful wavy gray hair stirred like moon-ripples on water as she shook her head patiently.

"Let her come," she said resignedly, "the others cannot be long now, and, mayhap, if I let her tongue start fair at a gallop, I may finish forty winks ere it slackens to a trot."

Thereinafter, swaying with an odd sidelong waddle of the hips in the fashionable gait which was supposed to emulate the grace of a swan or a young elephant, there came over the marble inlaid floor strewn with silken carpets from Khotan, a truly marvellous figure. Being somewhat stout in the body--though the face, still charmingly pretty was curiously unmarred by fatness or flabbiness--the extremity of the modes in which the figure was dressed did not become the wearer. The graceful dual garment (almost diaphanous but for its exceeding fulness, cut to the ground at the sides, but literally yards long in front and behind) instead of, when swept back by the walk, clinging in soft folds from hip to ankle and lying on the ground behind in a billowing train with no wrong side, was ruckled about the fat legs, and huddled itself confusedly behind them, giving the appearance of a peg-top entangled in a handkerchief!

There was no lack of colour, or stitching, and sewings about the lady. From head to foot she stood confessed as one of the leaders of ladies' fashions, and the jewelled chatelaine at her waist held _kohl_ caskets and rouge-pots, even an unmistakable powder box, while a large mirror set in pearls shone ring-fashion on her thumb.

She salaamed in the very latest court manner to Aunt Rosebody, and came up from the semi-prostration, breathless but complacent, to meet the little old lady's keen eyes fixed on her forehead whereon, just at the parting, was stuck a tiny, round, vermilion wafer.

"What is that?" asked Aunt Rosebody pointing an accusing finger at her. "Hast become a Hindu?"

Azîzan Begum tittered. "La! madam. 'Tis the very latest fashion! One cannot, with respect to oneself and others, appear without it, in----"

"In the Râjpût harem," interrupted the little lady, her tone rising ominously. "Well! 'tis not far distant, Azîz, if thou hast missed the way thither. Just through the door, down the steps, across the yard and thou wilt find plenty of red *tikkas*; but not here!"

"Madam! I protest," expostulated the poor fat fashionable; "I have no desire--and 'tis worn by everybody at court."

"It is not worn here," repeated Aunt Rosebody with cool dignity. "So if the desire to remain finds place in the respected and respectable lady's plans she--she can wash it off! Ooma! a basin of water. Let it be tepid lest the lady should receive a shock--and--and see it be duly scented with scent of flowers; something that will make the respected and respectable lady smell less like a civet cat! 'Tis pity, Azîz, thou dost not keep to rose-essence after taking the trouble to invent it!"

"I protest," murmured the Bibi, seeking support on the floor, and adjusting the set of her veil and her folds generally with the sort of reflex action which exists still in the women of her type--that is to say, hopelessly courtesan despite their excellent wifehood and motherhood-- "'Tis the very latest of my perfumes, and all the latest fashionables--"

The elder woman's face took on seriousness beneath its impatience. "I am not of the latest," she said, "though in truth I be later in life's journey than they. Yet even in my youth"--her sparkling bright eyes roved contemptuously over the other's dress--"I did not clothe myself after--after Satanstown! And thou growest old, Azîzan! Thou hast a daughter--but where is she?--did not they say she was with thee?"

"The child was beguiled bathward by Lady Umm Kulsum whom we met," bridled the Bibi.

"The child?" echoed Aunt Rosebody; "Lo! she will be giving thee dates ere long--ha--ha!"

She chuckled over her own little joke, for the giving of dates is the first step toward a wedding; but the Bibi tossed her head.

"She is but eight, and I protest is quite a babe--not one thought of marriage."

Auntie Rosebody leant back and yawned. "Eleven," she said calmly, "or twelve maybe. 'Tis thirteen since the ill-fated caravan left Persia, and on the way thy child was born. Strange, surely, that such close touch on death as must have been thine ere thou and her father could have left her--as thou didst--to die in the desert, should not have brought thee some sense in life! How about the betrothal to Sher Afkân?"

Bibi Azîzan gave an affected little scream.

"La! there 'tis! Did I not tell her father that if he would insist on sending the country-bumpkin a platter of welcome that the old tale would be revived. La! 'tis too vexing! I could cry; and my sweet poppet whom I long to keep always as my little babe, my perfect innocent! I protest, madam, I would kill any bridegroom."

"Oh fie! marmie!" came a laughing voice behind--"Not Prince Salîm, I will wager!"

Both women looked round with a start to see, holding back the wadded curtain, such a vision of youth and perfect loveliness as the world shows but seldom; yet once having shown does not let men forget. For this small slender Eastern maid, comparable at her eleven years to Western fourteen, was to take her place amongst the beauty which has swayed the destiny of empires.

As she stood backed by the soft embroideries of the curtain, the delicate outline of her still childish figure barely concealed by the silver tinsel veil Umm Kulsum had thrown over her in laughter at her utter nakedness as she had scrambled out of the bath, she showed at once innocent, yet full of guile. There was not one false note in the harmony of her beauty. The cupid's bow of her mouth was curved into a mischievous smile as she looked at her mother half-jibingly, and at Aunt Rosebody half-defiantly.

"Oh! my heart! Oh! what words!" gasped the former, having recourse to her vinaigrette, while the latter looked at her nodding her moonshiny head.

"So!" she said; "So, Azîzan! That lets the cat out of the cupboard!"

But there was no time for more, since through the upheld curtain trooped the bevy of bathers followed by their maids. Then arose such a chatter as to places and pillows, such giggles, such laughter, waxing loudest round Umm Kulsum who, ready dressed, caught the silver tissued maid-ling about the waist, and danced round with her, whirling through the room, feet flying, hair floating, until--quite breathless--she pulled her partner down right on Aunt Rosebody's rug.

The little old lady looked at the perfectly bewitching face, and a smile quivered about her mouth.

"What about the Prince Salîm, child?" she asked accusingly. "What about him?"

Mihr-un-nissa looked arch in return and positively made a *moue* of uncontrollable high spirits before she put on an air of immense and demure propriety.

"Nothing, gracious lady! Am I not betrothed to Sher Afkân Khân?"

Bibi Azîzan let loose an absolute shriek.

"Oh! my liver! Ah! ladies! Heard one ever the like? Mihr-un-nissa how darest thou?--it is not true--it is a lie!"

A curious expression of untamed obstinacy came to the girlish face and gave it a character beyond its years.

"Lo! Marmita!" she said lightly; "when thou and Afkân's mother have settled whether I be betrothed or no, there may be talk of truth. Till then I marry no one."

Bibi Azîzan subsided helplessly, limply, amongst her cushions. To say more might only induce the *enfant terrible*, of malicious intent, still further to reveal the family strife; so there was room for Umm Kulsum's tactful raillery.

"What! thou wilt be an old maid like me! And without even a pilgrimage to thy credit! Fie! Thou art too pretty for Jehannum!"

Mihr-un-nissa laughed scornfully. "I would rather Jehannum on my own feet than Paradise on a man's coat-tails. La! la! I hate men folk!"

There was a general gurgle of laughter. The girl's face grew crimson-dark; her eyes filled with tears, yet flashed also and she held her ground.

"'Tis true," she cried, stamping her bare foot with an almost soundless yet curiously imperative smack on the marble floor. "I hate them--they think of nothing but themselves--and--and women! And I hate women too--I want to be a Queen, and I *will* be one!"

"Come hither, child, and let me look at thee," said Auntie Rosebody, suddenly holding out her hand. The supple young thing crossed to her proudly, and crouching low touched the small fine old fingers with her forehead.

"Thine eyes, child--thine eyes!" said the old woman. "Let me see thy fate in them."

So for an instant's space the great lustrous soft depths of Mihr-un-nissa's fathomless eyes were appraised.

"She might keep him--as he should be kept," murmured Auntie Rosebody to herself; but Mihr-un-nissa was thinking of the queenship.

"What does the Most Beneficent see?" she asked eagerly. "Shall I be Queen?--Queen myself I mean--real Queen?"

There was an instant's pause and in the silence which hung over the whole room the imperious young voice seemed to linger. Then Umm Kulsum, seeing a look of sudden recoil in Aunt Rosebody's face, laughed cheerfully.

"Ask the witch wives, Mihro, not us! Or stay! Lo Auntie! dost remember the red woman with her curious cry whom we saw at the tank steps but now, and bade come hither, since she claimed to be the royal bard? She is Brahmin and tells the stars, she said. Let us have her in if she is here and then Mihro can hear fortunes."

"La!" cried Bibi Azîzan catching at any side escape from what had gone before, "I can tell the ladies who the woman is. She is mad--quite mad--and----"

"The more suitable for this subject of Queenship," remarked Aunt Rosebody dryly, twisting her hair deftly to a topknot which greatly enhanced her dignity. "Ooma! see if one Âtma, singer of pedigrees, soothsayer, heaven knows what, waits without. If so, bid her enter. And bring me a violet sherbet such as my father--may peace be his always!--loved when he was aweary of fools; then Bibi Azîzan can have her say in peace!"

After which Parthian shot she sipped her sherbet in silence. She was inwardly amused at the cat which Mihr-un-nissa--an enchanting piece truly!--had so wilfully and deftly let out of the cupboard. In truth there was some excuse for such vaulting ambition in the child's extraordinary beauty. Pity she had not been a few years older--pity nephew Akbar would not put pleasure first and politics second in Salîm's marriage--pity! Ah! pity in so many things.

"May the Gods pity us, dreamers who dream of their Godhead!"

The old lady started at the quaintly apposite cry which seemed indeed to force the whole vestibule into a second's silence.

Âtma Devi stood at the far arches, her poppy-petal dress showing for an instant brilliant in the glimpse of sunlight let in by the upraisal of the curtain.

In truth her entry brought a new note to the chord of womanhood which vibrated in the atmosphere; a note that was foreign to its harmony. A quick sense of tragedy came to the comedy of laughing ladies. Something in Âtma's womanly face and figure that was in them also, disguised, tucked away, hidden out of sight but still recognisable made them recoil to silence. Perhaps it was the "Not womanhood" of the dark days before Sex shows itself--the Not-womanhood which, with the "Not-manhood," go to make up the Paradise Life in which there shall be neither male nor female.

Âtma felt the recoil herself as her dark eyes questioned the scene before them, challenging it in swift antagonism. For the past two days her thoughts had been concentrated on her search for some clue of Siyah Yamin. She had drifted about the bazaars, giving her curious cry, she had watched at street corners, and listened patiently through the hurly-burly of passing voices for some hint, some sound. Without avail; and time was running short; she would not have wasted one minute of it in obeying Aunt Rosebody's order to attend at the palace but for a dazed sense of duty. She, the King's Châran, must not neglect royal commands; even Siyah Yamin must give way to them.

Siyah Yamin! Siyah Yamin! Ye Gods! why had either of those two children who had played together, grown up to be women? Why should any woman-child grow up to be hampered by her sex, left helpless?

Âtma's thoughts as she stood mechanically shaking the hour-glass drum, paused; her eyes in the darkness to which they were becoming accustomed had found something which brought answer to her questioning.

It was Mihr-un-nissa, who, barely veiled by silver tissue, sate a little way apart from the others on a yellow silken rug; her slender arms were around her knees, her head was tilted back against the wall on which a flower garland of the inlaid mosaic seemed to frame her delicate face, as through half-closed lids she returned the singer's stare.

"Art thou a witch-wife?" asked the little maid suddenly, as if none but they two were in the room. "Lo! I am Mihr-un-nissa, Queen of Women. Tell me--shall I indeed be Queen not of them only, but of men also?"

The brushers and dressers paused in their avocations to look and listen. Something insistent, compellent, seemed to have come into the atmosphere. Even Auntie Rosebody paused in the sipping of her sherbet and waited for the answer to that still-childish voice.

And those two stared at each other, feeling vaguely akin; the woman who strove to forget her sex in a man's work, the girl who cherished it as a means of gaining a like power.

"I offer excuse for interference," came Râkiya Begum's rasping voice, "but soothsaying except by reference to the Holy Book----"

"'Tis but for fun, Most Noble," pleaded Umm Kulsum, who was invariably the smoother of difficulties, "and they did it at the Holy City, for I paid seven golden *ashrafees* to a woman with a crystal who told me naught that I did not know before."

The little ripple of surrounding laughter did not soften Râkiya Begum's sternness.

"A crystal," she said severely, taking a pinch of snuff, "is different. That hath, as all know, its gift of God in certain hands; but the looking at grains of rice and the counting of pease-pods is irreligious, and most derogatory to true believers. Therefore in the absence of our Lady Hamida----"

The acerbity of this allusion to an occasionally divided headship in the harem was interrupted hastily by a twitter from the elder Salîma who addressed her daughter nervously.

"In truth dear heart, Ummu, 'twere better not mayhap--the woman is Hindu."

Mihr-un-nissa, her head still tilted back against the garlanded wall, looked through her lashes, and her cupid's bow of a mouth smiled bewilderingly.

"I mind not that one fly's weight," she remarked cheerfully, casually, as if her likings or dislikings were the only question at issue, "Come good red woman, begin! My fortune, please!"

Âtma hesitated. Here was a household divided against itself, and beyond Auntie Rosebody and Umm Kulsum, whose status she knew, she was unaware of the position of the scented, languidly laughing ladies around her. Yet a false step might be fatal to future right of entry. It was a time for swift, decisive action.

"I tell no fortunes," she replied. "I look only in the magic mirror after the fashion that a pious pilgrim of Mahomed taught my father, and if God sends a vision, I see!"

It was a fortunate hit. Râkiya Begum sate stiff with excitement. "Not the magic mirror of ink, such as is used in Room? Lo! ladies! this is a chance indeed! and I, at the moment, in one of my-poor verses was using it as an allegory for the vast enlargement of the mind by literature! Good woman! Let us see the process without delay. What dost require?"

Âtma's native wit was equal to the occasion. "A drop of ink from the inkpot of the poetess must bring visions," she replied readily, and Khânum

Râkiya Begum smiled her approval. So the inkpot came and Âtma, her full red skirts billowing about her, sank to the ground opposite Mihr-un-nissa whose bare limbs, the colour of freshly garnered wheat overlaid with a faint tinsel sheen, showed almost white in contrast with the intensity of the scarlet. Then holding the inkpot high in her right hand the Châran began to sing softly:

Drop, ink! and hide my flesh
Cover my worldly ways
Then let God's Light afresh
Mirror God's praise
Drop ink! Drop deep
Cover in Sleep
My Night of Nights and bring the Day of Days.

A little pool of ink lay, with curved surface like a dewdrop, on her left palm as the song ceased.

"If the gracious child will almost touch the mirror with her left forefinger and complete the circle of magic by touching my right arm with her right hand," she suggested in a mysterious monotonous voice.

For answer Mihr-un-nissa's firm little fingers closed round her wrist tightly. "Aye! it shall not stir," she said coolly. "I want to know for certain-- no clouds and waves and mists--I want to know. Dost hear?"

Childishly imperative her eyes questioned Âtma's. "Nay!" replied the latter, feeling in a measure at bay. "The gracious maid must close her eyes. I, Âtma, will look alone into the mirror and see--if God wills--the fortune of the Princess."

Aunt Rosebody's laugh came sudden, sarcastic.

"Not Princess yet, woman! Not as yet," she continued, turning to Bibi Azîzan, "even in the inmost heart of the house of Ghiâss Beg, the Lord Treasurer."

"I protest," began the fat fashionable one feebly.

Âtma gave a swift glance round at the speakers and the little pool of ink in her palm wavered despite Mihr-un-nissa's almost fierce grip.

"How now, slave?" cried the latter; "I said no wavering."

"There shall be none, Highness," replied Âtma bending her brows over her task again. But the mention of Ghiâss Beg's name had brought back the thought of Siyah Yamin. For the only clue of any sort which the two days of search had given to Âtma was a possible connection between the Lord High Treasurer's House and that of the Syeds of Bârha.

They were distantly related by marriage. It was the faintest of clues but the thought of it filled Âtma's mind in an instant with a pressing desire.

Siyah Yamin! Siyah Yamin! She must be found! Time was passing! The very next morning the Audience would be held.

Siyah Yamin! Siyah Yamin----

"I see naught," she went on monotonously, forcing herself to words foreign to her thoughts--"I see, I see--what do I see? A crowd of banners waving. 'Tis a marriage procession! And lo! the bridegroom--Ohé! like the young Krishn for beauty--tall, slim, and fair."

"Thou liest," came Mihr-un-nissa's voice full of passion. "Thou dost not see it. Thou dost not----"

As she spoke she flung up the wrist she held so roughly that the ink drops spurted over Âtma's scarlet dress; then, with a sudden bound, she stood confronting her, a tornado in silver tissue. "Lo! I was looking too, and I saw no crowd, no banners, no bridegroom. All I saw was Siyah Yamin playing on the lute as she played last night when----"

She broke off with a sudden dismay, then laughing round defiantly to her mother went on recklessly:

"There! I have let that musk-rat go! but I did see her, Marmita, just as she sate last night when you and she----"

Bibi Azîzan's shriek drowned the rest.

Then came Auntie Rosebody's voice of horror; "Siyah Yamin! At--at thy house, Azîzan! This passes indeed! Go, woman, and venture hither no more!"

"I offer excuse," remarked Râkiya Begum who had risen and come forward in sedate annoyance. Her stiff brocaded petticoat looked almost regal, but her thin angular body still suffered from lack of attire, and her veillessness showed her scanty hair screwed back tightly, ready for subsequent additions. Withal she had a certain dignity of thin, harsh, high features and scraggy uprightness. "That question, Khânzada Gulbadan Kkânum is, as the lawyers have it, *sub-judice*. To-morrow the King decides."

"Decides!" echoed Auntie Rosebody wrathfully. "And if he does decide!--what then? You can't beat a drum with one hand, and all the other five fingers are in the butter! No! No! Marry her fifty times, Siyah Yamin *is*

Siyah Yamin. You can't hide an elephant under a hencoop. So there! That's my say!"

Râkiya Begum took a pinch of snuff. "And I say nothing. A wise man learns to shave upon strangers."

Meanwhile Mihr-un-nissa, her swift anger passing into amused wonder, stood looking at the ink spots on the scarlet dress, until suddenly her cupid's-bow mouth curved itself into a smile.

"'Twas thy fault," she said nodding her head. "Thou must have been thinking of her, for I saw her clear; but see--that for thy spoilt dress!"

She tore off a gold bangle from her arm and held it out. They were standing close together, almost unobserved, the rest of the company being more interested in crowding about the discussion which still went on regarding Siyah Yamin.

"Why wilt not take it?" continued the little maiden stamping her foot, as Âtma Devi drew back.

"Because I want a bigger boon," she replied hurriedly, seizing her chance.

"A greater boon?" echoed Mihr-un-nissa curiously.

"Aye!" almost whispered Âtma Devi. "If the gracious child--in truth her head well deserves a crown--would take this in exchange for me," she hastily wrenched off a thin silver band-bracelet all too small for the matured wrist on which it was worn. "Take it to Siyah Yamin--it--it is hers. See! there is her name upon it."

She pointed to a word engraved on the bracelet. Mihr-un-nissa took it and stood holding it, her unfathomable eyes full of malicious contempt. "So! there is a mystery! La! I love mysteries--they are so easy to guess! Yea! I will give it--and find out! Is there any message?"

"None."

The childish face broke into almost sinister smiles. "Then the bracelet means the message! What is it? Come, or go? No matter! I will find out!"

She slipped the bracelet round her own slender wrist and turned away nonchalantly, a veritable Queen of Women.

CHAPTER IX

Fling back thy veil, Beloved! Lo! how long

Shall it avail

To hide thy womanish nature, and so wrong

Thy beauty frail.

"Is it thou, Siyâla?"

Âtma holding the cresset high peered out into the darkness of the stair.

A tinkle of soft laughter came from the shadows. "So! thou hast not forgotten the old signal, Âto! yet it was years agone that I gave thee the bracelet, and thou gavest me thine. Still have I come for the sake of it! That is enough, Yasmeen! I stay here till an hour ere dawn; then fetch me."

The last was called in a low voice down the darkness and thereinafter followed the sound of retreating steps; yet still no figure showed in the circle of cresset light.

"Wilt not come in Siyâl?" said Âtma impatiently, "if by chance someone came and found us women----"

Another tinkle of laughter rose from the shadows and out of them stepped swaggering a slender youth, the very print and spit of fashion, made taller by a high-wound turban, his hand on the jewelled scimitar stuck in his tight-wound girdle.

"They would say that Âtma Devi had found a proper lover," laughed the masquerader. "La! Âtma, on my soul I do love thee!--thou art so monstrous serious, and thy large eyes have a fire in them. Be mine, sweet widow!"

"Peace, Siyâl! This is not time for jesting. Come in and let me shut the door. I have matters of privacy to say."

"Say on," retorted the other gaily, "but not here. And call me not Siyâl! I am thy true lover Sher-Khân. In truth, Âtma," here the voice changed to seriousness, "this disguise was necessary, seeing where I bide! In God's truth we bazaar women have to go for trickery to the chaste zenânas. I had but to tell Yasmeen I wished to go out and this"--she touched her costume--"was forthcoming *instanter.* Lo! I shall doubt every likely lad I see for the future as myself disguised!--who knows, indeed, but what I was born to be a man! Come sweetheart, I cannot talk here! Come with thy Sher-Khân."

She stepped forward and laid her hand on Âtma's wrist.

"Whither?" asked the latter, feeling as she looked at the feminine face set in masculine clothes the nameless charm of the woman in the man, the man in the woman. "And wherefore?"

The answer came short and sharp. "Because if I am missed they will seek me here first. Mihr-un-nissa knows, and she--she has no mercy when she feels power! We will go to my paradise. I have the key still. Lord! How I shall love it after this past fortnight of a virtuous cage! Lo! the dew of heaven is not a satisfying drink! So"--she snatched at the cresset, "follow me, sister--sweetheart--widow if thou wilt--woman any way! Bah! how dark it is--truly they say 'the torchbearer sees not his own steps.'"

Thus chattering in shrill whispers, she led the way. A key rattled in a lock; there were more stairs, then another door opened and they stood in Siyah Yamin's paradise.

A deserted paradise indeed! Dark, almost dreadful in its unseenness, with only a rustle as of dead, dried flowers and leaves coming to them with the faint breeze which blew in their faces from the darkness. A faint scent, as of withered blossoms came with it.

Siyah Yamin closed the door with a bang, burst into a perfect cascade of laughter, and then, out of sheer delight and devilry pirouetted and postured down the central walk singing as she danced a *ghazal* from Hâfiz:

Love! Love! It is Spring
Be thou of joyous heart
Truly the birds will sing
Roses be blossoming
Though we depart!
This is our little day!
This is the hour of play
Ere you and I be clay
Kiss me, my heart!
Kiss me alway.

With the cresset in her hand, its lights and shades falling on the high turban with its waving green ends, on the effeminate embroideries of her dandified dress, and bringing out into filmy clouds the long floating coatee of gold-spangled white muslin worn as a loose overall, she seemed like the very Spirit of Sex, neither male nor female, careless of everything save reckless sensual pleasure.

So, suddenly, the lithe body stooped and from the cresset in her hand one of the many little oil lamplets edging the paths and encircling what had been flower beds ere neglect and noonday suns had left them shrivelled, flickered into flame; then another, and another, and another, as swaying, posturing, singing she danced on into the shadows leaving behind her a pathway as of stars.

Ere she reached the pavilion at the further end and sank breathless amongst its silken cushions, a dim radiance was suffused over the roof showing the withered roses, the trailing dead tendrils of the scented jasmine, the litter of spent blossoms, all the lees and dregs of a past pleasure. The very table, low to the ground, its mother-o'-pearl inlaying all dust-covered, still held a half emptied wine cup or two, a leaf plate of half-rotten fruit.

"Lo! Siyâla!" said Âtma, suddenly looking almost tenderly at her companion, as she lay, bathed in the rosy light of the hanging lamp she had lit, "what art thou in very truth? Sometimes thou seemest to me of the stars; at times thou art very earth."

The courtesan laughed. "I am Woman," she replied, flinging her high turban aside and drawing the loose fallen tresses of her hair through her fingers lazily, settling them in dainty fashion on her shoulders, "I wait as I have waited all the long ages for the Man! Lo! I am ready for his desire. I am the uttermost Nothingness which tempts Form. I am Mâya, illusion and delusion!"

Her voice full of music and charm fell on the ear drowsily.

"And thou, Âtma," she went on, "shall I tell thee what thou art? Thou art that which seeks not--which gives and takes nothing in return. Thou art salvation. Yet thou canst not save--the Woman is too strong for thee. Thou lovest the King!"

The blood flew to Âtma's face. "Thou liest!" she cried hotly.

Siyah Yamin's laugh filled the emptiness of the roof. "Thy denial proves it, sister! Were it not wiser to accept thy womanhood? Ohé! Âtma! there is joy in drawing the strength of a man through his lips!--in making him forget high thoughts--in dragging him down, down to the very depths of--of Nothingness!"

Her small bejewelled hand closed on the empty air; yet Âtma shivered: that emptiness seemed to hold so much. She sate down on the steps and resting her chin on her hand remained crouched in on herself, silent, looking out over the dead roses.

"Lo! here is wine!" came the gay voice. "Pledge me in it, Âtma! Does not Hâfiz say 'the cloister and the wine shop are not far apart?' No more is thy woman's love from my woman's love. Why shouldst thou try to make it man's love?"

My love is a burning fire,
And aloe-wood is my heart,
The censer is my desire,
Oh me! how I shrivel and smart!
Yet the flame mounts higher and higher:
Oh! love depart!
Make not a funeral pyre
Of censer and heart.

The trivial song ceased. Siyâla slipping from her cushions had slidden toward Âtma, and now, her chin resting on the latter's broad shoulder, was looking up at the brave steady face with cajoling menace in her eyes.

"Why, and what willst thou, Âto? There is no third way. Woman must be as I--the eternal Nothingness which Something sought in the beginning; sought, tempted by the desire for Form; which men seek now tempted by the Woman Form they have made! Tempted by me, the courtesan, who drains the good from them and flings it sterile on the dust heap of the world! Or they must be as thou art not: instinct with Motherhood, draining the soul of man to hand it on in ceaseless conflict of sex, of Form and Matter through the ages. But thou, Âto? Thou wouldst be neither! Thou art mother of the past, not of the future. Thou wouldst stand aside and give the man part of thee--'tis in all women even in Siyah Yamin--thou wouldst give this man part which has come to thee through thy fathers, back all untouched by thy womanhood to the man thou lovest! Fool! There is no such love for us womenkind!"

"There thou tellest truth, Siyâl," said Âtma coldly. "It is not love. Did I not tell thee so? But I came not here for this. We must speak and speak quickly."

So the two women, half seen in the suffused light of the empty roof, sate talking while the little lamplets twinkled like stars, and every here and there one, growing short of oil, flickered and went out leaving a gap of darkness.

"Three!" counted the courtesan with a yawn as the mellow echoing notes of the city gongs chimed through the night. "'Tis time I were gone!"

She caught up her turban, coiled her long hair beneath it, thus stood transformed at once into effeminate manhood. "And Sher-Khân," she continued swaggering, "hath not had even one kiss--sweet widow!--the perfume of thy hair is wrapped round my living soul----"

"Peace, Siyâl," said Âtma, who risen, stood sombre, thoughtful. "Then I can do no more. I have warned thee. If thou swearest, I will speak."

"And I will deny--what then?"

"Then is my death----"

Siyah Yamin burst into a peal of laughter.

"Death! Trust the men folk--aye!--Trust the King to put a spoke in that wheel! A woman is a woman, and thou art too good looking! Lord! I shall laugh to see it, and thou so serious. Come! let us drink to our success before we go."

She seized an empty wine cup, then stood looking at it for a second, checked by the sight of it. It was a blown glass goblet damascened with gold. She held it to the light, her small child's face grown suddenly soft. "The cup of pleasure," she murmured to herself. "How long is it since *he* gave it!" So, with a laugh, she filled it to the brim from a flagon that stood near.

"Thy health, Âto, and thy lover's!" she cried lightly. "Lo! he who gave the cup was mine once; but Siyah Yamin will never lack for men, since she is woman!"

She raised the cup to her lips but did not touch it, then, with a sudden gesture flung it far into the shadows. It fell with a crash beside a withered rose bush, and the red wine trickled through the dry earth to moisten the roots below.

"Come, Âtma." she continued. "Nay! leave the lights as they are. They will outlast the stars anyhow!"

A minute later Siyah Yamin's paradise held nothing but the twinkling lights flickering out one by one. Yet she was right. The rising sun found some of them burning bravely and the rose-shaded lamp in the pavilion shone persistently on the silken cushions as if seeking for some one; perhaps for her.

*   *   *   *   *

The palace was early astir that morning, and little knots of men waited gossiping in corridor and vestibule.

"It is not politic," sighed Abulfazl, "the common folk well ask who is God's vice-regent on earth if a King's order is no order."

"'Tis the devil's own foolery," spoke up Birbal roughly, bitterly, "the long beards wag loosely already, and if Akbar gives them a field they will take a barn."

And in truth a certain ill-defined smirk sate on the concealed lips of the learned doctors of the law who stood in a bevy near the door. To them even consideration of the vexed question was a distinct score. It was a confession that the usurper of their office did not know his business.

To the general public assembling in force it was an occasion for curiosity; for something new which might pave the way to almost anything. Only the Syeds, their hawk faces clustering close together, their hands clutching at their sword belts, seemed certain of the future.

A burst of the royal kettledrums in the distance echoed finally over a dense crowd, packing the wide arches of the huge Hall-of-Audience, and stretching beyond them into the paved courtyard.

"If he wear the Luck still, it will be something to go by," muttered a weak-looking courtier, who by his very dress--curiously nondescript--his shaven chin and high green turban showed a desire to run with the hare and hunt with the hounds.

There were many such in Akbar's empire; men whose imaginations went so far with the King, yet whose hearts failed them before the strangeness of his dreams.

Another long, loud burst of wild music, and the King showed alone on the high raised dais, canopied and latticed at the sides with fretted marble, which opened at the back into the private passage reserved for Royal use only. By reason of the limited space in which he stood--the central archway rising but a few inches above his head--he looked larger, taller, broader than his wont, and as he glanced keenly over the packed multitude before him, he showed every inch a king. Yet he was conscious that he, alone of all his empire, saw strength, not weakness, in his readiness for reconsideration; that he, only, felt that the revocation of his order would be a greater display of kingly power than the original order itself.

Standing as he did in shadow, it took the crowd a silent second or two before it realised--what to it was a stupendous fact--that in this critical new departure of their King's he was prepared to defy Fate. He had deserted his luck. The tight wound turban of royalty did not show the dull glow of the great diamond.

A sort of shiver ran through the Hall, checked by the King's voice.

"Are the suitors and the witnesses in the case present?" he asked.

Abulfazl, stepping into the wide open square kept clear before the railed dais, replied in the affirmative.

"Then proceed."

The sing-song voice of the court reader filled the hushed air, but from outside, beyond the red-toothed arches, came the morning song of many birds. The sunlight filtered in with the song, making Akbar's attention wander. How trivial these petty questions of rights and wrongs seemed beside the great questions of Life in itself.

"Bring forward the woman. Let her swear that she is true and lawful wife."

The crowd swayed at the back. A domed red dhooli showed forcing its way to the front.

"Room! Room!" cried the ushers. "Room! Room! for the virtuous."

If it was virtuous, there was still something in the very fall of the swinging silk curtains, in the lift of the liveried bearers, which set men's pulses a-bounding. For it was Siyah Yamin's dhooli and she was inside. Would she unveil? Would they see her again, uttermost mistress of art, absolute owner of guile? A faint sigh of disappointment seemed to shudder through the crowd as, in obedience to order, the bearers set down the dhooli and removed the red domed cover, thus disclosing a muffled figure which rose and salaamed low toward Akbar. Something there was of ultimate grace in the salutation, which made remembrance still more clear, and sent a pang of resentment through many of those present that this perfection should no longer be public property. A cupola of chastity indeed! screened and guarded by veiled duennas! Not one in faith, but two! It was preposterous!--Siyah Yamin! the darling of the town!

"Woman!" came Akbar's voice, "wilt thou swear that thou art lawfully wedded to the exiled Jamâl-ud-din, Syed of Bârha?"

There was an instant's pause, then a gay clear voice with a bubble of laughter in it replied:

"Yea! I swear! even though Âtma---- Where art thou, sister? Disguised as yon duenna, I'll go bail!"

At her first word there was a faint scuffle, a flinging aside of a *burka*, a silver flash, and almost ere she ended the Châran's cry rang out

It is a lie
I, Âtma, I
Give it the lie
Ye Bright Ones see me die
Avenge the lie!

The death-dagger of Âtma Devi's race rose high in the air above the silver fillet on her loosened hair, and the next moment it would have been buried in the heart beneath the silver hauberk had not a man's voice--not kingly at all in its hurried command--cried quickly:

"Hold her!"

As she staggered back, her balance gone by Birbal's swift arrest of the blow, a mocking voice fell on her ear.

"Did I not tell thee so, sister! Thou art too good-looking for death!"

It had all passed so quickly that folks were still almost incredulously craning to see, when sudden silence came to that group on the clear square before the dais. To Siyah Yamin, muffled in her chaste veil, to Âtma Devi with her bare defiance, to Birbal's eager acute face as he still held back that hand with the dagger.

"Speak! What hast thou to say?" said the King through the silence.

"This," came the reply, clear, resolute, as Âtma Devi drew from out her bosom a folded paper. "It was the death word of the King's Châran."

"Take it and read," said the King, and Abulfazl stepping forward, took the paper. His practised voice sounded sonorously through the wide hall.

"Avenge the lie for which I die. Siyah Yamin is Siyâla, daughter of Gokal, Brâhmin, of Chandankaura, Râjpûtana. We are sisters of the veil. I saw her married with the Seven Steps and the Sacrificial Fire to the death-dagger of my race which grants no divorce. She is Bride of the Gods for ever and ever and ever. The Gods curse him who steals her from them. Ye Bright Ones avenge the lie!"

"Is this true, woman?" asked the King, sternly.

From behind the veil came the gay mocking voice, "Let her prove it."

By this time the first shock of surprise was over, and men had begun to turn to each other, questioning and appraising the validity of Âtma's plea.

"And even if she can prove it, Oh! Most-Illustrious," began Budaoni, who from his translating work was cognisant of Hindu customs, "even if this evil woman was dedicated to the Gods, what then? She has read the creed, she hath become Musulman--she is duly married."

"If the Most-Illustrious will hear me," put in Birbal bowing low--"hear me, Bhât, Brâhmin, as one with knowledge and authority, I will tell the Most-Just that this is no ordinary dedication of a girl to the service of the Gods. *Deva-dasis* there be--aye! even those married to a dagger or a basil plant, on whom rests no life-long, death-long tie. But this is not of those!-- Married with the Seven Steps to a Châran's death-dagger! Accursed be he--- -"

"Accursed be thou, Hindu!" cried a voice from the crowd, and in an instant hands found sword-hilts and faces grew fierce.

"Sire! He is right," called Râjah Mân Singh. "The woman belongs to the Gods--who claims her, takes her through my body!"

"Idolater!" rose an answering sneer, "what Islâm claims is God's!"

But behind these voices in the packed mass of the crowd, men looked at each other dubiously; Hindu at Mahommedan, Mahommedan at Hindu. Should they claim this woman or let her go?

"If this slave may offer opinion," came Abulfazl's sonorous voice above the growing clamour, "the question must wait for proof."

"Enough!" said Akbar sternly. He had been standing with bent brows staring at Âtma, and at the veiled figure beside her, lost in thought. Then he turned to Birbal. "On thee, Maheshwar Rao, called by me Birbal, the burden of inquiry shall rest. Speak. As thou wilt answer to thy Gods, if what yon woman"--he pointed to Âtma Devi--"says be true, would this marriage to the dagger hold against all others?"

Quick and sharp came the answer. "The marriage is inviolable, sacred for Time and for Eternity."

"Then there must be proof. What proof hast thou?" His voice softened slightly with the words.

Âtma Devi standing tall and straight flung her left arm skyward. "I have none! None; save my own word. I saw it--we were children and I cried because she left me. Yea! I remember the bitterness of my tears."

There was a sudden gay laugh from the veilings at her side, a sudden wreathing and curving of draperies, and in an instant the woman within them stood revealed; revealed, not as the late wedded bride, not even as Siyah Yamin the courtesan, but as Siyâla the dancing girl of the Gods. Her nut-brown body, bare save for the tiny gold-encrusted bodice following each swelling line of her bosom, rose, seductively supple, from the innumerable fulnesses of the thin white muslin skirt which after clinging close to the loveliness of curve from hip to knees, fulled out like a bursting flower weighted by its heavy banding of gold tissue. She wore no veil, but her loose flowing hair was wreathed with jasmine chaplets, and round her neck, floating with each exquisite movement of her arms, was a multi-coloured gossamer silk scarf, rainbow hued, evanescent, ever-recurring, holding in its loopings, its doublings, something of the absolute grace of a coiling serpent.

And through the wide hall packed full of men instinct with anger, malice, hatred, and all uncharitableness, there ran, swiftly, at the mere sight of her, a common admiration, a common tremor of fear and hope.

Even the King stepped back from her pure womanhood.

"Lo! Weep not Âto! Wherefore should any weep; when all life is for laughter!" she said, and her polished voice sounded mysteriously sweet. "Great King! she says truth. I am Siyâl belovéd of the Gods, beloved of the Godhead in the man. I am no man's wife. I am no man's mistress. I am free to have and hold."

She flung both arms forward to the crowd and the rainbow scarf leaping up formed a halo round her head.

"Come! Come!" she murmured deeply, almost drowsily, "but seek not to bind. Or ever you were, I was. Yet I am yours!" Her eyes flashed down upon those liveried bearers of her dhooli, servants of her courtesanship. "Raise me shoulder high, slaves," she cried, "so that all may see Siyâl the Belovéd of the Gods, the beloved by men."

So shoulder high she stood smiling while a hoarse passionate breath surged through the vast assembly.

And then, suddenly, she set up the oldest chant in the world, the golden jingles about her feet clashing to its rhythm, the heavy gold bracelets sliding and clashing on her arms as she waved them in the dance of the devaad-asi--

I am the dancer Prakrit,
The wanton of change and unrest,

And the sound of my dancing feet
Roused the Sleeper self-em-meshed,
And the eyes that were blind with peace
Looked out and saw I was sweet,
So the worlds whirled to my feet
And Life grew big with Increase.
Death danced in the arms of Birth
And Tears were coupled with Mirth
And Cold things hurried to Heat
And Heat to Flame and Fire,
Till the whole world, racked with desire,
Kept time to my dancing feet.

"Prakrit! Prakrit!"

She paused in her swift twirling and the long sinuous end of her silken scarf which had floated round her undulating, almost alive in its likeness to the clutching creeping arm of an octopus, hovered in the air for a second then fell on her outstretched arm in delicate desireful folds.

Something like a faint sigh breathed through the audience. There was no other sound. Every man was spellbound, as swaying, posturing, yielding, she went on, allure in her eyes, her voice--

I am the Woman Prakrît,
The Keeper and Wanton of Sex,
And the clash of my dancing feet
Is a lure that ruins and wrecks.
Men's lips touch mine and desire
The Nothingness that is sweet,
And their souls flock to my feet
To die in a kiss of fire.
And I give them Death for Life,
And I bring them Sorrow and Strife,
As I suck their senses away
As they follow and follow for aye
The fall of my dancing feet.

Prakrît! Prakrît!

"Prâkrîti!--Prâkrîti!--Prâkrîti!"

The answering cry came multitudinously. But on it came the voice of the King.

"Syeds of Bârha! Do you claim this woman or shall she go?"

There could be but one answer, with that unveiled, unabashed figure, challenging every eye, flaunting before all men, making their very bodies and souls thrill to the cadence of her dancing feet.

The Syeds' hands felt their sword hilts sullenly, but their spokesman had no choice of words.

"Let her go. We of Bârha harbour no harlots--no idolaters."

So through the audience, in obedience to her sign, the servants of her courtesanship carried her, seated, discreetly smiling, decorously salaaming. But once outside, the crowd which followed her to Satanstown caught up the song she had sung and bellowed it to the skies, filling the lanes and byways with the tale which, told so many ways, brings the mind back at last to the beginning of all things--to the "Sleeper sleeping self-em-meshed."

As the procession passed a narrow turn, two men dressed as natives, almost of native complexion, yet of such curious dissimilarity of features from the crowd around them that the eye picked them out instinctively as strangers, stood back on a high piled doorstep to escape the crush.

"*Vadre retro Satanas*" muttered the taller of the two, crossing himself and thus giving a glimpse of a violet ribbon on his breast hung with the Portuguese Order of Christ. Its white cross charged upon a red one glistened for an instant in the sun like silver.

They were Jesuit missionaries, and the smaller of the two, as he watched, crossed himself also and murmured under his breath, "God help us! She is like a Madonna!"

And, in truth, Siyah Yamin silent, possibly fatigued by the excitement, seated with her childish face upraised, her eyes seemingly full of wistful thought fixed on vacancy, as if somewhere out of sight lay something very precious, looked innocent enough to touch that other pivot of feminine life, Motherhood.

And I give them Death for Life,
And I bring them Sorrow and Strife,
And I suck their senses away
As they follow and follow for aye
The fall of my dancing feet.

Prakrît! Prakrît!

The chorus bellowed out to the skies, as the procession swept on, leaving Father Ricci and Father Rudolpho Acquaviva to continue their way to the little mission chapel which Akbar had built for them.

So they went on their way, while in lessening sound came the chorus which holds the Secret of the Sin for which all religions promise forgiveness.

It brought a vague, throbbing restlessness to the hot air.

CHAPTER X

Opportunity flies, O brother.
As the clouds that quickly pass.
Make use of it now, for another
Will never be yours, Alas!

--HAFIZ.

"Birbal! Lo! It is always Birbal. May God's curse light on him for an infidel!"

Prince Salîm's young, sullen face lowered gloomily, he flung aside the half-tasted sweetmeat he had taken from the golden basket which was always held within his reach by a deaf and dumb slave.

"Ameen!" murmured Mirza Ibrahîm piously.

Khodadâd who in the *petit comite* of the Heir-Apparent's innermost circle of friends was enjoying the newly imported luxury of smoking, puffed a cloud into the scented air, smiled, bowed gravely; finally yawned. In truth the Prince wearied him not a little with his childish petulance, his hasty resentments, his invariable failure to take action; for he had just enough of his father in him to desire power, to feel aggrieved at his own subordinate position, yet not sufficient to make him set his desire above comfort, even above family affection.

They managed such matters better in Sinde. There, since time immemorial, fathers had killed superfluous sons, sons had killed a superfluous father, and brother removed brother without ridiculous reference to relationship.

Khodadâd looked at the Heir-Apparent negligently through a blown ring of tobacco smoke and appraised him critically. In a way, it was true, this great lout of a lad formed the most convenient nucleus round which conspiracy against the King might gather, since he would carry with him the sympathy of the Orthodox, that is, of at least two-thirds of the court.

But if he would not move he must be left behind, and conspiracy must go on without him. It was nothing to Sinde who sate on the throne of India, so it were not Akbar with his strong hand on the throat of all rulers who chose to rule in the good old fashion. If Salîm could be squared well and good, Sinde would help him to his own--on condition. But if not? Khodadâd's sinister face grew more sinister.

"That ended it anyhow," continued Mirza Ibrahîm who was recounting the events of the morning; for the Prince was a late riser and seldom attended audience. "His Majesty appealed to the infidel, who was backed, of course, by other idolaters such as Mân Singh."

Prince Salîm shot a savage glance at the speaker. "Have a care, fool," he cried, "Mân Singh will be of my house when I am married."

Mirza Ibrahîm spread out his hands in apology. "This slave's tongue slipped over the tangled knot of matrimony," he replied suavely. "But as I say, the King, forwarded by Birbal and others of his kidney began to inquire, the firebrand of a madwoman--she was a picture for looks as she stood breathing defiance--by the prophet! I envied the idolater his hold upon her!--began on childish tears, and ere one could cry rotten fruit there was Siyah Yamin, true daughter of the devil, outraging everybody and making each man's skin thrill to her dancing feet--even, I dare swear, the King your father's, if he be human enough for such frailty!"

Prince Salîm gloomed round from another sweetmeat.

"Some men stand above humanity, Sir Chamberlain," he said sullenly, "as some who call themselves men sit below monkeys."

Mirza Ibrahîm lifted his eyebrows in courtly surprise, bowed, and went on undisturbed. "In truth the jade was superb; so they carried her back shoulder-high to Satanstown, where half the young blades still linger, hoping for a smile. But not I. The madwoman is my quarry! Strange one can look fifty times at a woman and only fancy her the fifty-first."

He spoke calmly as one who took his *amours* rationally.

"And the Syedân? What said they?" asked the Prince.

"What could they say, with that dancing daughter of the devil all unveiled. In God's truth they breathed the more free, knowing themselves rid of the necessity for, sooner or later, sewing her into a sack and committing her and their honour to the silent bottom of the nearest river."

Khodadâd laughed suddenly, immoderately. "It will be a jest to hear the tale of how the virtuous mothers of Bârha received the Darling of the Town as daughter-in-law! Let us appoint a time for it! What say you, my Prince?"

Salîm frowned his silence; he was in a virtuous mood that morning, having as yet hardly recovered his rebellion after the check his father had given to it.

Ibrahîm looked at Khodadâd with a covert sneer, and took up provocation.

"The Most Illustrious Prince had better ask of Birbal what the Syedân said or what Akbar did; since he, only, was present at the secret interview."

Prince Salîm burst out with an oath, "Curse Birbal! I would to God the jesting hound were dead!"

Khodadâd's evil face came up alert, eager from his smoke-wreaths. "Is that, in truth, the wish of--of the Most Excellent the Heir-Apparent to the throne of India?" he asked, and there was something in his steady stare which made Salîm shift his eyes evasively.

"What good were death," he grumbled. "'Twould but make him and his advice grow in grace with my father, as do all folk who die in sanctity. If thou couldst kill the King's trust in him, that would be different."

"It, also, might be compassed," suggested Khodadâd suavely; but once more Salîm said nothing. Ibrahîm concealed a yawn by putting a scented sweatmeat into the cavern of his mouth, then proceeded with his daily task of poisoning the Prince's mind against authority.

"Yet, seeing that our gracious King Akbar gives up his Luck--as folk say he hath--to the infidel, Birbal's wisdom may yet be needed, so, 'twere a pity----"

"His Luck? What mean you?" asked the Prince quickly.

Khodadâd shrugged his shoulders lightly. "The diamond, Most Noble, was not in the kingly turban at the audience, and folk say--with what truth I know not--that it hath gone to the English jeweller to be cut Western fashion."

Salîm's heavy face became vital in an instant with a curious mixture of anger and fear. "Gone!" he echoed. "My father has no right!--it is mine to wear also when I am King. I tell thee 'tis an heirloom of luck----"

"Mayhap the luck will not be cut out of it, mayhap it is but talk after all," put in Ibrahîm deftly, diminishing the immediate wound, so that its venom might have time to work. "Remember the saying: 'The truth none heed; lies are the world's creed.' Time enough for trouble when your turn comes; meanwhile let us sing!"

He let his hand stray idly to the strings of the latest fashionable instrument which stood by his side. It was a sort of guitar, shaped like a peacock, real feathers being let into the frets to form a tail.

Nothing on earth is hidden; in the field
The little buds of ruby or of pearl
Burst into flowers so tinted, and the blaze
Of diamonds in hard marble heart concealed
Waits for Time's touch on all things to unfurl
Their stony shroud, and give them back the rays
In which gems glisten as they were always.

The tinkle of the *satara*, and the high trilling voice filled the quaint arches of the building in which the Prince lounged idly, surrounded by all the luxuries of young and sensual life.

It was the Pânch-Mahal, or Five Palaces, that puzzle to archaeologists of to-day, few of whom seem to know that it was built as a playground for Akbar's long-looked-for, eagerly-loved heir to many hopes. Here from sun or storm alike, shelter could be found; shelter that could bring with it no sense of being cribbed, cabined, or confined, since in these four column-supported and arcaded platforms, each superimposed on the next in lessening squares, no two things are absolutely alike. Carven capital, fluted pillar, and scrolled entablature each tell a different tale, and in the wide aisles, open to every wind of heaven, a child might learn, almost as it might learn from nature, the unending mutation, the ceaseless variety of life.

Whether it served its purpose who can say? One thing is certain; Salîm as he lay sullenly, resentfully searching the long processions of bird and beast, fruit and flower, magical monsters and mythical men that lay carven before his eyes, seeking therein more cause for rebellion, found himself assailed on all sides by the memory of an eager-faced teacher who called him son.

His father!

Yes! A deep, unreasoning, jealous affection lay at the bottom of half his unreasoning revolt.

So, as he lay divided between resentment and pride, the sound of many hoofs outside disturbed the sleepy afternoon air, a swift step took the steep stairs to the second story in its stride, and Akbar showed at the stair-head, unannounced.

He was in riding dress, with untanned leathern gaiters to the knee, his white cloth jerkin buckled tight with a broad leathern belt. On his grizzled hair he wore a close-fitting leathern cap cut like a chain-helmet. It was devoid of all ornament save a heron's plume at the side. His lean figure and alert air made him look years younger than his age, and his entry brought instant change of atmosphere to the perfumed indolence of the young Prince's court. Akbar's quick eye took in at a glance the sweetmeat baskets, held appetisingly near by slaves, beautiful or quaint, the scent fountains, the fighting avitovats, the dice-boxes and all the other paraphernalia of luxurious sloth.

"Come, boy!" he said sharply, "thou canst not stay idling here till bed-time! I come to challenge thee to a game of *chaugan*. Elders against Youngers, see you, and I and Birbal will----"

He turned affectionately as he spoke to the latter who had followed him more leisurely. But the very conjunction of names was sufficient for Salîm. His lustreless eyes flashed sudden fire, he was on his feet in a second.

"So be it, noble father!" he cried. "Since being foe to you makes me foe also to Râjah Birbal, I am content."

Without a moment's pause Khodadâd was on the Prince's heels in provocation. "Nay! most puissant Heir to Empire," he cried, with a sort of servile swagger, "filch not my foe from me. Firsts pair with firsts, seconds with seconds. So I, Khodadâd, lieutenant of the Prince's team, claim Birbal as my compeer to stand or fall together in all things."

There was no mistaking the utter unfriendliness of the challenge. Akbar stood frowning, but Birbal, suave, sarcastic, only smiled.

"Not in crime, Tarkhân-jee! I bar crime! 'Tis one thing to murder or steal without fear of punishment, another even to lie with a bowstring about one's neck! So, seeing the most excellent of lieutenants through being Tarkhân hath a supremacy in sin, I pray so far, to be excused; 'twill but bring Khodadâd one step nearer to judgment." He turned on his heel as he spoke; then continued nonchalantly: "Will your Majesty choose sides?"

"Nay!" replied the King, making an effort to restore good-humour. "Shaikie shall choose his, and a cast of the die as ever settle mine--save only for thee."

"May he be accursed!" muttered the young Prince as he flung aside his deftly-piled and jewel-strung turban, to don a close-eared leathern cap like his father. His mind was full of vague anger against that father. Had he indeed parted with the Luck of the House, leaving him, the heir, forlorn of hope? That must be Birbal's doing; Birbal with the sneering, bitter tongue, which found out the joints in one's armour with such deadly skill.

It was already late afternoon. An hour, or even less would see the rapid Indian dusk settle down over those wide plains below the Sikri ridge; but as yet the sun's slanting rays shone on the *chaugan* ground, catching the gilt spikes of the red boundary flags and the red and gold boundary ropes which were held at intervals by pages dressed to match in red and gold. Within the oblong thus marked out, the glittering white and gold and red and silver teams loosing their lean, low, be-tasselled ponies in preliminary canters, or gathering in knots to discuss the tactics of the coming game, made the scene show like some richly jewelled square of embroidery stretched out among the dusty levels.

Closely akin to polo, *chaugan* was *par excellence* the game of Mogul India; and Akbar excelled at it, holding it to be "no mere play, but a means of learning promptitude and decision, a test of manhood, a strengthener of the bonds of friendship."

It differed chiefly from the modern form of the game in having no set goal, the whole of each end of the oblong being counted as one. So, as a single flourish from the Royal *nakârah* sounded, ten riders ranged themselves at the farther end of the ground, eager, alert, their mounts (and themselves) hard held, all eyes--even those of the ponies--fixed on the ball which was held high in the King's right hand. On either side of the tense, vibrating line stood a pony, one for either team, its rider holding it by the reins ready on the instant to fling himself into the saddle and ride out to replace anyone disabled in the game. Beyond these again, at each corner, was a group of other ponies, other riders, also ready, when the gong sounded every twenty minutes, to ride out and replace two players in either team, thus ensuring a constant supply of fresh blood, fresh zest for the fight.

"Are you ready, Sahibân?" shouted the King, and with the cry dashed forward. The tense, vibrating line, giving a wild whoop, was not a second behind him, and so, tassels waving, sticks carried like lances came a veritable tornado of a charge that swept up to the centre of the ground where a red patch of brickdust showed set four-square.

Ralph Fitch, who with his companions was watching the strange new game, (perhaps the first Englishman who saw polo played), felt his pulses bound with excitement at this forward dash. "They be sportsmen, anyhow," he muttered under his breath. "Bravo! bravo!"

For Akbar's nimble little bay Arab pony, who played the game as keenly as its master, had propped on the red delivery point and stood quivering with the arrest, while its rider, holding back in his stirrups for all he was worth sent the ball spinning skyward with an awkward twist on it, then gripped his club, held till then with his reins.

"*Hul-lul-la-la-la-la-Harri-ho! Ari!--Nila-kunta!*"

The confused cries rose from the wrestling knot of caps, sticks, tassels, hoofs, and swinging arms which in an instant gathered, a whirling nebula of potential force about that nucleus point of a half-seen, falling ball.

"Ibrahîm!" shouted Khodadâd, whose vicious chestnut, hard held, flung itself high in air, almost unseating its rider, "to the left or the King has it."

So, swift as light, aid and prevention hustled each other, all so quickly that a snapshot would hardly have registered the contest, until a click, faint yet loud enough to fill each heart with joy or anger told that the King's stick catching the ball fairly ere it fell had sent it away in a clear swooping flight.

"He has it--ride! ride!" rose the cry from both sides and away they went helter-skelter, pell-mell.

Too late, however, for either side to intervene, for the ball driven with a will, dropped, rebounded, fell again within a foot of the fatal line at the end and so easily, softly, trickled over it.

"Well hit, father!" called Prince Salîm forgetful of anything but sheer pride in the King's prowess. His face, nevertheless, lowered again as in accordance with custom the defeated five rode back along the sides of the ground toward the starting end, pausing every twenty paces to pirouette their ponies and to salaam to the victors who, when the conquered had reached their places, rode triumphantly at a canter down the middle to take up theirs.

But consolation comes in all games, and the next throw-up decreed that the King should--not unwillingly--make obeisance to his son after a hard tussle.

The third goal also went to the juniors, for, whether due to the replacing in the King's team of Râjah Mân Singh by that inferior player his cousin Bhâwun Singh, or to a trifle of lameness in Akbar's little Arab, certain it is that after much swinging and driving of the ball backward and forward the cry arose amongst the spectators "He hath it--Khodadâd hath it this time!" And there was the Tarkhân, his eyes glued on the ground, deliberately trundling the ball along safe clipped in the crook of his stick, while the Prince and Dhâra beside him rode off all attempts at rescue.

"He hath bird-lime on it," muttered Birbal, as he swooped down fruitlessly. The ball trickled on deftly and even the King galloped forward to defend the goal, but it was in vain, for in the final *mêlée* someone--in the dust and glamour--God knows who, gave the final impetus, and the victors and vanquished wiped their streaming foreheads ere recommencing another struggle.

It began on both sides with almost fierce determination.

"God's truth! It stirs the blood!" gasped Ralph Fitch. He had seen many wonders at the court of the Great Mogul, but none so germane to his temperament as this. It was a game worthy of Englishmen he thought almost prophetically; since its lineal descendant, polo, has made India bearable to generations of an English garrison. So while John Newbery's eyes wandered over the jewels of the spectators around him, and William Leedes found his attention too much concentrated on the King's figure for due grip on the game as a whole, it was Ralph Fitch, who despite distance, dusk, and dust, cried excitedly:

"He hath it again--the Sindi hath it once more!"

True enough. Through the looming medley of dust, men, horses, Khodadâd (by many considered to be the best player of *chaugan* this side the Indus), showed ahead, trundling the ball as he might have trundled an iron hoop in a hooked iron stick. But this time he had the King to contend with.

"Back Birbal! it will come back!" shouted Akbar suddenly, and Khodadâd's thin lips set firmer, his wrist stiffened itself in downward pressure as just ahead he saw a faint inequality of the ground. No! the ball should not rise nor swerve, not even if the hammer-head of the King's stick lay ... so ... close ...

Ten thousand devils!

It was but a quarter of an inch, but it was enough for dexterity--and, like a lofter at a bunkered golf ball, Akbar's club was underneath--the next instant, played backhanded, the ball shot rearward to Birbal's keeping.

Khodadâd riding back amongst the defeated with a wrist which still felt the forceful grapple of Akbar's, cursed under his breath. He had been bested, and everything else was forgotten for the moment in pure personal anger. The thought of revenge rose in him unhampered even by care for personal safety; for was he not--as Birbal had taunted him with being-- Tarkhân? Unpunishable that is till he had told his full tale of crime. The Hindu dog might have to learn this to his cost!

The dusk had fallen. Here and there among the throng of spectators beyond the boundary ropes the twinkling light of a wandering sweetmeat-seller showed dimly amid the dust, and high on the towering palaces which backed the ground a few faint gleams from a lamp within gave outline to some latticed window, or corbeilled balcony.

"The game stands drawn," said Prince Salîm, wiping the sweat from his brow. "It grows too dark for more."

"Dark! 'Tis never too dark for victory," cried Akbar gaily. "Let us have out the blaze-balls, Shaiki! 'Twill be a point in thy favour, young eyes being sharper than old; so choose thy team and mine shall choose itself."

Either way they were likely players who ranged themselves in line while the blazing ball of *pilâs* wood, soaked in oil was handed to the King in the earthenware cup of a pipe stem.

He held it aloft flaring. "We play for life or death, gentlemen," he laughed, as with a bound his favourite countrybred mare Bijli, the fastest pony in the royal stable, answered to the spur.

"For life or death," murmured Khodadâd giving the rein to his mount, a chestnut Sindi stallion almost oversized for the game, but savagely keen in the playing of it.

By this time a perpetual film of dust lay square over the ground showing lighter than the undimmed dusk around it, and the watching eyes of the spectators strained into it, seeing now a faint star of light as the blazing ball sped onward, now a cloud of darkness as the huddled riders followed on its track. Not all of them, however; one rider held aloof, evidently biding his time for something which every instant of growing darkness would favour. It was Khodadâd, Tarkhân. A sinister indifference possessed him. If the chance came, as come it might, he had made up his mind to take it. A purely accidental collision would at least serve his purpose of personal revenge without much personal risk, his being by far the heavier horse, while its rider, of course, would be prepared for the shock.

Yes! if the chance came.

Like a skimming meteor the ball shot to the right of him and the King's voice came close on it. "Ride! Birbal, ride!"

Which of them was on the ball? No matter, thought Khodadâd, either was fair quarry!

He dug his spurs into the vicious chestnut and cut across to take them on the flank.

Birbal! Yes, that was Birbal's little gray. All the better since there could be no doubt as to who would have the worst of it. The Hindu pig would at least get a fall heavy enough to send better men to Jehannum.

Khodadâd's malicious chuckle ceased abruptly. A lean bay head showed close to his stirrup leather, and he realised in an instant that he was observed. Yes! he was being ridden off--ridden off by the King, damn him!

Well! let him try! Two could play at that game!

He jagged fiercely at the chestnut's tight rein and, overborne, the bay head yielded a point. But the pace of the brute was the devil. What right had even Kings to ride racers at *chaugan?* If once it crept past the stirrup level ... Curse it...!

Another fierce jag overreached its mark, the vicious beast he rode threw up its head, flung out its feet, so losing half a stride, and Khodadâd, beside himself with sheer temper, struck it madly over the ears with his polo-stick. That finished it. With a scream of rage and fear it plunged forward almost knocking over the smaller horse by force of its superior weight, but the next instant it was on its hind legs beating the air vainly, while the little bay at full racing stride swept under the battling hoofs. Only, however, to find itself in fresh danger. A horseman unseen till then had been creeping up on the right in support of Khodadâd.

Akbar who had been giving Bijli the rein in reckless devilry uttered a sharp cry as he recognised Salîm. Collision was inevitable, and the wonder as to which would suffer most flashed through the King's mind as after one vain, almost unconscious, tug, he realised the position, flung his stick from him, dug spurs to the bay and gripping it all he knew with his knees, rode straight to the crash. It came, but as it came Akbar's arm clipped his son, and borne on by the fierce impetus of Bijli's pace the two shot forward-- Akbar underneath--over the bay's head to lie stunned for a moment by the fall.

The King was the first to speak. "Thou art not hurt, Shaikie?" he gasped, the breath well-nigh pommelled from him by the Prince's weighty body.

"Not I!" gasped Salîm in his turn, beginning to realise what his father had done for him--"but--thou--thou art bleeding."

"From the nose only," replied Akbar cheerfully, as a crowding *posse* helped him to rise, "it was thy foot did it--God sent as much strength to thine arm. Nay gentlemen! we are unhurt!"

The assurance was needed, for already on all sides the cry had risen: "The King is down--the King is killed!" and folk were, in the dusk and gloom, pressing round a figure which still lay prostrate on the ground.

And those on the outside of the ever-thickening ring could not see that it was only Khodadâd knocked out of time for the moment by that backward flung stick of the King's, which had caught him fair on the cheek bone and felled him like an ox.

Akbar walked over and looked at him contemptuously.

"Lo! Tarkhân," he said briefly to the man struggling back to consciousness in Ibrahîm's arms, "ride not so--so *reckless* again, or ill may befall thee, Tarkhân though thou be."

CHAPTER XI

Sing me a ditty, sweet singer I sue
Afresh and afresh, anew and anew;
Sing of the wine cup the red roses brew
Afresh and afresh, anew and anew.

Sing of my sweetheart close claspt to my side
Love's lips to her lips in secret confide
Kisses to credit that still remain due
Afresh and afresh, anew and anew.

Cup bearer, Sâki! Boy! Silver-limbed, slim,
Cross thou, I pray thee, my poor threshold's rim,
Fill up my goblet and fill my soul too
Afresh and afresh, anew and anew.

How shall the guerdon of Love's life be mine
When thou deniest me the red rose's wine?
Fill up! and in thought my Beloved one I'll view
Afresh and afresh, anew and anew!

Breeze of the morning that flyest so fleet,
Haste thee! Ah haste thee, to her happy feet
Tell her the tale of her lover so true
Afresh and afresh, anew and anew.

Siyah Yamin paused, ending the song--which echoes and re-echoes through every harlot's house in India--with a gay flourish of her small fingers on the drum which had been throbbing a monotonous accompaniment.

She looked more like a piece of confectionery than ever in saffron and white and silver, and her indifferent laugh rang through the arches of her balconied room and out into the wickedest alley in Satanstown without a hint of anything in it save pure contentment. Contentment at being set free from unwelcome trammellings, contentment at being once more the Darling of the Town.

As for Âto, serious old Âto, with her mock heroics, she, Siyâla, bore her no grudge for having supplied an excellent opportunity for dramatic effect. Of course the "memory of tears" had precipitated matters somewhat, but the dénouement was foreordained. Had not she come prepared for it with her dancing clothes, her dancing feet?

Thus she lay lazily, contentedly, among her cushions and watched Mirza Ibrahîm and Khodadâd smoking their drugged pipes in her balcony. Her house was the rendezvous of all evil things and scarcely a plot was hatched without her knowing something of it. So, after a time she rose, silently as a carpet snake, and crept behind their backs. Then she laughed.

"Hast not hit on payment yet for thy scarred cheek, Khodadâd?" she asked derisively. "Lo! it spoils thy beauty, friend, and I have a mind to pass thee off as damaged goods to Yasmeena over the way. She is not bad as a mistress, though somewhat too stout. But there! 'When the stomach's full the eye sees God.'"

"Daughter of the devil!" muttered Khodadâd succinctly.

Siyah Yamin's childish face grew hard and clear as if it were carved in crystal. "Bandy no names, O Gift of God," she said disdainfully, "Who made me, made thee. Are there not ever two splits in a pea? Yet would not I sit still with a firebrand in my face." She pointed at the red mark left by Akbar's polo stick.

"Neither do we!" broke in Ibrahîm angrily. "Leave us to our talk, fool. We will hit, this time, on some plan with which no woman's lack of good faith can interfere."

Siyah Yamin yawned imperturbably. "What would you?" she replied. "I am better as I am, as the rat said when the cat invited him out of his hole. Thy party purpose did not suit me. But blame me not with the luck that lies ever with the King."

"Curse him!" muttered Khodadâd sullenly, and the courtesan gave another evil little laugh.

"Yea! even at *chaugan* thou hast no chance," she went on maliciously. "'Tis a pity he was not killed. Lo! being so stunned thou couldst not realise what the mere rumour of his death meant, or thou wouldst regret thy failure still more. The bazaar rang with the news for half-an-hour, half groaning, half cheering. *Then* was the time for action, not now, when the blind giant of India, formed of fools like my friends here, is ready once more to drive home Akbar's javelin head where it lists to go! God! did you but hate him as I, Woman, hate him the Man!"

"What wouldst thou do, harlot?" asked Ibrahîm turning on her sharply. "What couldst thou do?"

She half-closed her sleepy-looking eyes, and stared out into the sunshine in which the lane below lay festering. Not a hundred yards away, in the sunshine also, lay the high road from the great stretches of fields where the peasants toiled uncomplainingly, to the palace where the King dreamt his dream that was born out of due time, and along it the workers were passing bringing in the fruits of their labour. Piled baskets of green-skinned melons, red earthenware pots of milk, creaking wains of corn. For them life was simple, untouched by the imagination of either evil or good. For them even the gossip of their town-bred neighbours was unreal, fantastic.

"What would I do, pandar," replied the courtesan slowly, her eyes brightening in measure with her words, her voice gaining strength from her evil fancies, "If I believed that the Luckstone of Akbar brought luck as thou dost, it should be *mine!* Stay! It should be mine and bring discredit on the beast Birbal to whose charge 'tis given. Hold! interrupt me not! I see further--such thoughts come with the thinking. Aye! I would make Prince Salîm the thief, and so force him to revolt! See you not? See you not? Akbar's every thought of empire is bound up in the boy--that would be revenge indeed! There is no tie so strong as the tie of blood; loose that and the ship of a man's mind may go adrift. Make his son the thief I say, by guile if thou willst; but make Salîm the thief!"

Her large eyes had grown larger with her evil dreamings. They sate and looked at her as the fascinated bird looks at the snake.

"Impossible!" murmured the Lord Chamberlain, feeling nevertheless an answering quiver of assent.

"Naught is impossible to ultimate guile," she went on, every atom of her seeming to gain in vitality as her dream of deceit unfolded itself to her ready mind. "Where is the diamond kept--dost know?"

Khodadâd spoke then; he was gathering initiative from her malice. "He knows," he said, nodding his head at Ibrahîm, "as Chamberlain he must know."

"Where it cannot be touched," retorted the palace official, sullenly. "In the Hall of Labour, guarded, besentinelled, day and night. No chance of theft--save by deep treachery. And there is none to bribe. Shall I offer a price to virtue-ridden Budaoni, court preacher, who works there at his translations? Or blazon our attempt abroad by approaching the Râjpût soldiery or the King's paid artizans?"

Khodadâd's face fell. In truth bribery in such a stronghold of the King's as the Hall of Labour where the best workmen were employed at fabulous wages, seemed hopeless. But Siyah Yamin's took on a sudden expression of amused contempt.

"So!" she began, "but they are men; that is enough for me. And one of them is Diswunt--Diswunt the King's crippled painter----"

"Aye!" assented the Lord Chamberlain still more sullenly. "Diswunt who is devoted to his master. 'Tis next his studio the Englishman's lathe is set up; farthest therefore from the door, farthest from treachery."

Siyah Yamin stretched her beautiful arms in an all-embracing gesture and leant back against the wall that was grimed by a hundred, a million such contacts with vicious humanity.

"What wilt give me for the diamond, Ibrahîm?" she said suddenly, "a thousand golden pieces? I will not take a dirrhm less. 'Twill serve to pay the crazy painter for his likeness of me. Hast seen it? No?" She clapped her hands, and sate up with an odd expression of doubt, dislike, and desire on her small, childish face. "Then thou shalt see, and--and condemn it. What? Drum-banger?" she went on sharply as Deena's wicked old face showed at the stair-head in answer to her call. "How now? Where is Nargîz?"

"Gone out, Princess, leaving me the while devising a new devil's dance for my Lord Chamberlain's delectation this evening. He entertains the King's friends!"

Siyah Yamin interrupted a malicious leer at Ibrahîm with scant courtesy.

"Peace, fool! Go fetch the portrait of me Diswunt painted, these gentlemen would see it."

"Well?" she added when, a minute or two afterward four pairs of Eastern eyes were gazing at a picture which offended every canon of Eastern art. Here were no tiny smooth surfaced stipplings, no delicate dottings of jewellery no faultless complexion, no plastered hair. Even its size, its composition were unconventional. This was a life-sized face--the face and no more--peering out of a white swathing veil which filled up the small oval panel on which it was painted. But it stood there, propped against the humanity-grimed wall, a veritable marvel in the fierce determination to be quit of all convention which showed in its every touch.

The fighting quails called from their shrouded cages below, the sounds of the bazaar drifted upward, and on these sounds came Ibrahîm's sudden contemptuous laugh.

"Thou shouldst keep it as a scarecrow for unwelcome lovers," he said idly. "By God! Even hot lust would fly from such a *churail*."[111]

Siyah Yamin flushed angrily and bent forward to look at the picture more closely. Something there was even in its outrageous originality which she, as woman, recognised as true.

"The lad meant well, being my lover," she murmured softly, then her eyes turned to Mirza Ibrahîm with a whole world of malice in them.

"Thou shouldst get him to paint such an one for thee of Âtma Devi, friend; it might serve to heal thee of--of her scant courtesy--to say nothing of her bruises!"

The Lord Chamberlain grew purple with rage. "Curses on her!" he cried. "How didst hear? Did the jade dare to tell----"

The courtesan interrupted him with absolute contempt. "Truly thou hast a poor purblind brain concerning women, Mirza. Couldst not see, man, with half an eye that Âto is not of those who speak of insult? Nay! 'Twas old Deena yonder--who spends half his time with vice and half with virtue--who, when thou wast attempting to thrust thyself upon her, saw thee put through the door, and trundled down the stair like a bad baby! Fie upon thee, sonling!"

The raillery of her voice matched the derisive shaking of her jewelled finger as he rose sullenly, muttering curses and swearing to stop the old drum-banger's loose lip. "Aye! Thou canst do it with a handful of gold," yawned Siyah Yamin. "Deena's mouth just holds twenty good gold pieces. I have had to gag him myself ere now. Farewell then, conspirator! I will take a thousand of those same myself for the King's Luck, not one dirrhm less!"

Mirza Ibrahîm stood arrested at the stair head. Angry as he was, he knew her wit, and a glance at Khodadâd's face showed that he knew it also.

"How wilt thou compass it?" he asked sullenly.

She looked at him jeeringly. "By my wits, friend. Have I not all the vice of all India at my finger tips? Is not Pâhlu the subtlest thief in Hindustan amongst my brethren? Do not the stranglers, and poisoners, and beguilers rub shoulders with virtuous gentlemen as ye, in this my house? Nay! Leave it to me, Mirza, leave it to me, the courtesan!"

She lay softly laughing to herself when they had gone, until Deena the drum-banger coming up the stairs with laboriously secret creakings whispered: "Mistress Âtma Devi hath been waiting below for a private interview this hour past. Shall she come?"

Then she sate up, suddenly serious.

"Âto!" she said. "Yes! let her come--let her come!"

There was an almost malicious content in her tone, for she realised that here was metal worthy of her steel, that in the coming interview she would have no crass, heavy man's brain and heart to deal with, but a woman's. Dull they might be, it is true, yet would they be full of intuitions, of sudden unexpected grip on motive, and sudden clarities of vision. Yet for this alone, Âtma Devi might be useful to her in the immediate future; since she would need every atom of knowledge, every possible fulcrum, ere she could lay hands on the King's Luck. Aye! Âtma might help, though she was for the King; but that made it all the more imperative, all the more worthy skill, that she should be bent from her purpose, and be made unconsciously to work for the King's disadvantage.

So once more the whole vitality of the courtesan leapt up toward evil.

Woman against Woman! Aye! That was it! Woman glorying in her serpent-bruised heel against Woman treading on the serpent's head. Woman the Temptress, against Woman the Saviour.

Dimly she saw this--the unending conflict of the World--as she gave greeting with a mysterious smile on her baby-face to the tall somewhat gaunt figure with the harassed, perturbed look in its great grave dark eyes.

In truth, no imagination could have conceived a more subtle antagonism than lay between those two women as they sate for a second in silence, looking at each other across Diswunt the crippled painter's picture which still stood against the wall.

Something there seemed to be, indeed, in this man's ideal of the woman he loved, of his endeavour to solve the mystery of woman's dual nature which jarred upon the nerves of both these types of Womanhood; for as their eyes met, Siyah Yamin laughed hurriedly and pointed. "Dost recognise it?" she asked.

Âtma Devi's straight brows showed level and steady as she looked.

"Aye!" she answered, then added swiftly: "Lo! Siyah, with that before thee, I marvel thou canst be so unkind--to a poor lad who loves thee."

The last words came softly, lingeringly, for love was still to Âtma the one thing worth having in the world, though she denied it strenuously. The craving for it lay behind all her claims to Châranship. Vaguely she knew it, vaguely she was ashamed of it.

"Not more unkind than he who would fain thrust deformity upon *my* love," retorted the courtesan airily. "Lo! Âto! even thou, with all thy fine feelings, couldst not love crooked legs and a hunchback--the King hath neither! Then wherefore should I be kind?"

"Wherefore indeed," assented Âtma, disdaining her own flush. "So why not give him dismissal instead of keeping him, as thou dost, on the rack? See you, I speak warmly, in that he had his food from my father's house for service done before the King found him drawing dogs upon a white wall with a burnt bone, and reft him from us for teaching. Thus it grieved me to see him, but now, so distraught, so----"

"But now?" echoed Siyah Yamin sharply. "What! Hast been at the Hall of Labour?"

Âtma's face fell. "Nay! Not there. No woman finds entry there! Else had I seen for myself and not come to thee, seeking news." Her troubled eyes sought Siyah Yamin's almost resentfully.

"News?" echoed the latter, craft growing to her face. "What news? Somewhat that Diswunt would not tell thee? Out with it Âto? Tell me thy end--God knows but it may fit mine, since, so they say, extremities meet."

"Aye," assented Âtma sombrely. "That is why I seek thee. Hate and love are not far distant with us womenkind."

Then, suddenly she reached out a tense, nervous hand to lay upon Siyah Yamin's smooth round arm.

"Lo! Sister! thou hearest all things here, and I--I hear nothing! What news is there of the King's Luck? Hath he in truth yielded it to the Englishman?"

Siyah Yamin stared for a second, then burst into a perfect cascade of high-pitched laughter.

"Said I not truly," she gurgled, "that extremes meet! See! I will send for a cooling sherbet, and I will tell thee all!"

It was not all, it did not even approach the truth, but it served her purpose. So she sate, watching the effect of each word, and Âtma Devi listened, weighing each word, both with the same indescribable intuitions of their sex, appraising this, discounting that, until at last the latter rose, tall, dark, menacing, to look down on the other, crouching like a coiled snake among her cushions.

"Yea! as thou hast said, Siyâl, true loyalty would lend itself even to theft, or rather to the snatching of luck from ill luck, and the protection of the King from evil magic; and so I will tell Diswunt--I, his mistress by inheritance. And to give it to the keeping of the Beneficent Ladies as I have said were well done. The Lady Hamida, the King's mother, carries his honour close day and night, even as she once carried him. And Khânzada Gulbadan Begum hath wit more than most men, so I will aid if I can, being bound also to the King's honour. But hearken, Siyah! Lo! draw thy veil so-- let me have it." She sank to her knees and leaning forward caught the loose end of the courtesan's tinsel veil and flung it round her own head also. "Now let us swear once more, as sisters of the veil, to be true to each other until the death--until the death--dost hear?"

Taken by surprise Siyah Yamin shrank back from those blazing eyes, paled, faltered; finally, compelled thereto by the grip of a nature stronger than her own, muttered faintly:

"I swear."

"Till the death?"

"Till--death."

After Âtma had gone the courtesan sate for a while as if half-paralysed; she had gone further than was safe, seeing that she was to use Âtma as a tool; a half-crazed tool. Then she looked about her. The heat of the day was waxing. Below her the bazaar, becoming drowsy, was leaving a thousand wickednesses to welter and fester under the noon-tide sun while it slipped from them for a while in sleep; leaving them restlessly active, ceaselessly on the move like molecules in a sunray; thought hustling thought, intention seeking desire, making evil ready for the awakening of men to find a new stimulus to wrongdoing in the coolness of the afternoon. It was always so. Evil grew day by day. There was nothing else alive in the whole world.

So by degrees courage and confidence returned.

"Send for Pâhlu, the prince of thieves," she said "and bid Pooru, the false gem-maker, be here when I awaken. Meanwhile, let Deena take this to Diswunt at the Hall of Labour."

She sate for a second, pen in hand, cogitating half amusedly; then with a sudden smile wrote in delicate curvings a verse from Sa'adi's "Lamp and the Moth":

Oh! fearful tearful lover! Cease to sigh,
Passion's worst pangs thou knowest not--as I.
Leave pining, leave lamenting and be bolder
Woman yields readiest to those who hold her.

So, swallowing a perfumed pill of opium all sugar coated and silvered, she, too, slept in her balcony.

CHAPTER XII

Live in the living hour,
Fortune is fickle.
To thy lips, laughing flower,
Let good wine trickle.
Who hoardeth wealth to leave
He is a ne'er-do-well.
Who lives to rail and grieve
He is an infidel.
Rest in thy cypress shade,
Fill the cup higher,
Drink to each merry maid,
Drink to desire.
So saith the cup bearer,
So sings the lyre.

--HAFIZ.

The Hall of Labour lay deserted as if the artificers who worked in its surrounding arcades had taken profit by the wisdom of Hafiz which came trilling from the furthermost, sun-saturated end of the long parallelogram of roof in which Akbar's especial artificers laboured at especial tasks.

It was a quaint place this Hall or rather Roof of Labour, for it was set high between the higher palaces which rose around it on three sides. The fourth was arcaded as were the others, but in dummy fashion, that is to say with the shallow archways filled in with brick work--and gave on the wide plains of India, which were, however, invisible because of the height of the wall. Most things, indeed of the outside world were invisible from the Hall of Labour; you had to go through the sentry-guarded door opposite the hidden plains before you could get rid of a certain sense of imprisonment, of absorption in duty. The artificers in the cell-like workshops on the left hand of the doorway, were, however, better off in this case than those on the right, since the superstructure above these was but cell wide, and so from their farther ends, high, unattainable windows, partially bricked up, let in a cross light on lathes and crucibles, paint-brushes, and even inkpots; for in one of them near the door Budaoni, the historian, used to sit most days engaged on his uncongenial task of translating the Hindu scriptures, and glaring at another writer over the way who was copying the translation of the Gospels for which Akbar had paid the Jesuits a round sum of money. Money not quite honestly earned, since the text was deftly doctored to suit Jesuit dogma! But even if this had been known it would have mattered little to the jealousies of the rival writers.

Farther down this left hand side worked a chemist employed in testing atomic weights, an engraver busy over a ruby intaglio, an experimentalist attempting to prove the properties of quicksilver in the transmutation of metals, a worker in gold on crystal, and so on; till at the end came an empty arcade with shut door, then William Leedes's workshop, and on the other side the studio of Diswunt the crippled painter. He was especially favoured, for in addition to the high window which, like those in the other cells gave on the Court of Dreams--on the opposite side of which stood the King's Sleeping Palace--he had a corbeilled balcony overlooking the Indian plain; at least so much of it as could be seen by reason of the towering Arch of Victory which thrust itself skyward from its great plinth of steps. Looking downward, one could see them receding in sharp angles almost to the bottom of the rocky ridge. No place here, therefore, for escape or entry, so Diswunt was allowed the luxury of light, even when his great wide door was shut. He kept it so constantly; for he was morose by birth, embittered by the accident of it.

And yet the idle rhymes of Hafiz came to his lips as he sate irresolute, thinking of the paradise one woman had promised him if he did something--a mere trifle!--for her; of the hell with which another woman had threatened him should he fail to do the same thing. It was too bad to have duty and pleasure on the same side; and against them--what? Only loyalty to the man who seeing him--then a mere beast of burden--as he paused in the bazaar to make, with a bit of the charcoal he was carrying and a white-washed wall, a spirited sketch of a dog gnawing a bone, had sent him for training to the Court School of Painting. That, after all, had been but a sorry action! Diswunt looked distastefully at his work--a portrait of Akbar small enough to go into a ring--and his whole soul went out to charcoal and a white wall.

For the misshapen lad whose face had the brilliant, bizarre beauty of strongly marked feature which so often goes with physical deformity, was without doubt part of the sixteenth century crop of genius, of which so much has remained to the world, so much more has passed out of it, unwitting even of itself.

His eyes, as he sate listlessly, were dull with the hemp he drank habitually to deaden the depth of his discontent.

For Akbar had not been able to uphold, against the whole artistic verdict of his court, his own opinion that the "portrayal of real life gave special facilities for true education since every touch that went toward the likeness of reality must make the painter feel his own impotence to bestow life, and so lead him to a right appreciation of the immeasurable dignity of the Creator."

They had been brave words, but they had ended in stipplings and blobs of white paint to imitate pearls!

Yet there were some who thought as he, Diswunt the King's crippled painter thought. He shivered as he remembered the day but a week ago, when the infidel jeweller next door, with whom he had scraped up an acquaintance, had replied to a question he had asked in the lingua franca of mixed Portuguese and Arabic which served as court jargon for strangers.

"Nay friend! such missals, such pictures as these Jesuits bring are but monkish work. There be other painters over the black water. Lo! I studied for a while under one in Italia. Stay! I bethink me to have backed yonder chart on the wall with a copy. Turn it round and see!"

See! Diswunt had seen little else since! It was only a bad copy in red chalk of a torso by Michael Angelo, all blurred and half effaced, but it had been a master key, opening the door of real art to the lad, driven half crazy by dreams and drugs. Since then he had closed his door, and the stippled face of Akbar had not received a single touch; but the back of that closed door, which was made after Indian fashion, of plain whitewashed wood nailed to a strong outside frame-work, showed the cloudy smearings of much charcoal.

Should he, or should he not? It was close on noon. The silence told that the artificers were putting by their tools. Stay, they were beginning again! How was that?

He set the door wide open and carefully fastened it back, then looked out. The reason of this brisking up to business was evident, for the King, followed as usual by Birbal and Abulfazl, was crossing the court. Not that he noticed the general activity; his objective was William Leedes's workshop; for it having been notified that the first facet of the diamond had been duly cut, he was keen to see it. But the sight of his protégé Diswunt at his door made him forget his hurry, to pause and say kindly:

"Come thou, with the artist's eye, and help Akbar hold his own with these ignorant ones who have it that dulness equals God's luck." He flashed round half-contemptuous raillery even at Birbal.

"Nay sire!" retorted the latter, "If the Light of the World will pardon his slave, we do but hold that the King's Luck equals Brightness."

But Akbar's quick imagination was already caught by the angular speck of clear dark sheen which showed like a shadow on the dull radiance of the uncut diamond, as it lay matrixed in the cutter's lathe. So dark, but so clear.

"It is like a door," he cried exultantly. "Look! Diswunt, is it not as a door through which one might pass and see what other folks see not."

"And therefore desire not!" put in Birbal quickly. "My liege it is not yet too late. Let yonder flaw made of man remain as an outlet or inlet for Akbar's dreams; but let the remainder be, as it has always been, a sign of sovereignty to the people. Ask Abulfazl here. What thinkest thou Diwan-jee, is there danger in this thing or no?"

"There is the chance of it," replied the King's Prime Minister, slowly. "I can say no more, no less."

But Birbal was more vehement. "It is more than chance; it is certainty. I have my finger on the pulse of the people. Already it beats irregularly. Had I but the power----"

"Peace! Birbal," said the King, sternly. "Thou hast it not!" Then turning to William Leedes he continued as if nothing had been said. "And the next?"

The jeweller pointed to the mathematical diagrams at which he had been working.

"That is as fate and figures will have it, my liege. I labour to lose as little as may be."

Akbar's eyes twinkled, he gave a boyish laugh. "For fear of cutting out the King's luck? Lo! that should satisfy thee, Birbal."

"Not one whit, sire," replied the latter stanchly. "Birbal knows his own mind; and by all the gods in Indra's heaven, had I not been put in charge of ill-luck by the King's order--I--I would have stolen luck for him."

He laughed lightly giving his usual slight shrug of the shoulder; but Diswunt turned away suddenly and stood looking out on the sunlight.

Should he, should he not? It meant paradise, it meant escape from hell according to two women; but *this* was a man; and the King's best friend, the keenest intellect in the court.

"I stay!" he said curtly to the sentry who came to keep watch and ward while William Leedes went out for the mid-day recess.

"Best not!" remarked the latter casually. "Art needs rest, and thou has been at it ever since thou didst see Michael Angelo. Lo! were I to work unceasing at my problem I should grow crazy with angles and take a month where a week would suffice."

"Take the month an thou willst" retorted the cripple ill-humouredly as he banged to his door.

So there was no hurry! He had a week wherein to do the little thing that was asked of him. Only to wile the jeweller from his cell for one brief minute.

It was, however, but two days afterward, that he stood at the lintel of William Leedes's workshop. Something had gone wrong with the latter's calculations and he had lingered after the Hall of Labour had emptied. The lad's eyes were bloodshot, his hands were trembling with the hemp he had drunken. And then suddenly he walked over to the diamond. "Truly, as the King said, it is like a door" he murmured, "a door through which men could see--but these men can see naught. Though every line is true--they cannot see it."

"Cannot see what?" asked William Leedes abstractedly from his compasses.

For answer Diswunt gave a wild jeering laugh and clutched the jeweller by the wrist.

"Come and see it; *thou* canst see! Come, I say--nay! thou must come and tell me if I be fool utterly."

His door, set wide, almost elbowed that of the jeweller's, and, overborne by Diswunt's wild appeal, William Leedes found himself on its threshold.

"Not that! not that!" almost yelled the lad, his half insane, reckless laughter echoing loudly through the arches. "Didst think I brought thee to see the pattering of flies-paws. Stand forward a bit--so forward----"

The wide door, as he set it aswing, enforced his demand; and what it brought to view as it swung, astonished William Leedes to forgetfulness and left him silent with admiration.

It was a hunting piece in rough charcoal. A buck standing at bay amid a herd of hyenas; but there was something more in it than that and William Leedes involuntarily crossed himself.

"Thou hast a devil, Diswunt," he said at last, and once more the half-mad painter's high, reckless laugh filled the arches.

"So! thou canst see! Dost mark the Tarkhân's sneer, the Chamberlain's cold glare?"

It was true. Something in the noble poise of the stag's head was reminiscent of the King, and each one of the savage beasts surrounding it recalled by some witchery of touch or line the foremost of the King's enemies.

"Lo! yonder is the stupidity of the Makhdûm," went on Diswunt punctuating his words by that high laugh; "yonder the self-satisfaction of Budaoni, the fat foolishness of Ghiâss Beg." He paused, almost as if listening to the faint echo of his laughter in the roof. Then sudden seriousness came to him.

"But he will escape them, *now*. Dost see the javelin to the right yonder-- that shall save him and his Luck."

The last word came curiously clear as if intended to awake remembrance. It did so.

"By'r Lady!" cried William Leedes, "I had a'most forgot." He was back in his workshop in a moment to find the diamond matrixed as ever in its place, with the darker sheen of the first facet showing full of promise.

But Diswunt stood at the lintel and looked out, not at the sunshine but at the door of the empty workshop next to William Leedes. It quivered slightly as if wind were behind it, or as if someone were gently closing a bolt.

CHAPTER XIII

Whirr spindles on my rushing reel
Leap thread from out my fingers feel.
Time dwindles! Fate will cut the thread
Sleep dead! Before her grinding wheel
Kindles life's spark again for woe or weal.

Birbal paused on Âtma's threshold listening to her deep voice backed by the burring hum of her spinning wheel, and as he listened he shivered. This thought of unending life aroused from death or ever the tired eyes were fast closed appalled him. Not for him such slight slumber!

Then he knocked. There was a sound of quick uprising from within, a swift echo of footsteps and then Âtma's voice at the door said with a breathlessness in it:

"What is't? Hast brought news--is all well?"

"Well or ill matters naught" he replied cavalierly. "Open! I come from the King."

But the phrase had lost its charm, "Go thy way, Chamberlain of Princes!" came the mocking answer. "Once bit, twice shy."

"Thou mistakest, sister" urged Birbal, who knowing Mirza Ibrahîm's reputation, had no difficulty in guessing the cause of Âtma Devi's refusal. "I am Maheshwar Rao, disciple by birth of thy dead father."

The reassurance was deft, and the door held ajar upon the chain showed Âtma's figure, tall, low-browed, defiant.

"What wants my lord?" she asked, and her voice trembled as if from some secret perturbation. "A kiss like my Lord Ibrahîm, ere I turned him out, close clipped in an embrace for which he cared not? Yet enter--in the King's name enter to the house of his Châran."

Something there was of strain, of anxiety, in face and manner, that made Birbal's keen eyes seek round the roof for its cause. Then he laughed. "Nay! I seek no kisses, widow, where a lover has just left his lips."

She stared at him haughtily. "What means my lord?"

He pointed easily to a pair of man's shoes which stood in a corner beside the door. "Smagdarite's, sister! Ah I have your secret. He is here, for yonder are his shoes!"

Âtma's eyes following his, grew puzzled in their anger.

"Shoes!" she echoed superbly. "I see them not, my lord."

This time the laugh came more coarsely. "None so blind as the blind beggar! Bah! woman, do I not know what woman is? He is here I say--hath been here always, and thou didst delude me last time with the child's voice."

He paused, for suddenly a tremulous sweet song as of some mating bird rose on the air.

My singing soul has its nest
Near the great white Throne
Where the roses of Paradise rest
On its Corner Stone,
And the scent of those roses seems
To bring idle dreams
Of Life and Love and the Endless Quest.

Oh bird! arise
Lift up thine eyes
To the Heaven that lies
Beyond Paradise.

Once again the man who doubted all things felt a thrill almost of fear; but Fate promptly gave him back his self-confidence, for a voice behind him said as the song ceased.

"If my lord seeks me, I seek my lord."

He turned to find the *rebeck* player on the threshold; but with bare feet. So the cynical laughter rang out this time in frank amusement. "Well designed, musician! But the shoes lie yonder." And then he hummed gaily the refrain of a popular song.

Love to her mind
Came like the wind,
All stealthy as the cat is.

But those not blind
Next morn will find
Footsteps beneath her lattice.

A flickering smile showed on the *rebeck* player's lips. "My lord has learnt that of lust in the bazaar. If he desires to learn of love he should go--to Bayazîd!"

The faintly inflected play of words was out of keeping with the man who made it; but the vague questionings concerning him which for days past had been in Birbal's mind seemed to have vanished with his first look at the miserable, almost squalid figure, the dull eyes, the deathlike mask of the face. What could the fellow be but street musician? Except--since women were incomprehensible--the widow's lover!

Something of curiosity, however, remained.

"Bayazîd?" he echoed haughtily. "What knowest thou of the drunkard who calls himself King of Malwa?"

"That he is King of Musicians, my lord, and this slave's master. He could tell my lord all concerning love. Aye! even as well as the Sufi from Isphahân."

Those dull eyes seemed to take on a leer and Birbal stared at them, startled back into questionings.

"The Sufi? What dost know of him?" he asked quickly.

"Naught!" replied the musician evasively. "Save that the servants said he sups at the river palace this night; he and another king--Payandâr of Sinde mayhap."

He looked up again with that leer in his eyes, and the wonder died out of Birbal's. The man was palpably a trickster; palpably trying to play on credulity--credulity in Birbal, prince of doubters!

"Then will they sup in hell, slave," he said curtly "since Payandâr hath been dead these fifteen years. So farewell, Smagdarite, lest I disturb love. Stay--let me see thy talisman once more."

"This dustborn atom in a beam of light resigns it," came the reply, and for an instant Birbal stood paralysed by dim remembrance. But the green stone on its greasy skein lay in his hands, all inert, without perfume, without, charm.

It was like nothing so much, he told himself, as half chewed cud, and he tossed it back contemptuously, a gold piece following it.

"That for thy pains. Farewell, widow! Luck to thy love!"

He turned to go, but the *rebeck* player who had stooped to pick up the coin, still stood in the doorway, and the sun flashing on the gold he held betwixt finger and thumb seemed for a second to blind Birbal's eyes to everything else.

"If the Most Excellent desires to hear of love," came the musician's voice softly, "he might go to the King Bayazîd's river palace--this night-- when the moon is waning. The river palace, my lord, when the moon is waning."

The words echoed down the stairs after Birbal who seemed not to hear them. They had, however, the opposite effect on Âtma Devi; who all this time had stood silent, apparently engrossed in listening. Now she roused herself and turned accusingly to her companion.

"So thou has been here all the time, and it was to thee the child talked in gray dawn and gray dusk! Wherefore did I not see thee?"

"Because thou wouldst not, sister! Because thy mind has been elsewhere--whither God knows." She started and looked at him half-fearfully but he went on unregarding. "It is what the will wishes to see that is seen. To all else we are blind."

Something in the words seemed to strike a new note in her, and the half savage, half anxious look on her face vanished. "Yes! mayhap I have been blind," she muttered to herself despondently. "But wherefore--Oh ye dear Gods! wherefore am I blind!"

She turned to lean over the parapet, as if to rest her eyes, her very heart, upon the dim blue distant haze betwixt earth and sky.

"Because thou wilt not see the Truth, sister"--the voice seemed to her to belong to that dim earth and sky--"because thou hast denied love. Yet naught else will save the King."

She gave a startled cry but, looking round, saw that the Wayfarer had gone. "May Shiv-jee protect me" she murmured to herself. "He is magician for sure. Yet is he wrong. I am no woman, but the King's Châran, I have done my duty!" So, clenching her hands she sate and dreamed for him of safety, honour, empire.

Birbal, meanwhile, dreamt the same dream as he plunged into the increasing intricacy of cabal which centred round his master. So he gave no thought at all to so contemptible a person as the opium-drugged, song-besotted Bayazîd who still styled himself the King of Malwa, though he had fled from royalty for the sake of a dead dancing girl; as if any woman were worth such a sacrifice! True, the tragic tale of Rupmati, the poetess, musician, singer, ultimate artist, who had made her King forget even statesmanship for seven long happy years, had its æsthetic beauty. One could picture the consternation of the dove-cot when Adham Khân, Akbar's general and foster-brother put the royal lover to flight; picture still more easily, knowing Adham Khân's nature, his defiance of orders, and the proposals he made to Rupmati. While the rest was pure poetry! The beautiful woman dressing herself as a bride is dressed for the conqueror's assignation, and then leaving nothing but dead flesh awaiting him on the couch strewn with flowers. That was fine! But Bayazîd? Even though Akbar's own hand had brought retribution on libertine Adham's head for this and other offences, he, Birbal, would never have come cringing to the Emperor's court, to spend his time in singing love *ghazals*. That was contemptible.

And yet as the day wore on, the memory of the *rebeck* player's words returned inconsequently, almost annoyingly. What was it to him, Birbal, if Bayazîd had a supper party or no? He had other corn to parch. And he parched it consistently until, late on in the evening, having excused himself, he knew not why, from an entertainment at the palace, he fell asleep peacefully.

The gongs were sounding eleven when he woke suddenly to a new resolve, which admitted of no reconsideration.

He would go to the river palace. After all, there might be something in what the *rebeck* player had said--he might be in the right. At any rate there was no harm in seeing. He clapped his hands and ordered his fast trotting bullocks. But the river palace lay some miles away in an orange garden down by the sliding yellow stream which flows past Agra and it was nigh on midnight ere he reached its wide open gateway. Bidding his râth await him outside, he passed inward. A sentry slept in the scented shadow of the archway, so he went on unchallenged into the scented garden where the faint shadows of the waning moonlight slept also across the broad paved walks, and on the conduits of running water that was hastening to slake the nightly thirst of the sun-wearied plots of pomegranate and orange trees on which the ripe fruit hung obscure. The dim clearness seemed to show the darkness; above all the utter darkness of the great pile of the palace.

No signs here of a supper party! The fact whetted his curiosity, and he went on, feeling himself the only live thing in a world of drugs and dreams.

In the hallway another drowsy servant showed, curled up half asleep upon the floor.

"Your master?" asked Birbal.

"Roofways," came the answer with a yawn.

The whole place seemed opium-soddened; there was a cloying savour of poppy and dead roses in the narrow turret stairs which led upward; so narrow that the stone wall on either side was polished by the elbows of the passers up and down.

The first floor was dark save for the fading moonlight seen through the open window archways, so he went up again, until the wide roof set amid the encircling shadowy trees through which the pale gleam of the river showed, lay beneath his feet.

And overhead were the stars beginning their watch of the night.

One seemed to have fallen from heaven to burn in a silver filagree shrine, in shape like a domed mausoleum, which was the only thing dimly visible in the darkness; that, and still more dimly the lute with broken strings which lay before it illumined by the twinkling light.

"Bayazîd!"

He stood and called; till from the night beyond the light came a chanting, drowsy, half coherent voice--

None knows the Secret! Therefore take the cup
Lightly with laughing lip and drink it up.
Though it be heart's blood!--just one little sup
So ... That is good!... Now die!

"True wisdom, Hafiz, prince of poets," murmured Birbal as he went forward and called again.

This time the answer came from near, "Yea! I am Bayazîd. Welcome friend!"

He was resting on cushions behind the shrine and the light from its little lamp showed him, long, lank, listless. But the wide eyes in which burnt the dull fires of the Dreamgiver, recognised the visitor, and the man who had been King of Malwa roused himself to give salutation with stately ceremonial courtesy, and motioned Birbal to a seat beside him. As the latter sank into the cushions they gave out a scent of roses, and swift memory-- swiftest of all for perfumes--made him look round hastily; but the roof showed no sign of other living soul.

"It is good of my lord to come so far and so late," murmured Bayazîd. "In what can I help my Lord?" The words came drowsily. He seemed in danger of falling asleep once and for all.

"I came to see Payandâr, King of Sinde," said Birbal sharply. If that did not rouse the besotted fool nothing else would. The result was, in its way, excellent. Bayazîd sate up instantly and laid his hand on Birbal's arm.

"What of Payandâr?" he queried, his face working. "What of the Master of Love? Does he indeed live, as some folk say?"

"That Bayazîd should know, better than some folk," replied Birbal dryly, "since he was to have supped here to-night."

"To-night" echoed Bayazîd. "Nay, not to-night, or she would have told me. She knows the Secret now!"

Birbal laughed lightly. "As we shall all know it--or not know it some day! As Payandâr knows it also, since he died in the desert."

A sudden bitter exaltation came to the half-seen haggardness of the face, the voice rang almost militantly.

"Aye! in the desert, driven thither as we dreamers of love are driven ever, by lust--man's lust! Lo! thou knowest of my own seven happy years-- of my songstress who sang of love--of the viper who slew her and slew the King in me. Ohí Rupmati, Rupmati! Were it not that thou comest to me ever in the song of birds, in the breeze of the night, in God's sunshine and in his flowers, I too would seek the desert and save myself from the deadly companionship of my kind. So I wait for thee and thy broken lute." He sank back into his cushions stilled by the very violence of his emotions; but after a while his voice went on more and more drowsily. "That the world knows. All know the tale of Bayazîd and Rupmati. But who knows the story of Payandâr? Shall I tell it as she told it me? How he loved a Rose in a garden of roses; naught but a gardener's daughter--and he a Prince of the Tarkhâns. What do the Tarkhâns know of Love? But he knew. He loved her--aye! though he was Heir. So, vile utterly, his father betrayed him. A bastard younger brother did the deed one night in the Garden of Roses, and when dawn came the Rosebud had been plucked, despoiled! He left Kingship, and died mad in the desert--so they say! But Love cannot die. Even in the Wilderness there is a Rose Garden ready for it. So he took the Rosebud thither, plucked, despoiled, soiled, bruised, and broken. And out of Death came Life. Out of Lust came Love, though the child was a crippled thing, despoiled, spoiled, bruised, and broken by its birth. But Death came also to the Rosebud in the Rose Garden of Love, amidst the perfume of roses. Is it not even now in the air? Is not the darkness full of the Essence of Love. Ohí, Ohí Rupmati! let me hearken to thy broken lute."

Was it fancy, or mingled with the faint sighing of the night wind amongst many leaves, and the fainter rush of the sliding river was there a sound as of jangled music?

Birbal sate arrested for a second, then, seeing from the supineness of the figure beside him, that all hope of further speech with the drug-eater was over, rose impatiently and made his way downstairs, asking himself why he had come.

He paused astonished, however, to find the lower story no longer dark. It was, on the contrary, brilliantly lit, servants were flitting about, and in the central room, whose twelve arches gave on surrounding arched aisles, which in their turn gave on overshadowing trees and river gleam, a supper cloth was laid for two.

And by all the Gods! The figure which sate there holding a cup of wine in its raised right hand was the Sufi from Isphahân!

CHAPTER XIV

Bring wine and I will read
The riddle of this life of mine;
The old stars' wizardry, the shine
Of new moons wandering overhead:
All this, I'll read with wine.

--HAFIZ.

For an instant Birbal was speechless, then he recovered himself.

"Who art thou, man of many faces?"

The question came peremptorily, the answer suavely.

"Thine host; for the rest, as thou art, a mere wayfarer on the limited path of life. Combining the two, this slave ventures to offer refreshment. Cupbearer! Wine of Shirâz, and scent the goblet's edge with rose.

Mechanically Birbal drained the beaker, and the good liquor tingling to his finger tips, he faced his familiar world again, incredulous as ever.

"So," he said, as following the Sufi's sign he seated himself among the cushions at the other side of the supper cloth. "It is, as I thought, the Wayfarer. How many disguises hast thou O Bairupiya?[112] Musician? Envoy? Sufi?" then a thought struck him and he gave his little contemptuous jeering laugh, "mayhap King Payandâr also--but that he is dead."

"Aye, dead!" assented the Sufi gravely, "and the dead being but the cast-off garments of the living, count not in disguise."

"But wherefore----" began Birbal.

His host smiled. "Let me quote the King of Poets to my lord--

"Ah, soul of a man live free
Of the Wherefore, the How,
For the passing moments flee.
Drink deep of the wine cup now,
Drink deep, for He who is Wise
He hath the Seeing Eyes,

He knows the Secret that lies
In the Hows and the Whys.

"Cupbearer, yet another wine of Shirâz and scent the goblet's edge with the roses that grow beneath the vine."

The echo of the chanted song died away; then suddenly he reached out his thin brown hand--the index finger wore a ring set with a marvellous emerald, the surface of which was close covered with fine flowing hieroglyphics--and laid it on Birbal's in familiar grip.

The latter started, turned pale. "Thou art the devil,--juggler, with thy tricks!" he muttered faintly. "How didst learn the sign-manual of my race, secret, inviolate?"

The Sufi laughed. "There is no devilry to the Hindu in being the outcome of many incarnations. Mayhap in my past I have been Bhât-Bandi and my lord----" he paused. "What matters it? 'Tis but the trick of memory. Birbal forgets, this slave remembers. Aye, friend! 'tis but a trick indeed! I juggle with men's eyes, and they with their own senses."

He clapped his hands, gave a swift order in some unknown tongue, and as if by magic the servants disappeared, extinguishing the lights as they vanished, leaving those two alone in the rosy radiance of a lamp that swung above the supper table. Its downward light left their two faces in shadow.

"Listen, my lord!" said the Sufi rapidly. "I will waste no time in words. I am here at Akbar's court, a spy. Wherefore, or who my master is, seek not to know. Mayhap time will show. I spy on Prince Dalîl of Sinde--dost know him? Khodadâd Tarkhân, boon companion of the Heir-to-Empire. Start not! I watch him, I wait for him, not for myself only, but for Sinde--for that unhappy country which counts on Akbar's aid, aid which will not come if the assassin's dagger--if conspiracy--succeeds. Dost see? Dost understand? Lo! I am Sinde incarnate--waiting, watching."

He paused again and in the brief silence Birbal could hear a long sobbing breath. The lamp had grown dimmer, and to his half startled eyes its radiance seemed to leave the white-robed figure to chill shadow. He too caught in his breath as a thought came to him.

"But that Payandâr is dead," he began whisperingly, "I should deem----
"

"Aye, he is dead!" echoed the other, almost menacingly. "But though he died in the Desert--as thou hast heard from Bayazîd--Love, Unconditioned, Ineffable----"

A sudden distaste to the man who spoke, to the whole tenor of his talk, boastful, as it were, of some hold on the Unseen not known of commoner clay, seized on Birbal.

"Keep that for the King, holy man!" he said decisively. "Birbal talks not till dawn of Wine-cups and Roses and the Beloved."

"Perhaps 'twere better if he did," replied the Sufi boldly. "Nathless I did not bring thee hither to talk of love, but to tell thee by my arts that the King's Luck is stolen."

The impulse to start, to rise, was strong for an instant; then memory came to calm the man of the world.

"Impossible" he said quietly. "I saw it to-day. It is in safe keeping--the worse luck perhaps."

A jibing laugh echoed through the arches.

"So even Birbal hath superstition! But listen! Stay, I will tell thee common truth. I go nightly to swing up the palace wall to Akbar's balcony. Wherefore? Because, my lord, I pass not far from a certain window where Mirza Ibrahîm and Khodadâd Khân hatch conspiracies; and there is an iron stanchion by the side of it with which even a swinging dhooli may find rest--and listen! Dost understand? So I hear all, even their hours of meeting; and I am spy, a man of many faces--as thou knowst. I was there but now--and the diamond is stolen. I meant when I bid thee come hither, simply to warn thee, since to thy charge----"

Birbal rose then, his eyes full of impatient disregard for the trickster, the juggler--the man who pretended to supernatural knowledge, and found it--or said he found it--by common spying!

"Why dost thou tell me?" he asked quickly. "Thou sayest thou art friend to Akbar. Thou art no friend of mine."

There was a pause; a faint hesitancy came to the shadowed face before him, as of one who, playing many different parts, finds them mixed up in general confusion. Suddenly he seemed to grip himself, the real man behind so many disguises of the unreal.

"Yet are we both friends of Akbar's aim, that is Unity. Thy hand, Birbal! let us swear troth for that!"

That slender, brown, outstretched hand with the green glint of the emerald on its index finger seemed to have a compelling power. Birbal's sought it and the result was startling. The man whose whole life was one long claim for individuality, realised in a second that so far as his impact on that clasping hand was concerned, he had lost all sense of personal touch. Flesh seemed made one with Flesh, with all things.

"*Tat twam asi*" ("Thou art that!")

The fundamental creed of the East overwhelmed him as he stood. Then suddenly he was alone again.

Alone in the darkness, save for the faint glimmer of the toothed arches that gave on the shadowy gloom of overhanging trees and sliding river.

"Wayfarer!" he called. "Wayfarer!" "Juggler! Where art thou? Sufi! Spy!"

But there was no answer. He stood for a moment dazed; then he felt his way for the stair, and called again. A steady snore came in return. The drowsy servant he had questioned on entering was evidently now fast asleep.

No wonder! he told himself as he made his way outward to his waiting râth. The whole place was full of dreams; the very roses in the garden had lost their scent through slumber. As he passed down the garden path, he caught himself yawning, though his mind was broad awake.

Therein lay the puzzle--the body slept, the soul----

He turned at the outer archway to give a last look at the palace. To his intense surprise it was ablaze with lights from basement to roof, and standing in a balcony of the second story which gave on the sliding river, he could see quite distinctly, a figure looking out over the gleam of the water. The face, melancholy beyond words, was deathly pale, and seen in profile only, looked like a cut cameo. Its drooping eyelid half hid the lustreless eye, the long black hair, escaping from the high green turban outlined the narrow contour of forehead and cheek, then fell in ringlets on the sloping shoulders, green clothed, and hung, as was the turban, with festoons on festoons of emeralds.

The light struck them; they shone coldly green, incomparably clear.

The emeralds of Sinde surely! No other regalia held----

As the thought flashed to Birbal's mind, the lights flashed out and he was left to the scentless darkness of the garden, to a half muttered curse at the untrustworthiness of his own senses when in the grip of-- of what?

As the trotting bullocks made their way back to Fatehpur Sikri, the puzzle of what had held him recurred again and again, even amid his turmoil of thought regarding the diamond. The tale he had heard could scarcely be true--he had seen the gem safe, but a few hours back; yet the fact that such a conspiracy was on foot was quite credible, and might necessitate still greater care, and at once.

The gray dawn was breaking into day, when, having roused William Leedes without ceremony and carried him to the Hall of Labour, they entered the sentinelled laboratory to find the diamond gleaming as ever on the lathe.

It was a relief. Birbal sate down on the jeweller's stool and breathed again. Despite his incredulity he felt that his whole being, mind and body, had been impressed by the mountebank's manner. He had actually allowed it to overcome his reason.

William Leedes, still but half awake, in utter ignorance of why he had been brought thither, stood for a while stupidly, awaiting a remark. Finally he ventured to ask what was required of him.

"What?" echoed Birbal lightly, recognising with his usual craft, that the less said about his fear the better. "Only that the King is eager to know somewhat of the second facet."

The jeweller's face fell. "Therein lies the puzzle," he said "and I have not yet solved it. The thickness of the stone is great--almost too great, and to cleave it would be to remove, mayhap, too much. Yet without it to find true axis--the sun as we call it in the trade--is a problem that defies at present my geometry."

"Hast tried Aljebr?" asked Birbal, roused instantly to interest. "Show me thy work, sir jeweller, mayhap I can help."

Passed master as he was in the Eastern science of Algebra, they were soon at work with signs and figures.

"That comes more nigh it," said William Leedes, hopefully taking up a small style and going to the lathe.

"Were I to make this point the axis and----" the lathe spun round, then stopped suddenly as he bent to look closer.

"It--it scratches," he murmured, too astonished for bewilderment.

Birbal was by his side in a second, had wrenched the gem from its holding and had it at the light.

A scratch indeed!

In an instant his subtle mind followed the trail unerringly. The trick of a false diamond which he and Abulfazl had urged upon Akbar had been played here. But how? Who was the culprit? His knowledge of humanity, of the world and its ways, instantly exculpated the Englishman from implication in the theft. But had he been careless? That was a point for inquiry; but now, this instant moment, what was to be done? what had best be done?

"Sit silent on yonder stool and work out thy problem, fool!" he said in a whisper to William Leedes, who stood gaping, ready to burst out into speech when it came back to him, "and leave me to work out mine. This is no diamond. 'Tis a false gem made, I swear by Pooru; but to whose order? And for what purpose?"

He paced the little workshop, every fibre of his keen wit vibrating to the tense pressure of his thought. Then he laid his hand suddenly on the amazed jeweller's shoulder.

"When didst thou leave it--only for a moment? Speak truth."

But William Leedes brain had already begun to work slowly.

"Diswunt!" he said mechanically, "he showed me."

The next minute they stood looking round the painter's empty studio. Through the corbeilled balcony they could see the miracle of dawn being enacted, but in the wide, cool, airy room was nothing.

"What did he show thee?" asked Birbal menacingly. For answer William Leedes threw back the door. It fell into its place with a clang of chain upon staple, leaving disclosed no hunting scene; that had been fiercely rubbed off, leaving gray clouds upon the whitewashed wood; but on this indefinite background, limned in with large lines and splashes of a curious scarlet was the figure of a woman. A woman standing, her feet moving in a rhythmic dance, her scarf floating in serpentine curves.

"Siyah Yamin!" cried Birbal under his breath, and stooped to read a legend, dashed in roughly--with the brush, apparently, that still stood half immersed in a bowl, where lingered dregs of the same curious ghastly crimson scarlet pigment with which the portrait was limned.

It was only a verse from Hafiz.

Each man has his gift; to one a cup of wine, to another the heart's blood; so ask not life from the picture on the wall.

The man of wit, of intelligence beyond most, stood looking at the picture in silence. Then he bent to pick up a scrap of crushed paper which lay before it.

As he smoothed it out his face was a study in distaste which grew to quick sympathy as he read. It contained but a few words from Sa'adi:

Wide is the space 'twixt him who clasps his love
And he who watches for her door to move.

And below this in flowing curves:

"Watch no longer, cripple! Gulamâr hath consolation if 'tis needed."

Birbal crushed it in his hand again and walking straight to the corbeilled balcony looked out. In the dawn light a confused, dark bundle as of clothes lay on the angled steps of the Arch of Victory. The distaste vanished from Birbal's face. He stood looking down, infinite pity in his eyes, as he quoted softly:

Yea! He who made me from the clay
And set my soul within it and alway.
Pities and pardons, and enfolds me ever
In His beneficence. Shall I not lay
My heart back in His Hand?

"He--he hath killed himself," cried William Leedes, who had followed to look also.

"Nay, she hath killed him--he painted her in his heart's blood," replied Birbal grimly, stooping for a closer look at the nigh empty bowl, the incarnadined brush.

"Yet I fail to see," began the jeweller, when his companion swept him into silence with a rush of contemptuous irritation.

"Fail to see? How shouldst thou see, strange-bred as thou art from the uttermost guile of India--this old, old India that was guileful long ages before thy island came into being? What canst thou or thy kind know of the bottomless deceits, the dregs of many years, the sediment of many men which must underlay the smooth levels of India? But I, Brâhmin, Indian bred, I see all; and I see here the wagging beards of Mahommedan doctors, virtuous, tradition-bound; I see the lawless desires of libertines like Ibrahîm, the deep designs of Khodadâd--misnamed mayhap! But under all I see the ancient harlotry of womankind. Aye! even what they call Love--misnamed again! Yea, I see the scented balcony in Satanstown where this----"

He pulled himself up and laid his hand compellingly on the jeweller's arm. "But of that hereafter. For the present keep council if thou lovest life. To you and to me only is that gem no diamond. Cut an hundred facets on it an thou wilt; but if its falseness be found out, ere *I* will it, thou diest. Dost hear?"

Then his tone softened a little. "Stay! this scrawling must not stand to tell its tale. Water and this brush, sir jeweller, will send it flying--do this for me--and for *thyself*."

He paused, to give another look at the lad's last work. "Lo! there is genius in it, for 'tis the jade herself. Poor fool! pity he had not read the master to better purpose."

So he passed out with studied carelessness humming as he went another bit of the wisdom of Hafiz:

Wisdom is wearisome--very!
Bring the noose of wine for its neck,
Let us drink, my friend, and be merry,
There's nothing to fear or to reck.
The sun is wine and the Moon's the cup;
Pour the Sun to the Moon and we'll drink it up. And be merry--be merry--very!

CHAPTER XV

I have oft said it, and again I say
That I, poor soul, did never choose my way,
But like taught birds, in hooded darkness heard
What was the Master's will, the Master's word
Bramble or rose whate'er His order gives
I take in joy--knowing the Gardener lives.

--JAMI.

Auntie Rosebody's face showed pale above her wadded pink wrapper in the light of the little cresset that was set upon the floor. Her small hand shook as she reached it out mechanically and took something that was held out to her by one of the two women who, close-wrapped in their *burka* veils, squatted opposite to her. She did not look at this something, she simply held it fast in her closed palm.

What else could she do at two o'clock in the morning, when she had been aroused from innocent slumber to decide, in an instant, the part she would play in a conspiracy to preserve her nephew the King's Luck, and increase that of her beloved grand-nephew the Prince Salîm.

Decide it! When she could scarcely gather her senses together sufficiently to understand what the woman told her: the woman with the polished Persian periods, the persuasive voice, which stamped her, what she was, courtesan. The other voice she vaguely recognised, so, after a time she challenged it.

"Thou art Âtma Devi, the mad fortune teller," she said, catching at any straw of reality in this whirlpool of dreams.

"I am the King's Châran" came the reply. "Therefore, as the Most Beneficent knows, his honour stands for my life."

True! There was reassurance in the thought, besides that which came from the glib list of respected and respectable names that fell from the other glib mouth. Khodadâd's was not amongst them, neither was Mirza Ibrahîm's; for Siyah Yamin knew her company. She was too wise even to betray her own identity and strove to keep the polish from her periods as much as she could as she talked on and on of the safety of the King, of bewitchments, of the immense value it might be to the Prince in the coming Audience of Nobility if luck and favour might be assured to him by the secret wearing of the talisman.

Even so much she protested, should be sufficient reason for the Most Benificent assuming custody of the great diamond, even if she returned it afterward. It would be as easy to replace the false gem with the true one, as it had been to replace the true with the false. But once the bewitchment of the foreigner was broken, the King himself would likely give thanks to God and to his great-aunt. Here was her opportunity!

Poor Auntie Rosebody's eyes wandered helplessly from one *burka-ed* form to the other. She could not even think what "Dearest Lady" would have said. Her mind held nothing but the fact that she, the Lady Hamida, and the whole harem had, but that very afternoon, discussed with tears the question of this cutting of the King's Luck, and that even Hamida had applauded her impulsive assertion that to steal the gem would be allowable under the circumstances. And now, here it was stolen, and in her very hand. It was like the Day of Resurrection!

"And the Prince will need fortune," came the glib voice, "since for these two nights passed, he hath undoubtedly been in Satanstown with Siyah Yamin. And that angers the King. So, those who send us, say 'twere better if the King, his Royal Father, were to give him some distant post of honour--as indeed is but his right. But this can be compassed but by favour, and for this purpose the wearing of such a talisman is potent."

Aunt Rosebody groaned. Did she not know it! Were there not instances without number even in her own family of such influences? If she could only consult someone--even Hamida. But the women were urgent. Except in the safe keeping of the Beneficent Ladies, and under promise, the diamond could not be left.

Then it was that the little lady reached out her hand and took what was held out to her. After that there was but a short whispered conference, and then Aunt Rosebody was left feeling as if the whole round world was tight clasped in her small hand, while the women stole back, as they had come, protected by the Lord Chamberlain's order.

"Well!" asked Siyah Yamin, when, safe beyond the walls, speech was possible. "Art satisfied, Âto, now that thou hast seen the King's Luck out of my evil hands? Ah! Fie on thee sister, for thy threats, thy unkind thoughts of poor little Siyâla, who, heaven knows, has had more curses than cowries out of the business. Yet but for me and my pet thief Pâhlu, who between ourselves nigh starved waiting in the empty workshop while Diswunt was making up his mind--the King's Luck would still be--where it ought to be!"

Âtma's face grew troubled. Ever since the deed had been done, she had, woman like, become afraid of it. It was this vague fear which had made her insist on accompanying Siyah Yamin, so that she might see for herself that the gem had been given into the hands of the Beneficent Ladies. "Think'st thou so in truth, Siyâl----?" she asked reproachfully, "and yet thou hast not ceased to assure me" She broke off, then added "And but for me, sister, Diswunt's mind would never have been made up. It was I----"

Siyah Yamin burst into a low laugh as she disappeared between the curtains of her waiting dhooli. "Give him good reward, then, sister, after woman's fashion. Lo! I have given him mine already."

Something in her tone made Âtma stoop and hurriedly open those closed curtains that were heavy with stale scents. A glimmer of gray dawn-- for it had taken time to persuade Aunt Rosebody to action--showed faintly the courtesan's face set in the white folds of the *burka* she had thrown upward for more air. Perhaps it was a memory of the portrait thus framed which made Âtma repeat herself. "I wonder thou canst be so unkind to a poor lad who loves thee."

"Unkind?" echoed the courtesan with the zest of a child who kills flies. "Death is no unkindness, and they will give it him, doubtless, if he hath been unwise. For he will not blab--that I know--he loves too much!"

She was right. Even as she spoke Diswunt was seeking the Great Silence.

The wind of dawn which found his face as he fell, found her soft babyish face also; but it brought no message, told no secret.

Âtma stood watching the dhooli as it swung off toward Satanstown with a rising dread at her heart. And yet she had acted for the best, and when all was said and done the King's Luck was in good hands.

Siyah Yamin said the same thing to the two conspirators Mirza Ibrahîm and Khodadâd, whom she found waiting for her return anxiously.

"Yea! Yea! Yea!" she answered yawning. "Lord! how we apples swim! She will put it as talisman in the Prince's turban. The rest is not for me. Lo! I have done my work."

"And more!" spoke up Khodadâd after a vain look at his companion to urge him to the task. "Why hast thou taken the woman Âtma into thy confidence? It may spoil all. Why hast thou done it, I say? For that we will have answer now, will we not Ibrahîm? Thou hadst no right----"

Siyah Yamin yawned again.

"Because, fool! without her I could not work!" Then she smiled suddenly. "Lo! there is something betwixt me and old Âto which mankind wist not of, and which I--understand not. But see you, gentlemen, if I need a scapegoat she is ready to hand. And if that please you not, go! But quarrel not over such trifles in the making of plans, my friends. Time runs short and as the proverb says,

One can hear snakes bickering,
By the long tongues flickering.

So this advice I give--silence."

As usual she had the last word.

Poor Auntie Rosebody was at the same moment giving herself the same advice. Sleep had of course, been effectually banished from her eyes, and she was still sitting with the little packet she had received from the women close clasped in her hand. She had held it for so many minutes-- nay, surely hours!--that it seemed to have become part of herself, and her thoughts had long since left even the question as to whether she ought not at once to summon the King and give it back to its rightful owner. The only point with her now was how she could manage her part without help. She had made up her mind not speak to Hamida. One never quite knew what she might think or say. But was there no one else? Aunt Rosebody felt as if she must burst without speech; but it must be speech with silence. And except at night time, it was almost impossible for any one to have a private interview with any one else in the woman's house. It was full to the brim with idle hussies, eunuchs, actual spies! Naturally if she wanted audience of Hamida Begum, she could claim a private one; or even of Râkiya--here the blood flew to Auntie Rosebody's face. No! it should never be old Râkiya, with her hemistitches, her girding tongue, her ill-bred remarks about dead saints! Gulbadan Begum was a good hater and the mere thought of confiding in her enemy quite flustered her. Yet she could not wait for discreet nightfall. What was to be done must be done at once, that very morning; since the festivities that were to commence the six weeks revelling in honour of Salîm's coming marriage were to begin that afternoon. And then, suddenly, a thought struck her. Umm Kulsum! Little Umm Kulsum who was such a tower of good sense and sympathy! She would tell her. Yes! she would tell her, not in the dhooli going to the bathing steps. There they might be overheard by the duennas who walked beside it. That was the worst of being a woman--there were spies everywhere, even upon the bathing steps. But out on the water, right away in the tank, under the azure-silk sky of heaven--there she could ensure solitude!

Aunt Rosebody heaved a sigh of relief. Ah! it was very well of Râkiya Khânum to jibe at indecent youth, but it was something to be able to swim and so get away from old cats!

And so it came to pass that Umm Kulsum coming up to shake her head like a wet spaniel after her dive through the arches, nearly went to the bottom from sheer affright of what she saw in Auntie Rosebody's face.

"Don't" cried the little lady, catching her by the hand and thus largely adding to her imminence of sinking. "Now do listen, Ummu. But I think, my dear, you had better turn on your back and float, for what I've got to tell will make your liver melt, for sure."

So side by side, hand in hand, they floated in the warm, morn-lit water, Auntie Rosebody's gray hair mingling in snaky fashion with Umm Kulsum's black locks while the former told her tale. And more than once the elder woman had to adjure the younger one to keep a straight back and float decently, since some of Aunt Rosebody's revelations were disturbing.

"And now O Umm Kulsum, pilgrimess, mind you, to holy Mecca, save my soul from sin--if thou canst--and tell me, above all, if I be asleep or awake."

The confused appeal brought silence for a moment whilst those two brave, superstitious, affectionate women's faces stared into the azure blue.

Then Umm Kulsum said softly, "It is God's will. He has sent us to do this thing, and we must do it. Yea! Auntie, even if they kill us we must save the King's Luck, and buy favour to Salîm."

"Oh Ummu!" sobbed Auntie Rosebody. "How glad I am I told thee! Thou art wisdom itself and thinkest even as I do. We are two splits to one pea."

And so two set, determined, and in their exaltation, supremely happy, faces showed ducking and bobbing as they swam and made plans. Ummu was to set to work at once and make a seed-pearled and gold-embroidered brocade bag for the stone, which should deftly disguise its shape, and Aunt Rosebody was to say it contained a precious relic from Mecca, and insist on the scapegrace wearing it concealed in his turban for the day. After that? Why ... why...? After that all would depend upon the fortune of the Prince.

So little Umm Kulsum retired to her violet garden in hot haste to dry her hair as usual, and then, having dismissed her maids, began work in the solitude of the secluded spot set round with low walls and orange trees.

She had thought it all out, had seen that time pressed, and so without remorse cut a bold snippet out of the pearl-edged embroidered hem of her very best overcoat which she had told her tirewomen she meant to wear. The damage would not be seen if she wore a thick veil, and a very little sewing, but a few pearls deftly applied, would make of the precious piece a relic holder as good as any in the palace. So her round simple face grew absorbed in her task, when a rustle in the orange tree above her made her look up.

She saw another laughing face looking down; a face that with its orange-coloured veil showed like a ripe fruit amongst the burnished green leaves. The next instant Mihr-un-nissa's lithe, still-childish figure had swung itself to the ground and her forefinger was wagging roguishly at Umm Kulsum's hasty and futile effort to conceal her work.

"Oh fie! Ummu. What! secrets?" came the mocking voice. "Dost not know," here it took on a ludicrous likeness to her mother's, "that only ill-bred young women degrade themselves by duplicity." Then she cuddled close and looked at Umm Kulsum with a perfectly ravishing smile. "Say, sweetheart! is it a love letter?"

Umm Kulsum gave a little shriek of horror. "Go to! thou art a bad girl, Mihru! How didst come here? And how darest thou even mention love letters?"

Mihr-un-nissa cuddled closer. "How? Because I needed to see thee, Ummu--Auntie Ummu I shall call thee, dearest. So when they denied me, I crept out by the window and along the wall. Mother is at the reception, but I needed thee. And as for love--Ah! Ummu! I *have seen him!*"

"Seen whom?" asked Umm Kulsum stolidly. Her mind was busy with likely lies, for she knew the penetrating wit, the cold clear-sightedness, of this child-girl.

"Why!--my man, of course," came the reply with sage noddings of the pretty head.

Everything save horrified outrage flew from Umm Kulsum's mind. "Thou--thou shameless one!--thou canst not mean it. And if thou hadst--by chance--to dare to say it. Mihr-un-nissa Begum, say it is not true!"

The pretty head nodded again cheerfully. "But it is true, Auntie Ummu, and it was not by chance. I climbed into a tree--thou knowest I can climb trees--and saw him over the wall as he came to sup with father. And I like him. He hath a kind, strong face. And--lo! Ummu, one can be queen of a man's heart."

As she sate there, her small slender hands closed on each other as if she held something very precious, a mysterious smile came to her eyes, her mouth. Years younger than her companion, in all things of womanhood she outpassed her utterly. So, as she paused, sudden shame came to her.

"And dost know, Ummu," she went on, a fine blush invading her cheeks that were the colour of ripe wheat, her hands unloosing themselves to plait and replait in her confusion the fold of Umm Kulsum's best overcoat which lay beside her, "I--I think he saw me for--for he smiled-- though he walked on sedately as a gentleman should. But I am not sure his eyes----"

She paused abruptly, gave a little shriek, "Oh! Ummu! thou hast cut it-- thy beautiful overcoat----"

She held up the accusing gap in the hem, and her young face took on swift, keen interest. "So--thy secret! Come out with it, Auntie!" She snatched at Umm Kulsum's work and held it out derisively. "An amulet-- nay! a relic holder!" she cried gaily. "Lo! Umm Kulsum Khânum! it must be for thy lover to wear--in his turban likely."

Umm Kulsum gasped, and leant back against the orange bole helplessly. "Truly, Mihru! thou--thou art a witch!" she murmured feebly.

The expression on the girlish face intensified into absolute cunning. "So--then it is for some one's turban--Prince Salîm's I dare swear--to bring him luck with his father. Ohí Ummu! I have hit it! Tell me, sweetheart, what goes in it? Come! let me have a look at thy face"--for Umm Kulsum in sheer dread of those piercing inquisitive eyes had swaddled herself hastily in her veil. "What thou willst not. Then it is something worth knowing. I will find out--but la! that scent of ambergris portends my mother's passing. I must begone, Auntie Ummu, ere they seek for me. Farewell--and--and good luck go with thy Prince. He needs it!"

She had swung herself into the orange tree once more and was gone, leaving Umm Kulsum with a beating heart. It was an ill chance, and the girl was as a wizard with her guesses; but seeing that the Audience of Nobility was to be held that night, there was small chance for Mihr-un-nissa's wit to do harm. And the Prince would be under solemn promise to bring the talisman back next morning without fail.

Whether he intended to keep the promise or not, certain it is that he made it, while Auntie Rosebody's voice shook over the oath she administered, and little Umm Kulsum stood by trembling in her very marrow. And when the young man had gone off, all duly dressed for his part in the festivities, sulkily carrying with him the well wishes of every woman in the harem in addition to that mighty talisman which they all looked at from a distance with awe, those two poor conspirators retired together and wept on each other's neck.

"I will fast to-night O child!" said the old woman ruefully. "God knows it may be my last; but he may spare thee, being young."

Umm Kulsum only sobbed the more. Why should she add to Aunt Rosebody's anxieties by telling her of Mihr-un-nissa's visit? And after all, the girl had wished the Prince good luck! Something at least should come of that.

And ere many hours were over something did; for, as Prince Salîm walked back through the Palace Gardens, Fate beckoned to him, and from that time forth until his death he never forgot the call.

It happened on this wise. Vaguely disturbed, he dismissed his retinue in an ill temper, and despite the heat of the early afternoon sun sought solitude. Wherefore, who knows?

Had the conspirators gone so far as to tell him that he carried with him the King's Luck, and that he had but to declare himself to find following sufficient to give him the sceptre? Or had they merely begun to prepare the way for such telling in the future? Certain it is that he was moody, thoughtful beyond his wont. In half an hour or so the festival would begin by a grand illumination; the festival which would bring him marriage, if his father ...

That break in his thoughts seemed to end every subject for thought.

If his father--if his father...?

The noise of the firework makers and lamp sellers who were at work in the principal paths, annoyed him, so he wandered off into the more private ones, amusing himself idly, almost unconsciously, with a pair of doves he had taken, as the only silent companions--he had said bitterly, in the court.

If his father--if his father...? The question obsessed him.

Whether he knew actually that he carried kingship with him, certain it is that his thoughts were with himself, as king. What he would do, what he would say, what he would think.

If--this thing--were to happen, *now*, would he marry this Râjpûtni? Not--by all the twelve Imams--if she were ugly! And, as his friends said--they were all Mahommedans--the first wife should be of Islâm.

He had wandered farther than he knew, and without realising it had entered the garden belonging to the women's apartments. But it was empty; the hour was early and every one busy dressing for the festival. So he went on unhindered. It was cooler here in the pleached alleys, and perfumed too. Out yonder in the sunlight the very scent of the flowers seemed burnt up.

Yes! If he married----

The onyx-eyed birds of love he was carrying fluttered and fretted. Were they too, dreaming of liberty. Curse the brutes! Why could they not keep quiet, and give him a chance of making up his mind.

His eye caught someone, a slip of a child it looked, wrapped close in a creamy veil sitting beside a fountain. Some coolie's daughter, no doubt, waiting for her father to finish work.

"Here, hold these birds, child," he cried peremptorily. The figure did not move and with another curse on its stupidity he strode up to it, thrust the pigeons into its lap and with a brief order to hold them fast till his return, strode off again. Something he must settle, he felt, before he met his father in the Audience of Nobility.

Vague, instinctive affection and loyalty had to war with passionate desires for power, with the thousand and one poisoned thoughts which, day and night, were put into his mind diligently by those who sought him as their tool.

When he had disappeared into the thickets of pomegranate and orange, there came a sudden little laugh.

"Oh! birdies! birdies! What a stupid stripling!"

The shrouding veil which she had hastily drawn round her on the appearance of the Prince, slipped back, and Mihr-un-nissa's dimpling face was buried in the opalescent feathers of her captives. "Nay! no struggling! Sure thou art better here than with your sulky, fatling Prince--though see you, my birds, he is not so ill-looking when he is seen close, as the squirrel said of the spider when he had dismembered him! But he is not a patch on Sher Afkân. La! how Ummu squirmed when I spoke of him. What sillies women be, as if one might not use one's eyes. Ohí! Now I have it! 'Tis the talisman in his turban gives the Prince his air. Have a care! Mihr-un-nissa, lest thou fall in love with him and desert true friend. And yet----"

She paused, looked down at her own face mirrored in the water and what she saw there held her.

It was true what the woman told her. That was no mere wife's face--it was the face of a queen--a real queen----

The birds of love fluttered in her listless hold. Lost in her dreams she scarcely noticed that one, eluding her slack grasp fled joyfully to coo his pæan of liberty from an orange tree hard by.

Was it worth it? Was it worth it? What was all the power in the world worth to a woman, as she--the girl upon its verge--imagined womanhood?

"My birds?" The Prince had returned. The imperious voice roused her; roused her temper also.

"Here, my lord," she replied curtly.

"What? Only one?" The voice was angry now; almost ready for a curse.

She set, as it were, soul and body into cold ice.

"Sire!" she answered, with chill courtesy, "one has flown."

In the shade of the trees, her face, averted, was unseen, and of her figure, crouched in upon itself instinctively, the Prince saw nothing but childish outlines.

"Stupid fool," he cried roughly. "How? Damn you! Tell me how."

She was on her feet in a second, facing his anger fearlessly, her own blazing hot in defiance of all things. Aye! even this fading Prince who dared to call her fool!

"So! my lord!" she cried defiantly and from her outstretched hands the second dove flew circling to join its mate.

Salîm stood startled into silence. From the orange tree the doves were cooing. The perfumes of the garden rose up around them. Overhead blazed the brazen sky.

But the Heir-Apparent of India saw nothing save that first glimpse of the woman who as Mihr-un-nissa, Queen of Women, Nurmabal, the Light of Palaces, and finally as Nur-jahan, the Light of the World, was to play so large a part in his life.

He was too much taken up with the love which, like the doves, had flitted from the listless hand of Fate even to attempt to detain the girl, when with a sudden sweeping salaam, a soft sweet, "Your servant, Mihr-un-nissa" she turned and fled.

At least, she felt, he might as well know who she was.

CHAPTER XVI

A thousand ships have foundered here before
So lost, no chip of them came back to shore.
I, too, on those waves wandered many a night,
Till terror plucked my sleeve, and cried "No More!
Back to the land! God's wide horizon rings
Thee and the worlds. Thinkst thou the King of kings
To compare by conjecture? Ah! poor wight,
Wisdom itself, wists not His hidden things."

--SA'ADI.

When Mihr-un-nissa fled from the Prince in the garden, she did not fly far. Just round the corner waiting for her return, stood her covered palanquin, her dutiful duenna. For Mussumât Fâtima had long since given up attempting to control her young mistress. To begin with, she had found out that Mihr-un-nissa was not as other girls. She was wild as a young hawk, but there it ended. Except in so far as uttermost mischief went, she was to be trusted; there never was any fear of love letters or any improprieties of that sort. So, if she chose to fancy sitting beside a fountain by herself in the women's garden, where was the harm? She was a mound of sense; so much so, that on this hot afternoon (heaven knows why the child had insisted on coming out--to ruin her complexion, doubtless, if she could--but she couldn't--from the crown of her head to the sole of her foot there wasn't a speck or a freckle) no one could blame a body for dozing in the dhooli and dreaming.

"La! child! How thou didst frighten me," gasped Fâtima, as a tornado of yellow and purple draperies flung itself breezily on the top of her fat person.

"Oh! Futtu! Futtu!" panted the girl, half laughter, half tears. "I have seen him!"

"What, again!" shrilled the duenna, waking instantly to a sense of her responsibilities. "Impudence! knowest thou not that paper boats don't float for ever, and that who lacks modesty lacks conscience?"

"Oh! have done with second-hand wisdom," said the girl, superbly. "And it was not him--It was the Prince--Prince Salîm."

Fâtima let loose a shriek. "Oh! my liver! An' thou darest to tell me! 'Tis bread and water for a week, miss----"

"And I spoke to him and he spoke to me," continued the culprit, calmly; out of sheer perversity, reversing the order of events.

Fâtima let loose a louder shriek. "What! Lo! the noose is round thy neck, and mine too! May the devil be deaf! If folk hear----"

But the girl who had drawn aside with distaste and was now seated half in and half out of the palanquin, interrupted the duenna contemptuously. "Futtu, thou art a full-weight fool. Why dost not remember it needs skill to do wrong instead of making thy nose red with wrath?"

Suddenly she stood up, a curiously defiant figure. "Lo! I am sick of saws and sayings. I want to know at first hand! And I will know. Call the carriers. I go to Âtma Devi. Lo! I have tried, as thou knowest, to see in the ink again; but it comes not. I lack the charm she said; she shall teach it me. Nay!" she continued stemming Fâtima's rising flood of denials, "See here, fool. If thou deniest me I go straight home, and tell--not *my* mother, she would be pleased--but Sher Afkân's, and then----" She clasped the old woman's neck with both hands and squeezed it tight. "Does it feel nice, Futtu?" she asked solicitously.

So it came to pass that just as the sun was setting, its last rays sparkled on Mihr-un-nissa's jewelled hair, as she sate on the Châran's roof waiting for the drop of ink to fall into her palm. She was more woman than child now, since she had watched the birth of desire, and of something more than desire, in Prince Salîm's eyes. So that was love! A queer thing, at best, it must be to feel as he must have felt, before he could look so poor a slave. If that was love, she could not give it back. What! give homage to a lout of a lad? And yet the Queenship! Oh! if it had been Akbar himself, then she would have known what to do, for he was King indeed! Or if--yes! if it had been "*him*," for he was a man indeed!

> Drop ink and hide my flesh,
> Cover my worldly ways.
> Then let God's light afresh
> Mirror God's praise.
> Drop ink, drop deep,
> Cover in sleep

My night of nights and bring the day of days.

This time the chanted words thrilled little Mihr-un-nissa through and through. For once--and perhaps for the first time in her young life she was in deadly earnest. But, once again poor Âtma's mind was far from her spell. Ever since Deena that morning had brought her word of Diswunt's death, regret, remorse had warred with her defiance. It was strange. What did it mean? Had he regretted? And wherefore? At times absorbed with fear lest she should have betrayed the King, she had been ready to seek out Birbal and tell him the truth, risking her own life. But there was her promise, her sisters-troth with Siyah Yamin. That cut both ways. It forced her to silence, so long as the courtezan kept troth. And had she not? Had not Âtma Devi seen with her own eyes Aunt Rosebody's hand close on the diamond? Could it be in better keeping?

"If the gracious child will complete the circle of magic," she began, when Mihr-un-nissa's laugh rang out disdainfully.

"What! to see what thou thinkest? Not so! What I shall see, what I shall do, is of my own gift. Stand back woman!--touch me not!"

> Drop ink, drop deep,
> Cover in sleep

My night of nights and bring the day of days.

She chanted the words lingeringly and for an instant there was silence while those two women, the fat, worldly duenna, and the passion-distraught denier of her sex, listened and looked with long-drawn tense breathings. It was deadly earnest to them also. Would she see? Could she see? Such things were, they knew, beyond the magic frauds of fortune-tellers.

And then suddenly the sweet round voice rose eagerly.

"I see! Holy prophet! I see--It is the Prince; but Lord! how fat he hath grown and how old--I think he is the King----"

Fâtima under her breath muttered "An old King's better than a young Prince."

Mihr-un-nissa flashed round on her. "'An egg to-day's better than a hen to-morrow,' so there! saw-sayer!" Then she looked again. "Sher Afkân this time. He hath a scar upon his face that suits him well, and a drawn sword."

"'The soldier gains his bread, by the risking of his head,'" murmured the irrepressible Fâtima.

"'Lie you must, or your belly will bust,'" quoted Mihr-un-nissa shamelessly, too interested, really, to do more than fling a reply in this war of wise sayings. "Lo! clouds--clouds--nothing but clouds again. What's this? Crossed swords and someone fighting for his life. Holy Prophet! save him! save him! Clouds again. That is my face grown old--and I am all in white," the girl's voice seemed to shrink in on itself; her eyes, startled, looked indeed as if across the chasm of the years she saw herself as she would be. "Surely I am widow--and there's the King once more." She drew back from her own hand as she might have drawn back from fate. "Then *he* was not killed," she muttered in a low whisper. "It must have been the--the other. Oh help! help! help!"

She started to her feet, and as if in answer to her scarce audible cry, a violent knocking shook the door.

"Open! Open! in the King's name, open!"

The command reduced even Mihr-un-nissa to the conventional quiet which on such occasions sinks on an Indian woman's house, when those are within who should not be seen.

You might have heard a pin drop.

"Âtma Devi, Châran of the King, open to his demand," came Birbal's voice, clear, unmistakeable, followed quickly by the order--"Break open the door, slaves, I must see if she be within ere seeking elsewhere."

There was no time to lose. Instinctively Fâtima, holding fast to her charge and dragging her with her, fled noiselessly to the closed door of the slip of a room where Zarîfa lay sleeping, and Mihr-un-nissa herself seeing no other way out of the *impasse*, allowed herself to be dragged, as stealthily, as noiselessly.

None too soon, for as the latter motioning her duenna arbitrarily to the farther corner of the darkness was limply closing the door so as to allow a crack for hearing, a crash told that one bolt of the outer one had given way, and Âtma Devi's voice rang out--

"Hold! I will open to my Lord Birbal."

His voice in return came through from without. "So thou wouldst spare thy lock, widow! See that thou spare thy life also! Slaves--get you gone--await me on the landing below, and if I call, come."

A moment after he was facing Âtma Devi, his face pale with contemptuous passion.

"No lies, widow," he began at once. "I have come for the truth. Old Deena, the drumbanger, hath blabbed somewhat! I have gathered more in the bazaars. Thou art in this plot of the King's Luck, or thou knowest something of Siyah Yamin's part in it. Speak or----"

The flash of the poniard he held met an answering flash, as Âtma slipped forward, the death-dagger of her race ready on the instant, her passion roused instinctively at the sight of his.

"The King's Châran," she replied haughtily, "knows how to die--knows how to protect the King's Luck; and as for Siyah Yamin she is my sister of the veil. Between us lies troth--to death."

That had been her chief thought during the past few hours. It had indeed been her consolation in the vague regrets which had assailed her. Siyah Yamin was hand-fast to her. The courtesan had repeated the oath solemnly when Âtma Devi in restless anxiety had gone to her again; what is more she had given words of warning against Birbal, against the faction which he and Abulfazl represented. She had stigmatised them as self-seeking, as those who led the King astray. And had he not gone astray? Was there not, to begin with, this new edict forbidding widows to burn with their husbands? Would not the next step--if these two remained his advisers--be the forbidding of women to be widows indeed?

Every atom of womanhood in her, all tangled and torn apart by the plucking fingers of natural instinct and inherited ethics, rose up in revolt against herself, against everybody, everything in the world save that one thing--the King's honour, the King's Luck.

She stood surging in uttermost rebellion, and Birbal realised that a deftless word, almost a deftless look, would send the dagger of her race to her woman's heart.

So, realising also his mistake in having thus driven his last chance of discovery into such sharp antagonism, he shrugged his shoulders, strolled over to the parapet, and sate dangling his legs in his usual debonair fashion. But his keen eyes were on hers.

"Thy pardon, sister," he said. "Who can doubt that the King's Châran has his luck at heart, and it is for this, that I have come to thee. Now listen."

He paused and but for his intentness those keen eyes of his might have seen the faintest quiver of the door opposite him, as if someone behind it wished to hear better.

"The King's Luck, given to the stranger to be cut, hath been stolen from the lathe, and a false gem put in its place. Shall I tell thee how?" his questioning eyes found hers with a baffling stare in them and he went on. "A thief--Pâhlu, prince of thieves most likely, but I have naught against him as yet--managed entry to the empty workshop next to the diamond by scarce-seen clamps in the outer brick wall. He must have worked hard, and risked his life many dark, midnight hours; but he did it. The clamps remain. And doubtless he had a silken rope. Then Diswunt, the King's painter, beguiled the foreign jeweller out of his cell for a second or two. So the deed was done. But who beguiled Diswunt? Siyah Yamin doubtless. I have proof of that--but the boy was loyal. It would need some sense of duty, of devotion, to beguile him; that I know. Now, thou didst go to his house, not once but twice--of that, also, I have found proof. Wherefore? That is what, in the King's name, I ask?"

He paused for a reply, but none came, and his face hardened.

"Now listen further," he went on again. "Of another thing I have but too much proof. The court is astir. But now, I passed that hell-doomed cur Khodadâd, and he smiled at me--at me, his bitterest enemy! So he is content. Some plot is afoot, and the foundation of all plots is the Prince Salîm--they seek to oust Akbar and place the drunken lout, slave to his own passions and so slave to theirs, upon the King's throne."

Âtma laughed scornfully. "That will they never do--my Lord the King hath too many friends."

"And too many enemies, also," retorted Birbal. "Fool thou dost not see, thou dost not understand--thou art but a woman of whom men expect naught!"

It was growing dusk rapidly so a faint widening in the door-chink passed unnoticed.

"Now listen again!" he went on yet once more. "Thou hast been often to Siyah Yamin's of late, and Deena hath a tale of two veiled women at the Palace last night----"

There was the faintest flicker of a flinch in Âtma's eyes, and he was on his feet in a second, stretching out an accusing hand toward her.

"Thou wast there--thou and that accursed harlot--deny it not!"

She withdrew a pace and set her back to the wall. "I deny nothing, and I affirm nothing, my lord," she replied coolly, obstinately, though she felt torn in two by the conflict of her doubts.

"Fool!" he blazed out again. "I tell thee every second may be precious! Listen--if thou canst listen, being but woman! Not only the court, but within the last hour or so the soldiery, the people, show unrest also, and we may be undone this night! I myself can scarce understand.--It has come in a second like a miracle--as of some talisman----" his quick wit caught at his own words--"I have it!--The King's Luck! the Prince hath it."

In a second he had gripped both Âtma's wrists with his lithe hands and held her pinned to the wall. "Tell me, fool! All things rest on it mayhap--all things for which we have worked and hoped--for which he hath worked and hoped--the peace, the unity of India. Say! woman! Didst give it to the Prince?" Then seeing the utter obstinacy of her face, he realised the futility of wasting time with her, when he had found a cue which might lead to much elsewhere, and throwing her hands from him with a curse on all womanhood, he turned to go relying on his own keen wit.

But another keen wit joined to a mind capable of comprehension had been at work behind the chink. There was a faint scuffle, a muffled shriek, as Fâtima, who had heard nothing, made a dive at her little mistress's dress as she flung the door wide, and stepped out. Fate forced the duenna to grip the veil, so she only made matters worse; for Mihr-un-nissa stood bare-headed before the strange man.

Birbal, however, even in his hurry to seek help elsewhere, did not need such trivialities as veils to make him pause with instant consideration for the dignity of the slim young figure which barred his way.

"My lord," came the full rich young voice, "need not rail at all womankind. Here is one who will tell him the truth for the sake of Kingship. Peace! Âtma!" continued the girl, turning hotly on the Châran who would have interrupted, "thou understandest not, so be silent! My lord! I judge the talisman of the King's luck to be at this moment in Prince Salîm's turban. For at the palace this morning, I saw Khânzada Umm Kulsum sewing somewhat into a relic bag for this purpose, and she denied me knowledge. Nay! I am sure of it----."

She paused and Birbal asked quickly:

"Will the Queen-of-Women give reason?"

The girl's face suddenly dimpled into smiles, a mischievous twinkle took her eyes captive.

"Because the Most-Excellent the Heir-Apparent straightway came out of the Palace and fell in love with me."

A shriek of horror from Fâtima who was employed in attempting to re-enshroud the young girl's beauty emphasised the absolute impropriety of the remark, but Birbal bowed to the very ground.

"That is Luck beyond the Luck of Kings, madam," he said, "and reason beyond question. This Speck of Dust in the Court of Intellect gives thanks for the Truth, and withdraws his earthly clay"--he paused, for as he turned to go he saw the *rebeck* player standing on the threshold. "Back slave!" he cried at once impetuously--"this roof is sacred to a Queen."

But the musician's pale face lit up suddenly. "A Queen suffers no ill from the eyes of a King," he replied, fixing his gaze on Mihr-un-nissa. So for an instant they stood, measuring one another; then the man turned quickly to Birbal, "Come, my lord," he said, "the Sufi from Isphahân desires to see the Most Excellent!--when he can withdraw his earthly clay from the presence of the Queen of Queens."

Mihr-un-nissa stood looking after them as they disappeared, nodding her head with a superior air. Then, in sudden change, she clapped her hands together joyfully like a child. "That is good," she cried. "It is lovely to be called that. Lo! I would do most things for that--except marry the Prince! Yea! most things so that it was the Luck of a real King!" Something in her own words made her pause. "That must be safeguarded," she murmured, as if to herself. Then she wheeled round and caught the fat duenna by both hands and tried to force her to her knees.

"Kneel, Fâtima, or I will hurt thee! Kneel, dost hear? What! thou disobeyest me!" A stamp of her foot emphasised her order, and brought the fat duenna down in a hurry.

"Say! didst hear aught?" asked the girl superbly. "In the room, I mean, not here."

"Highness, not a word!" protested Fâtima; "but what I heard here-- what I saw here--have made me deaf and blind for ever."

"So much the better, Futtu, so much the better," nodded Mihr-un-nissa wisely. "Still 'tis always best to be on the safe side. So put thy mouth in the dust and say after me:

"May crows pick out mine eyes.

"Say! dost hear?

"May crows pick out mine eyes."

An ineffectual murmur came from the dust.

"May pigs devour my thighs."

The dust had evidently got into the speaker's mouth, for the words became more and more inaudible, as the stern young teacher went on:

"My heart rot carrion wise,
My liver be eaten with flies,
My lights blown up with sighs,
Myself, my son, and all that I prize
Burn in a fire that never dies
If ever I open my lips to say
The things I have heard and have seen to-day."

"So!" said Mihr-un-nissa when the formula was over, "that's done. And as for thee?" she passed quickly to Âtma Devi, who, half stunned by the swift mastery with which the girl had taken the whole business out of her hands, still stood leaning blankly against the blank wall and looked her curiously in the eyes. "Why wouldst thou not tell? And wherefore didst thou steal the diamond?"

Then as she stood childishly curious, comprehension came to her and she smiled half-contemptuously half-mysteriously.

"So, thou also lookest a slave," she said, "poor slave!"

But as she and Fâtima went whisperingly down the stairs, the faint clatter of their loose slippers mingling like castanets amid the soft swishing of silk, the jingling of jewels, she paused to listen to a bird-like voice singing:

Love dost live in the red rose garden?
Love dost grow from a red rose root?
Dost set thy springe with th' boughs that harden
Or twine it soft with the young green shoot?
Love! dost thou lurk in the red rose-bud?
Love! is thy throne in the rose-heart's crown?
Love! does the perfume of red rose flood
In on the soul till the senses drown?

Nay!

Love lives not in a garden of roses,
Root nor bough nor the young green shoot,
Bud nor chalice the perfume encloses
Of Love lying lowly at Love's own feet.
For Love is the Rose, Love is the Star

Love is the heart of things near and afar,
And afar--and afar--and afar!

Mihr-un-nissa shook her head, as the whispering descent began again. Of a truth Love was far, very far, away.

CHAPTER XVII

Yet when from off the table of God's grace
He gives what each may carry to their place
Satan draws nigh, "Even for me" he says
"A portion has been portioned in God's ways."

--SA'ADI.

The Most Illustrious, the Mighty in Power, the High in Pomp, the Exalted in Splendour, the Father of his People, the Conqueror of the Age, the Pole Star of Faith, the Sun of the World, Jalâl-ud-din Mahommed Akbar, Great Mogul, Emperor of India, sate enthroned on a dais which had been erected for the purpose of the festivities on the uppermost terrace of the Palace Gardens.

The violet blackness of the sky above him was ablaze with stars, as only an Indian sky can blaze, when the dust held in the atmosphere has been laid by recent rain. And, to the infinite relief of the town and all concerned in its welfare, rain had fallen--fallen in torrents, suddenly sharply, during the later hours of dawn, leaving every tank full, every street washed clean under the vivid blue sky which the storm seemed to have washed also.

Relief had come from heaven, but no one looked at the stars, for the blaze below held all eyes. A circle of Bengal lights so arranged that the King's head should show against them, shed veritable sunlight on his golden throne and on the white-robed figure that sate on it; for, as ever, Akbar was dressed with studied simplicity. True, the Benares muslin with its fine stitched edging of silver had taken years in the loom, the ropes of pearls he wore over it were worth a king's ransom, but there was no note of colour anywhere, and the turban, guiltless of all ornament save the heron's plume of chieftainship, showed dull without the calm radiance of the great diamond. Yet all things centred on the man who sate enthroned, because it was his thought, his imagination which had inspired the whole marvellous spectacle that was being held in the terraced garden surrounded by distant half-seen palaces.

And it was marvellous, indeed! The dais (behind which in darkest shadow rose the latticed vantage ground of the court ladies) was semicircular, round-fronted and was superabundantly lit by that crown of twelve Bengal lights (representing the twelve solar months) which hung like a halo round the man who claimed to be the Sun of his World. A big claim, but in this instance it was made with such magnificent straightforwardness, such clear perception of all that the claim entailed, as to disarm criticism. This dais, some ten feet high, rose from a semicircular round-fronted plinth which was lost in shadow, partly because of a projecting eave which prevented the light from above striking on it, and partly because seven equi-distant lights (representing the seven days of the week and in varying colours showing the tints of a rainbow) were so cunningly set in shades round the dais that their light left the plinth in darkness and shot out, in ever widening rays, through the garden, growing less and less distinct until at its farther end colour seemed lost in a general mist of light.

And in six of these rays, red, orange, yellow, blue, indigo, violet, widening with the light, sate, in ordered rows, on the red side the Hindus and Buddhists of the court, upon the violet side the Mahommedans, the Jains, the Jews. Only the central green ray, compounded of these two factors blue and yellow remained empty, showing nothing but a narrow marble walk bordered on either side by wide water ways, out of which fountains shot high into the still, dark air; shot, illumined so far by the lights, then, rising high above them, mere ghostly shadows on the darkness, to fall again in drops that grew iridescent as they fell.

There was no other illumination in the garden; but the distant palaces were outlined in every curve, every detail, by little soft flickering lamplets like stars.

The running water in the waterways came out of the dark plinth below the dais, and about fifty yards from it, ran under a wider crossways marble platform which ended the narrow pathway; emerging from this short hiding to fall rippling over a marble slope, where (safe-sheltered from every drop in deftly cut niches) cunning little coloured lamps shone, converting the whole cascade into a rainbow. Hence, united, the stream of the two waterways merged into one, and flowed to disappear from the garden through a low archway tunnelled beneath the palace; thence to find its way by underground passages to the tank at the bottom of the Sikri ridge.

Even as a mere spectacular effect the scene was striking, but once the inner meaning of it, so clear to the mind of the white-robed figure on the throne, was grasped, it became of absorbing interest as representing the vast empire which Akbar had so far succeeded in welding together. First the surging misty radiance of the crowd at the end; then, strengthening as each ray narrowed, the broad demarcations of the various religions professed by Akbar's subjects. Râjpûts in their red robes on the one side elbowing the Brâhmins in the orange of the ascetic; Shiahs in purple beside the Sunnis in indigo; while in the yellow ray sate Buddhists in their devotional colour; in the blue the Sufis, the Jews, the Jains, all the smaller cults that are to be found in India.

Between them, centring all, shone the green ray of the true faith, the perfect equality of toleration and freedom which was Akbar's ideal--and it was empty!

Perfect as the scene was, every soul in the garden that night felt a consciousness of vague depression, vague expectation. Eyes wandered as they were not used to wander from that central figure on the throne.

"'Tis the talisman which the scapegrace wears," whispered Aunt Rosebody ruefully from behind the latticed screen to little Umm Kulsum who was holding her hand--she had been holding it practically ever since the fatal moment, a few hours back, when they had seen the Prince walk away unconcernedly with the hidden diamond in his turban of state. "Oh! Ummu, I feel so cold down my back. But there is no remedy against one's own acts! Though why such temptation should be put in the way of an old woman only God and His Prophet knows! But 'tis always so. He had but one eye and the grit fell in it."

"We did what we thought best, auntie!" whimpered the Mother of Plumpness, "and we can take it back when the Audience is over--or we can die!"

Aunt Rosebody shook her head mournfully. "Dying is no good" she protested, "but why doth not the scapegrace come and have done with it! If oil isn't ready when the frying pan's ready, it had best go away!"

"In truth it appears long waiting, mayhap, for the last day," sighed Umm Kulsum tragically.

"Last day!" echoed Aunt Rosebody snappishly. "Lo! who wants a last day? Not I. Sure I am betwixt and between. Earth too hard, sky too far like the swallows. Please God they'll hurry up and let me get to my prayers. Lo! there goes Khodadâd with a smile on his face. True is it that lies only shine in the dark."

In truth Khodadâd stepped jauntily and his face shone with content as he passed to his place in the light-screened plinth where the court officials were gathered awaiting the signal which was to summon them to the dais above, there to range themselves behind the Emperor for the coming audience.

"It is nigh time," said Mirza Ibrahîm, who as Court Chamberlain had charge of the ceremonies. "Gentlemen are you ready?"

Then he bent forward to the newcomer and whispered something. The whispered reply brought such satisfaction to Ibrahîm's face also, that he stared with open contempt at Birbal, who lounging in, lazily late, was making his way toward him.

"My lord has nearly missed his chance," he said meaningly.

"Nay! Sir Chamberlain," replied Birbal coolly, "I am about to take it, and--and give it." He held out a paper as he spoke. "The matter is urgent, since as the Envoy comes with all the Insignia of Royalty, he must be presented before the Heir-Apparent. But such etiquettes are safe in the hands of a Chamberlain! For the rest, he and his retinue await reception at the gate."

"What is't?" asked Khodadâd in an undertone as he saw Ibrahîm's face change. But his own turned grayish green, as, over the shoulder he read the titular address:

"I, Payandâr Tarkhân of the House of Sinde coming by order----"

"Impossible," he gasped. "This--this is some jest of my lord Birbal's. Payandâr is----"

"There be other Tarkhâns so called besides the one who died in the wilderness," retorted Birbal slowly, "and this one comes as King--so he says. Read through the document, Mirza Sahib, and see if all is in order. If so, do the duty of Chamberlain; and be quick about it, for yonder go the royal *nakârahs*. The Hour of Audience has come. Gentlemen! to our places. I will inform the Emperor."

A minute later, the court officials stood in a serried semicircle behind the King, and the green light, the central light of the seven, had divided into two and shone guarding either side of a narrow marble staircase which was disclosed leading upward to the dais. At the foot of this stood Mirza Ibrahîm, reading aloud, in a voice which betrayed his agitation, the titular names and designations of the Amir of Sinde. His mind was busy with a thousand questionings. What did it all mean? And why had Khodadâd been so disturbed? Surely their plans were secure? Surely the Prince had been told of the talisman? Surely this knowledge would breed confidence--and so--with aid--defiance? Every one was ready. That very night might see conspiracy successful at last, the Prince, at last, forced into taking his part.

"Let the Royalty of Sinde, as represented by him who wears the Insignia of Royalty be welcome to the Court of the Sun of the World."

The words were spoken by Abulfazl, as Prime Minister. His face showed a slight astonishment which was reflected even on Akbar's. He leant forward as if eager to see the unexpected visitor, and all eyes followed his toward the dim radiance of the distant crowd. Something there was in the multitude of faces, half seen though deep-shadowed, which thrilled many of the lookers. But the thrill passed into something like an electric shock, as tearing the still night air with discordant clangour, an almost inconceivable clash and crash of copper kettledrums and brass cymbals seemed to crack the ears that heard it.

Instinctively almost every one present drew back from the sound, blinked, then opened eyes afresh upon the world of coloured lights and hidden imaginations. Even Akbar started, and Birbal, looking eagerly into his eyes, gave a quick sigh of relief.

So swiftly had the start come and gone, yet so real had been its effect upon every nerve, that people felt dazed, uncertain, waking as it were to the perception that a figure was standing on the crossway platform of marble above the rainbow cascade--standing almost alone, though backed by a confused crowding of retinue on either side the central waterway.

The only other figures really visible were two misshapen dwarfs, one in front, bearing a tasselled lance, the other behind, bearing a tasselled lance also. But both showed jet black from head to foot, and each carried, the front one on his breast, the one behind on his back a round, brilliant mirror. Or was it a brilliant light? Certain it is that as the dwarfs strutted forward, leading and following the central figure these round plaques shot out a dazzling brilliance, and for, an instant seemed to cloud all else.

The next thing that became clear was the vivid green of emeralds; such ropes of them, shining like young green wheatfields, in the green radiance shed by the central light of green.

"The emeralds of Sinde, sure enough," said Mân Singh half to himself, and settled down comfortably to look, as he sate heading the red ray of Râjpûts. But there were others in those converging rays who stared and said doubtfully, "Sure, yonder are Birbal's daughter's two dwarfs that all know!" Until hushed by some neighbour's contemptuous denial, they also saw their mistake, and looked with believing eyes. There was one man, however, who, though he denied strenuously grew grayer and grayer as he watched the slight figure with the long black curls resting on its sloping shoulders, and the slight beard scarce covering the thin narrow cheeks. "'Tis Sufurdâr for sure!" muttered Khodadâd fighting against fear--"it is but the emeralds that bring the resemblance--that is all!--before God, that is all!"

So, the green light in which the little group was enveloped growing greener as the three figures approached the dais, they advanced, until at the foot of the stairs, the dwarfs stood one to each side, the one who had walked in front wheeling to show his mirror also to the watching eyes.

To that confused crowd at the end of the garden these two shining spots glowed beneath the green lamps. That was all; and the familiar words of welcome given as Akbar motioned the representative of Sinde to the cushions beside him took all the strangeness from the scene. It was the beginning of the marriage festival; other Princes had sent, or would send their representatives. Sinde, no doubt to curry favour with the Mogul, had sent its Royalty by the hand of an envoy; but the great event of the evening was yet to come. For that was the reception of the Bridegroom-Elect, the Heir-Apparent--the man who might come to his own any day, since Akbar was ever reckless of his own life. Had he not escaped by a miracle being killed at *chaugan* but the other day?

So the whole assembly stirred as one man, when the Royal *nakârahs* sounded once more, and Prince Salîm followed by a right royal retinue showed, where the Envoy of Sinde had showed, on the marble platform above the rainbow cascade.

"Lo! Ummu!" whispered Auntie Rosebody, "we did the right thing. He looks the Archangel Gabriel. Let me go to bed in the dark, my day is full!"

And in truth the Prince had never looked better in his life. Perhaps the whole-heartedness of his plunge into Love's sea was the only reason why his hopes ran high; perhaps he knew of the talisman he carried, but carried it with no evil intention; perhaps again those hopes of his had gone further than mere Love, so that he saw himself master of the situation, able to give the Râjpût girl whom he had never seen the go by, able to do in future what he chose, what he desired. But certain it is that every eye followed his youthful dignity with admiration, and more than one looked furtively from the son to the father, appraising both. In that father's mind, however, was no hint of jealousy, only unmixed joy.

As he raised his son from his obeisance and kissed him on both cheeks, it seemed to him as if, at long last, content had come to him. The questionings which had so harassed him of late seemed to have fled. Here was an heir, indeed!

"How well thou lookest Shaikie!" he whispered affectionately in the young man's ear ere taking him by the hand and leading him forward so that they might be seen by all the populace.

A goodly pair indeed! The younger man, somehow--for this evening at any rate--with more personal charm about him; but the elder one even in his plain dress, his unadorned turban, a king every inch of him.

"Heralds! read out the Titles of this my beloved son, Salîm!"

Akbar's voice raised in command penetrated to the farthest corner of the garden and every ear strained to catch the honours that were to be showered on this Heir to Empire. Aunt Rosebody's face, flushed with anxiety grew crimson dark with sheer delight as she listened.

"Captain of Ten Thousand--praise be to Allah!" she commented breathlessly. "What! a Viceroy in the Northeast--now may I go to Paradise!--Master of Distinctions!--what! Sunshade and Fly whisk! Umm Kulsum! I go again to Mecca to give thanks--And the jewels--not *sir-a-pa*, head to foot!--not *sir-a-pa!*--Yes!--Now may they kill me--one can take two kicks from a milch cow! Unalienable--did I hear right--Ummu tell me! tell this poor old woman who--who--cannot believe--her ears."

"Unalienable, never to be neglected. Always to be considered by right, election, and consent Crown Prince." So far the Mother of Plumpness repeated in a trembling voice; then the two women fell on each other's necks and wept.

"Bring the well!" murmured Auntie Rosebody. "I'll drown myself."

And Akbar stood holding his heir by his right hand, full of a great triumph.

"Lo! I have given thee all, Shaikie" he said fondly, "art content?"

"Not all!" said a quiet voice beside him. "There is yet one honour withheld from this Peerless Prince, this Honourable Heir."

It was the Envoy from Sinde who as the representative of royalty stood on Akbar's left hand a step behind him.

Akbar flashed round on him haughtily. "What honour hath Sinde to suggest?"

"The honour of Brotherhood to the Sun of the World. The honour of the exchange of turbans!"

The converging rays of spectators suddenly seemed to quiver, as if some of their component parts stirred, but the Emperor stood still, his eyes upon the envoy's.

Then his own narrowed with quick thought. "Sinde is right," he said slowly, "there is no tie like brotherhood. It is the chain which links the whole world to One." He turned swiftly to his son withdrawing his hand from him and so for an instant standing apart, dissevered, independent.

The stir in the rays grew more evident, but his voice quieted it.

"Brother," it said, and its ringing tones filled the wide spaces, "let us exchange the sign of brotherhood!"

His own simple turban with its heron's plume was in his hand.

For an instant Prince Salîm hesitated; the next his more elaborate one with its hidden diamond was in his. It could not be otherwise.

"So!" smiled Akbar, giving himself up as he did always, to imagination, to sentiment, to dreams. "Take thou the inner place, Shaikie, next my heart--my arms are longer!"

Long enough any how to reach round Salîm's less sinewy ones and place the tufted turban of Kingship on the young man's head, where being a trifle too large it slipped well down over the ears and forehead.

"Thou must grow to it, little brother," quoth Akbar in fond pleasure. "As for me I must walk circumspectly lest my brotherhood fall!"

And in truth the Prince's turban showed all too much of the grizzled hair.

"Ummu! I will go back and say thanksgiving till dawn," faltered Auntie Rosebody behind the screen. "Truly what is to be, won't rub out. The Lord had it in His keeping, all the time, and we were wondering which side of the wall the cat would jump! So the King hath his own again, and Salîm hath more grace than the scapegrace deserves. Truly you may toil and sweat. What Fate wills you'll get."

The proverb might have been quoted by many another in the assembly had they been able to realise at once the full meaning of the little incident. But a sort of blank amaze settled down even on those conspirators who grasped at once that the chance of immediate defiance was over. Mirza Ibrahîm looked at Khodadâd, Khodadâd at Mirza Ibrahîm, and their glances betrayed one and the same thought.

This was no accident. Someone had split on their secret. Who?

"Come, my brother!" said Akbar, taking his son's hand and advancing toward the marble steps. "Now that the conferring of titles is over, let us pass to amusement."

The court ushers rushed to their places, the royal *nakârahs* sounded, and the cortège of the select few passed downward amid a seething shout of content from that dim crowd at the end of the garden. But above that strange sound like a surging wave, which seems to sweep along any densely packed mass of men, rose another.

This had a rumble in it, a sharp hiss, then a deafening low, long continued roar.

Akbar, who had just reached the narrow marble pathway, stopped dead and looked round him sharply.

"The reservoir!" he cried, "the reservoir above!"

His instinct was right. The rain of dawn had found some weak spot in the masonry and the next instant, bursting its hidden way beneath the dais and hurling great blocks of marble before it, a huge volume of water rose spurtling into the air.

"Run for it, Shaikie, run for it! Leap from the platform!"

The cry came not one moment too soon. Keeping within bounds by the very force of its onward impulse, the great wave of water, which would have hurled them down the marble cascade, but just touched their heels, as choosing different sides they leapt to safety.

Leapt turbanless, their ill-fitting head-dresses having tumbled off at their first start.

The general shriek of horror at the impending catastrophe subsided into confused babels of relief centring round the Prince on the left, the King on the right. So none noticed two men one on the right, one on the left of the wide central waterway who instantly started to race two half-floating half-sinking objects which, swept over the cascade by that wild impulse of flood, were now unsteadily swirling down to be engulfed under the low archway leading to subterreanean passages. And neither Khodadâd nor Birbal had eyes for anything save the prize of that race.

A sudden swerve to the left taking the Prince's turban with its talisman almost within reach of the enemy, decided Birbal. He paused a second. Then his low forward dive gave him a yard or two, and he rose to find his hand and Khodadâd's both clutching at what they sought. But his was the nearer.

"Not so fast, Tarkhân-jee," he jibed breathless, unable to resist retort, even in that moment of stress. "Beware stealing or thy list of crime is full! This is my master's."

Then the current caught him and hurled him almost helpless to the other side. Half a yard farther and he would have been sucked down into the archway, but a thin arm clutched at him and the clutch held.

A brief struggle and he stood beside the *rebeck* player, gazing at him stupidly, but half conscious of who he was. Only for an instant however; the next he faced Khodadâd who, backed by Mirza Ibrahîm was scowling at him across the water.

"Your pardon, gentlemen," he gasped politely, as before their very eyes, he calmly searched for and tore out the talisman which Umm Kulsum and Aunt Rosebody had sewn so deftly into the folds of Salîm's turban? "but I would fain see if this be my master's headdress given him in brotherhood by his son. Yes! of a surety it is. It will be kept, messieurs, the appointed time, and returned in due course--with the talisman--by all the gods! with the talisman--I wot not if it be a true or a false one--to those who gave it."

With that he turned on his heel regardless of the volley of curses from over the water.

But he rounded fiercely on the *rebeck* player's sardonic request to be remembered in that he had saved the master's life.

"Thou art the devil, juggler," he said and there was real fear in his voice. "Get thee gone, since, before God, I know not who thou art."

A laugh followed him.

CHAPTER XVIII

Longing for the Unseen as never one
Longed, passionate, for Seen; remembering none
From dawning to the setting of the sun
Save Secret Things unheard, unseen, unwon
No man shall know, till this world's life is done.

--SA'ADI.

"I would have sent for thee," said Âtma softly, "but there was none to send. The whole town was away at the festival--so I stayed." She sighed almost fiercely in her regret at having been let and hindered, though her eyes were tender, as she gazed down on little Zarîfa who lay in the Wayfarer's arms. It was bare dawn, and, in the shadow of the wall one could but just see the perfect outline of the sleeping face that nestled close to his pallid mask.

"She fails fast, methinks," added the woman in a lower tone.

"Aye! she fails--at last," echoed the man's voice. As if to give them both the lie, the whispered words brought a sudden smile to Zarîfa's face. Her eyes opened full of swift desire, her whole deformed body pressed closer to the breast on which it lay, and there was unmistakable appeal in the soft curved cheeks, the curved waiting lips. The Wayfarer answered it instantly and laid his to hers.

The kiss was long; his mask came up from it with a certain repulsion of expression, at once tender and cruel.

"Yea, it is true! She nears womanhood, and what hath she to do with its blessing, or with its curse," he muttered, looking at the face, which, satisfied, had sunk to sleep once more, a smile still hovering over it; then he laid the misshapen bundle of humanity he held--so small, so helpless, so apart from everything save limited life--on the string bed, whence he had taken it, and covered it gently with the quilt; for the air of dawn was chill.

Âtma stood looking down on the beautiful face, feeling a hot anger rise in her heart against all mankind.

"Thou didst never love her mother, or thou wouldst not speak so," she said scornfully.

The Wayfarer, who at the parapet was watching the slow growth of dawn, turned on her swiftly. "Not love her, woman?" he echoed passionately, fiercely. "That God knows! It is her father that I hate--it is for him I wait!"

"Her father? Art *thou* not then----?" began the Châran in surprise, but the *rebeck* player had recovered his calm monotony of manner.

"Her father truly," he said, "since of Love I brought her into the world, of Love I care for her, of Love I give her Love."

As he spoke his fingers were busy about his neck, and Âtma seeing him stoop over the sleeper, saw also that he left something in the ghostly half-seen folds of the white quilt.

"What is't?" she asked curiously, stooping also, conscious of a certain unreality in what had passed, in what was passing. She had sate up all night beside Zarîfa, unable to leave her, unable to get a message sent to summon any one; and so, unable to hear what was happening, when so much might happen.

The nervous tension of that night of waiting, of watching had been great; yet she had forgotten it when in the false dawn the Wayfarer had suddenly appeared. Since then she had been absorbed, as he was, in the child--this child of Love!

Ye Gods! What was it that exhaled roses? The whole air was full of their scent--her very eyes seemed to see them, crowning the sleeping head, hiding the scant contour of the deformed body: and to her, ignorant in a way, yet from her birth familiar with mystical thoughts, credulous of all mystical things, the sudden inrush of unreality brought small surprise but quick curiosity, and she caught imperatively at the Wayfarer's hand.

"Who art thou, Lord!" she asked simply. "In the name of this Rose of Love tell this slave."

The man drew back from her touch resentfully; his face grew more human, less deathlike, and Âtma watching it wondered at the change in it, and asked herself, if this were indeed the poor musician who played for the chance hearers of the bazaars.

"Thou hast spoken a compelling word, sister," he said, "so thou shalt be told. But guard the secret if thou lovest--any! I am Payandâr--whether king or hind matters little. Mayhap I am both, since I am Love incarnate and Hate incarnate. That is Spiritual Love which knows not Sex, and Earthly Love which lives by it. And I--doubtless thou hast heard the tale, told as a legend--I loved one who was to be my wife. But she whom I held sacred, my brother, of wanton wickedness, dishonoured. Yonder child is his--so the Earthly Love that is in me still, despite the Rose Garden of the wilderness, waits till the measure of his iniquity shall be full. It will not be long."

He stretched his hand out menacingly, and turned to go.

"Thy brother?" she echoed, "who----"

He stopped her with a sudden wild gesture.

"Ask not that, fool!" he cried passionately. "Lo! thou art very woman, cleaving to the detail, seeing naught of the spirit. Thou canst not even see that I have lied? I tell thee she *is* my child--the child of the sins which I, Tarkhân, inherited even as he did--the child of many sins that are in me, even as they are in him."

He stooped over the sleeper and kissed her on the forehead.

"Master!" said Âtma tremulously as she saw him cross to the door. "Must thou go? I have waited long--and now----"

"There comes one who will bring thee news, and I will be back ere long," he answered, and even as he spoke a voice full of importance, breathless with hurry, came from the stairs.

"Mistress Âtma! Mistress, I say. God send she be not out, or, if mischief come of it, I will be double damned for double treason."

The next instant old Deena the drumbanger, his drum hitched to his back like a huge hump, hustled the departing musician at the door and flung himself blubbering at Âtma's feet.

"Lo! chaste pillar of virtue! said I not ever ill service was as the feeding of snakes--one never knows but when one has to turn on them rather than that they should turn on thee," he began tumultuously, "but I have come! Yea! old Deena hath to remember his soul and if mistress Siyah Yamin----"

"Siyah Yamin! What of her," queried Âtma sharply even as she added, "Speak, lower, fool! Thou wilt disturb the child."

Deena made a grimace of apology, pursed his face up, looked at the sleeper, shook his head with elaborate regret, and then hitching his drum round to equalise his balance, squatted with his elbows resting on it, ready for a calm whispered recital of what he had come prepared to tell.

"There is no need to begin at the beginning," he said tentatively and was rewarded by Âtma's curt "Tell all, slave! I have been held here by the child all night and know nothing."

"Thank God for ignorance!" ejaculated the old gossip piously, and went on to recount the events of the past night.

Âtma listened quietly. She started and clasped her hands tighter when she heard how the King and Prince Salîm had exchanged turbans, but her long night's vigil had brought so many visions of what Birbal's wit might compass that she scarcely felt surprised. The story of the bursting of the reservoir and, the miraculous escape of the father and son, however, told as it was from the outside (for old Deena naturally knew nothing of the extraordinary import of the incident he was describing) roused her instant alarm.

"Prate not about their bareheadedness!" she broke in on his tale of how the two had stood before the multitude shorn of honourable headgear but mighty in monarchy--"the turbans man! the turbans! what of them?"

Deena's wicked old eyes lost their sparkle, his tone grew peevish. "Lo! mistress! wouldst spoil the picture. Doubtless they drowned. Who thinks of turbans when----"

Âtma was on her feet. "Bide thou here! I must go," she said hurriedly. She felt she could no longer stand inaction. All this had came about--if, indeed, it had come about "Yea! I must go to Siyah Yamin," she repeated blindly.

Old Deena laid a detaining hand on her red skirt. "Not there! mistress! Not there. Lo! thou hast not heard what I come to tell. Thou didst bid me begin at the beginning and I began; but 'tis not only scorpions' tails that end in a sting, and this one hath venom in it I swear. If thou hadst heard--Nay listen! mistress! 'Twas Meean Khodadâd and Mirza Ibrahîm who came raging to Siyah Yamin's half an hour agone. I had gone back thither after the show was over to have speech with Yasmeen and the hussy was virtuous and would not let me in. So, standing there I heard----"

"What?" asked Âtma fiercely, "Canst not speak without twists and turns?"

"Lo! Mistress! let my tongue follow my brain as the potter's donkey follows muddy breeches thinking them his master," replied Deena mildly. "I am at the very prick o' the point. They swore vengeance on thee for what I know not, protesting that thou and thou only couldst be the cause; and then they swore at Siyah Yamin for telling thee; but gingerly, for look you Siyâla is not one to threaten lightly--but she said--doubtless with that smile which makes a body feel like a camel without legs----"

"What said she, fool?" interrupted Âtma exasperated.

"That without the seeing of thee she could not tell; whereupon they said that if they saw thee----"

Âtma caught up a white cloth and wrapped it round her. "Stay thou here!" she said imperatively, "the child sleeps and I will be back in half an hour."

She was well down the stairs ere Deena ceased to call feebly! "Not so! oh mistress most chaste, not so!" and resigning himself to circumstances closed the door, hasping it lightly by the bottom hook and chain, then sate down beside the sleeping child.

"Even as a Peri," he murmured to himself as he looked at the face showing more clearly now in the coming light. "Truly God knows His own work--yet is there no mortal sense in sending such a countenance of beauty with no body to match it fit for hugging."

So he dozed off into the sleep which pure vice had taught him to take in snatches.

Meanwhile Âtma hurrying through the still deserted alleys felt her mind too much in a tumult for concentration; thus, as she almost ran past the high unarched doorways, the blank walls shutting out all things, the constant burr of the unseen hand-mills busy over their daily task of grinding flour came to join the unceasing burr of thought that whirled in her brain. Doubt as to her own wisdom had assailed her the night long, and now with this uncertitude concerning the fate of the diamond, she felt she could have killed herself for the part she had played in its theft. Why had she played it? Why? Why? The futility of fighting against Fate came home to her, as from a closed courtyard rose shrilly the voice of a woman chanting the song of the Grinding Stone and the Grounden Wheat:

Red Sandstone and red-husked wheat
Whirl in your dancing, part and meet
My right hand is your master,
What if the stone be rushed?
What if the grain be crushed?
Men and women must eat,
The cry of the child be hushed.
Whirl faster and faster,
God's right hand is our master!
What though Love mates with Lust,
Though Just yield to Unjust,
What care the Stone and the Wheat,
For men and women must eat,

The cry of the child be hushed,
So Dust grind Dust!

Dust grind dust! She smote her hands together and sped on. She could at least challenge these men for the truth, and tell them that they lied. She had told no tales!

And as she made her breathless way toward Satanstown, Mirza Ibrahîm and Meean Khodadâd were making their way back from it. They had gained nothing from Siyah Yamin save biting words and contemptuous gibes. She had done her part and there would be time to hold her fool when it was proved that Âtma had betrayed her. For herself, she did not believe it; and in so saying she for once spoke her real thought. She knew, briefly, that treachery was out of the question with her sister of the veil.

But the two men held, manlike, to what was on the surface.

"Fret not, Khodadâd," said Mirza Ibrahîm with a sinister smile, as they passed out from the courtesan's house, "there is no hurry to settle scores with the madwoman. I, being Chamberlain, claim her as the King's woman, and then----"

"Then may I go shares with thee, or take thy leavings!" muttered Khodadâd fiercely. "That may be thy revenge; but I am Tarkhân."

"Tarkhân or no, it grows too light for us now, Meean Sahib, so fare thee well for the time," remarked Ibrahîm significantly. And in truth the sky was beginning to show pearly over the pile of the city.

"Tarkhâns need no darkness for their deeds," retorted Khodadâd recklessly. His temper, as ever, had overmastered him, he was literally beside himself with rage and disappointment. These two confederates were fools! What man could succeed, bound hand and foot by chicken-hearted cowards like Ibrahîm, and the rest of them? But he--aye! he would take revenge, dawn though it was! for he was Tarkhân, accredited to evil deeds.

"To Siyah Yamin's Paradise," he said flinging himself into the palanquin which followed behind him. The madwoman lived in the same tenement. So much he knew, and the rest would come; if he had luck. If not there was no harm done. Pure devilry possessed him; he could not rest without some attempt at retaliation.

And so old Deena woke from his snatched snooze at whispering voices outside, followed by a steady calculated shouldering of the door, a slip of the ill-hasped chain, and the sudden consequent sprawl of half a dozen stalwart Abyssinians on to the roof.

"Back slaves!" said Khodadâd, his voice low and hoarse with passion that leapt up with the chance of satisfaction. "And close the door behind you."

Old Deena scrambled to his feet. "My lord! my lord!" he expostulated, every atom of virtue in him rising up scandalised at the intrusion, all the more so perhaps, because of his loose life. "This roof is the abode of chastity."

"Fool!" said the Tarkhân seizing him easily by the throat. "The woman--where is she? Speak low or I strangle thee."

"She--is--not here," gasped the old man--"Mercy lord! mercy!"

"Not here!--thou liest!"

Still holding Deena fast pinned against the wall Khodadâd's eyes flashed round the roof. There were no shadows now; the morning light clear and fresh filled every corner.

"Ye gods! and devils!"

The words came low, almost soft, with the sudden inrush of admiration, as Khodadâd's hands fell away from the old man's throat, and he took one step toward the bed.

"My lord! My lord!" cried Deena starting forward. "She is ill, she is a child--she is----"

He staggered back from the blow dealt him recklessly.

"She is beautiful--that is enough!" came with a chuckling laugh. "Wake, my houri! Wake up my peri of Paradise."

There was a faint scream, the mere cry, as it were, of a wounded bird. "Nay beauty! thou shalt kiss me! What! Scent of roses and no love? Pâh! how the perfume gets into my brain. Never but once before--but this is no time for the past! Nay! struggle not. Such beauty needs no veiling."

The little murmuring wail died to silence, and the half jibing voice was silent also. So, horror-struck, Khodadâd stood for one instant before the deformity he had unshrouded. Then with a curse he turned and fled.

Deena, still dazed with the blow, crept over to the bed and covered crippledom again.

"Little one," he crooned, "there is no fear--he will not come back."

But there was no answer, and he leant swiftly to listen for a breath.

"Little one! Little one!" he cried. He could hear none, and as he stooped his wrinkled face puckering into tears, a voice behind him said quietly: "She is dead! Lo! it was time."

Deena turned to see the *rebeck* player who closing the door softly, came to stand beside the bed.

"Dead! Dead!" blubbered the old sinner. "Yea! Yea! it is so--his kisses killed her--only his kisses."

"Whose?"

The question echoed and re-echoed over the roof instinct with a sudden new fire, a sudden authority, and it reduced Deena to snivelling submission.

"Only a kiss lord, only a kiss; but Meean Khodadâd----"

He paused struck dumb by the expression on the Wayfarer's face. Grief, horror, exultation showed on it, and over all a great awe as of one who sees a mystery.

"Khodadâd! Oh! Thou most Mighty! Khodadâd! It is the end."

CHAPTER XIX

Love sent music to sing Love's praise
So Harmony came to this world's sad ways.
Master of melody, Cæsar of sound,
Each chord he struck fettered reasoning,
Till man and beast by it quite were bound
Into friendship fast and companioning.
Yea! at the note of his crooked lyre
One wakened up, one was lulled to sleep,
And the whole wide world grew quick with desire
To dance and to die, to laugh and to weep.
At the burst of his blended melody
The heart of the wise knew the mystery.

--NIZÂMI.

"Lo I am true!" cried Âtma menacingly, "Art thou so also, O! Siyâl?"

She had been with the courtesan for full half an hour, time was running short, and yet she felt that she had gained nothing, and knew scarcely more than she had done when she had climbed the steep oil-greased narrow stairs to the balcony room. She had been eager then to face fact--if need be--keen to test the loyalty of her fellow conspirators; but now she stood baffled before Siyah Yamin's easy but inflexible contempt. That someone had betrayed them the latter said was indubitable; and as Âtma was the only outsider, she must be the culprit. Not necessarily a conscious offender. But, by all she held most sacred, did not Âtma know of some indiscretion, could she not, briefly, guess--and then the noisy, yet silvery laugh had rung out at the Châran's tell-tale face. Her tongue, however, had been loyal. She had refused to say a word. Not that she felt in any way bound to shield Mihr-un-nissa from the possible revenge of those whose game she had given away, but because it was out of the question to tell of the secret visit of a screened lady.

So Siyah Yamin had declined information except by fair barter; declined it with jibes and smiles; but now sudden pallor came to her face, she shifted her eyes uneasily from Âtma's half accusing ones.

"True?" she echoed, and, and her voice had a petulant ring in it. "Aye! as true as it befits womanhood to be! Lo! Âto I grow tired of my sex at times and would I were a man!" She pressed her hands close to her heart, then suddenly burst out again into her hard silvery laugh "And thou? sweet widow--dost not pine for thy lover Sher Khân? Is he not here despite these--petticoats?" She flounced out her clinging muslins.

"Peace, fool! So thou wilt not tell" said Âtma frowning, "then I must ask elsewhere."

"Aye! Ask!" jibed the courtesan. "There be many with tongues beside poor little me who will, look you, have confidence for confidence. Belike the Beneficent Ladies, or mayhap Rajah Birbal for the Envoy from Sinde whom some deem a mere simulacrum of a man, or even the Feringhi jeweller--to say nothing of the King himself."

Her eyes were keenly on the Châran's face as she spoke, but there was no flicker of expression to give her any clue. In truth Âtma was absolutely in the dark. She did not even know if the turban were lost or found. Her mind ran riot over supposition in either case. If the former, it could not remain lost for ever in those underground chambers. It might even now have drifted to the tank where a hundred hands might find it. She must go and watch. And yet, what use? The rather send divers to search below; if indeed any man would so adventure his life! And for this she must proclaim a cause, proclaim that she knew of the theft. And after all there might be no reason for this. Birbal, with his quick wit, must have saved the turban. He must; yet not even he could outwit Fate.

She smote her hands together again impotently as she ran, this time toward the roof which she had left too long. That feeling of neglected duty strangely enough, overmastered all others. She must go back to her immediate charge. Once there she would have time to think what she must do to find out the truth. For she must find it even if she had to go to the King himself tell him all and then repay herself for treachery by the death dagger.

But what she found awaiting her on the roof drove these thoughts from her mind for a time; only for a time--that Time which meant nothing to one brought up as she had been, in a philosophy which counts the past, the present, the future as one. For in India there is no hurry about anything; the wisdom of Isaiah is in every mouth, "He that believeth shall not make haste."

Yet as she joined in the woman's wailing over Zarîfa--for the news of death spreads quickly, and the neighbours troop in as to a festival--a dull wonder lay at the back of her brain, a vague resentment at her own ignorance.

In truth the resentment was scarcely justifiable, since many others concerned in the incident were feeling the same dull surprise.

The conspirators first of all, who found themselves once more deprived of their *point d'appui*. And Khodadâd the arch-plotter was strangely silent, strangely lacking in suggestion. As the day wore on, indeed he withdrew petulantly from all conclave, and taking Mirza Ibrahîm with him, plunged into pleasure at Satanstown. For something in that scent of roses on the roof, something in the look of that face sleeping so peacefully upon the pillow, had roused memory; and memory in her long slumber had somehow, from some subliminal consciousness in that unknown ego of which Khodadâd Tarkhân was the outward and visible sign, associated herself with regret. He told himself, lightly, that it was the shock of seeing deformity where he had expected beauty, which had unnerved him; but it was not that. It was the ineffaceable memory of Beauty itself.

Then in the Palace where Umm Kulsum and Aunt Rosebody had sate in the little balcony outside the latter's private room all the morning, unable to feel joy over the merciful escape of the Most High and their scapegrace darling because of the probable loss of the turban with its talisman; yet unable to feel sufficient grief over the latter because of bubbling gladness over the Brotherhood between those two dear ones (a Brotherhood that nothing must disturb, not even self-seeking confession of sin) on to all this had followed a dull wonder as to what was to be done next. For after noonday prayers were over had come a despatch by hand from my Lord Birbal, Chief Constable of the Kingdom returning in due course of etiquette to the givers, the turban they had supposed lost. And what is more, when their anxious fingers had privilege to pry, there was the talisman also, safe and sound.

The shock of relief kept them both silent awhile; then Aunt Rosebody cracked all her knuckles vehemently.

"So goes care!" she cried, adding piously, "truly we might have trusted God! His club makes no noise, and what's in the pot comes on the plate."

Then her face clouded. "But what is to be done next Ummu?" she asked feebly. Umm Kulsum shook her head.

"We might give it back to the woman."

"What?" interrupted the little old lady peevishly. "To a civet-cat from the bazaar of whom we know nothing?"

"There was the red woman also, auntie," suggested the Mother of Plumpness, "she seemed honest--at least when she came to----"

"Tell Mihru's fortune--a pack of lies!" sniffed her companion. "Canst think of nothing better, child?"

"Mayhap it might be wiser," suggested Umm Kulsum again, "to consult----"

"Consult whom?" shrilled Gulbadan Khânum, and this time the interruption was wrathful. "What would be the use of asking Hamida? All know her answer. 'Tell truth and shame Shaitan.' And as for Râkiya Begum with her spectacles and her etiquettes and her distiches, I would sooner die! Now it would be different if 'Dearest Lady' were alive----" She paused and her lively dark eyes grew limpid with sudden tears.

"We can go where she went for wisdom," whispered little Umm Kulsum consolingly, "we can pray."

Aunt Rosebody gave a grunt of satisfaction and dried her eyes. "Aye! there is some sense in that! We can pray and wait. 'Twill at least give us time to think out some plan for ourselves, and sleep brings wisdom; but Ummu, Ummu, I would give every hair I possess--and though they are gray they are not uncomely--that I had never mixed myself up with the King's Luck. 'Tis worse than the Day of Resurrection, for then a body will but have two roads to choose--up and down--and here! Lo! wonder grows like a white ants' castle."

In this feeling Aunt Rosebody was not alone. Birbal himself was in a similar state of blank surprise, for to him had come the most startling dénouement of all.

After the momentous events of the night he had felt himself entitled to a few hours' rest. He had had little of it by day or by dark, ever since he had discovered the theft of the diamond; for he had given himself up wholly to the recovery of the stolen jewel; but now that he had this safely stowed away in his waistband-purse he could spare leisure for comfort. So he slept the sleep of the just, without a dream to disturb him. Yet his brain must have been working, for, when he woke, it was to a sense that in the excitement of the moment of success he had made a mistake. Had he had time to consider he would never have given himself away to his enemies as he had done by showing them that he knew of the talisman. It was a tactical error; which might be partially rectified so far as some people were concerned. Therefore without further delay, he sent a message to William Leedes, at the Hall of Labour, to come up to him at once, bringing the false diamond with him. When this arrived it did not take long to exchange the true for the false, and then with due decorum to send the turban back to the Beneficent Ladies, who, he knew from what Mihr-un-nissa had said, had given it to the Prince. He calculated cunningly that this return would at least keep them quiet, and women were invariably at the bottom of every conspiracy.

He felt very secure, very confident, very complacent, and spent an hour or two in entertaining William Leedes with Eastern sumptuousness ere ordering the palanquins to take the jeweller and the diamond back to safe keeping in the Hall of Labour, whence he assured himself no thief in the world would have another chance of purloining it. In truth he had some reason for complacency; since the general outlook was clearing. These repeated failures must dishearten the enemies of empire, and the mere fact of the bond of Brotherhood between the King and his son--which had come incidentally by the way in the course of counterplot--added to the chance of Akbar being content with practical politics and remaining at Fatephur Sikri.

The only unsatisfactory item in past or present was the memory of the man who juggled with other men's eyes and ears. Who and what was he? A friend to Akbar at any rate, and for the time being, that was enough.

The wide roof of the Hall of Labour lay ablaze with afternoon sunshine as they entered it, and as they passed along the arcades, the workmen looked up and salaamed. The door of Diswunt's studio was locked and barred, and a sentry paced across that of the jeweller. Known though they were, it required the password ere William Leedes could produce his key, unlock the door, enter, then close and lock it again behind them.

Birbal gave a sigh of relief as he drew out his waistband-purse. "At last!" he said holding out the diamond. "Replace it on the lathe, sir jeweller, and once I see it there--lo! I will vow pilgrimage if needs be. Yea! I will cry 'Hari Ganga' like any drunk man in a puddle!"

He turned aside, out of sheer lightheartedness, humming a *ghazal* from Hâfiz.

Make fast a wine cup to my shroud
That at the latter day
My soul a good drink be allowed
To nerve it for the fray.

Meanwhile the jeweller's deft hands were busy. A few turns, a click or two, and William Leedes bent over the treasure joyfully.

"There it is, my master; with naught but a few days' delay in the cutting thereof! I must be all the quicker now, else the King will wonder. Yet have I lost as little time as may be, since the next facet is assured--it will run so."

The delicate steel point he held just touched the surface. Then it fell away from it, as the hand holding the instrument seemed to shrink back. The foot, too, left the treadle, and the spinning pivots slackened speed and sank to rest.

"What is't?" asked Birbal, turning hastily.

The jeweller's face was white, his very jaw had fallen.

"It--it scratches" he muttered faintly "there is some mistake."

There was no mistake about the scratch however. It showed distinct, and wrote the truth without a shadow of doubt. This was no diamond; it was a fraud, like the other!

For an instant Birbal's head whirled. Then helplessly he fingered his purse again. Could he by chance have made a mistake and sent back the wrong one? Impossible; and yet?

He sank on the jeweller's seat and covered his face with his hands. For once his wit was not quick enough to grasp the situation, and-- clogging thought!--that dim suspicion recurred despite denial--Had he by chance made a mistake?

So Âtma as she sate apart on the roof watching the Mahommedan woman prepare Zarîfa's body for the burial which was to take place at sunset had no monopoly in confusion and wonder. She could take no part in what was going on. She dare not, from fear of defilement, even touch the dead child with a kiss, but she sate jealously watching that every ceremonial was duly carried out.

"Lo! she is lovely as any houri *now!*" chattered the Dom women who had come in to perform the last offices, as they bound the corpse with gold tinsel to the string bedstead on which it was to be carried to the grave. "'Tis a sin, for sure, to have more body in death than in life; but what will you? Mayhap Munkir and Niker[13] seeing her look so, may not ask questions, but give her a decent body for Paradise--sure she needed one poor thing!"

So they stood looking down on their handiwork. And in truth the crippled child looked very beautiful. The *rebeck* player, saying it was the custom of his tribe, had hired from somewhere a low, oblong, lidless coffin, more like a deep picture frame than anything else; and in this, as it lay on the bed, these tirewomen of the dead, had so disposed draperies, and pillows, and whatnot, that all the curves of the budding womanhood showed beneath the face that remained more beautiful even in death than it had been in life. It was covered only with a fine network, for the veil was draped carefully on either side the slender neck. One corner of it, and a loop of jasmin chaplet fell over the dingy worn gilt of the coffin frame.

"Lo! many will envy Death his bride and send regrets after her as she passes by," said the oldest of the Domni, nodding her head wisely. And it was so.

For as the two bearers--it needed but two for that bier--shuffled at sunset-tide with their light burden through the crowded bazaar, more than one careless eye grew to sudden interest. And one spectator, an idle reckless looking man who sate on a sherbet-seller's threshold joking with a light woman in an upper balcony, ceased his sarcasms to murmur a stanza from Hafiz; for he was rhymster too.

No more from poet's lips
Shall love songs pass
She who once garnered them
Is dead--alas!

There were few mourners. Only the professional wailers, and the *rebeck* player, who with bent head, followed the bier making mournful music as he went. Âtma, of another creed, still held aloof, walking veiled and stately some way behind. And all around them slipping aside to let the dead pass, for the most part careless almost unheeding, were the living; buying, selling, gossiping, chaffering.

Âtma drew breath more freely when they were through the city gates, and the bearers stepped out more quickly over hard stretches of sand and waste hillocks set with thorn and caper bushes toward the little cemetery which the musician had chosen. A few gnarled *jhand* trees decked with coloured snippets of cloth tied there by many mourners, a few nameless roly-poly concrete graves, a sprinkling of tiny turrets showing where someone was laid--someone whose resting place was unknown to all save the women who came thither every week to mourn--marked the spot. A dreary lonesome spot, in truth. But the westering sun showed warm and red over the desert horizon, and the chipping notes of the seven-brother birds sounded cheerful as the family flitted from one tree to another.

The grave was already dug and the diggers stood by waiting for their day's pay. It was a wide deep grave, looking as if it had been cut out of yellow rock, so dry, so even were the sides. And the low arch of the long niche on one side in which the corpse was to be laid as in a coffin, was as regular as if built in with unburnt brick. To Âtma's surprise, the floor of this niche was set thick, as by a coverlet, with roses. She glanced hastily at the *rebeck* player, but he was already immersed in the prayers with which an attendant priest had greeted the little procession. She listened gravely, repeating to herself meanwhile the formulas--so few, so simple--of her own creed.

And yet when, after saying aloud the prayer for benediction, the *rebeck*-player stood forward, raised the sad gracious figure from the coffin, and stepping into the grave laid it gently in the niche, she shivered as she saw him stoop to gather up a handful of earth.

"We created you of dust and we return you to dust, and we shall raise you out of the dust upon the day of resurrection."

The words seemed to her almost horrible. To be left lying alone in the desert, waiting, waiting, waiting!

For what? For yourself--the old mean self of which she was so tired.

Ah! better surely to find rest at once in the Great Self which pervaded all things!

"Wilt thou not throw earth also?" said a voice beside her, "then throw flowers. These are the roses of love."

The *rebeck* player pulled aside the kerchief covering a flat basket which one of the Dom women had carried, and lo! there were roses red at their hearts, pale where the sun had kissed them. Their scent filled the air.

"Yea! lord," she said meekly, "I will throw them."

The priest, the bearers, the Dom women had disappeared, their task done. Only the grave-diggers chattered to one another as they filled in the grave.

"Lo! she would have been ripe for kisses soon and now the worms have got her," said one discontentedly.

"Ballah! friend!" quoth the other. "Lovers die, but love dies not--there be ever other food for lust in the world!"

"Throw them into thy life also, sister," said the musician, suddenly. "There is no fear or blame in love."

So as he stood watching the shovelsful of earth hide the roses which covered little Zarîfa, he played softly on his *rebeck*, and sang a whispering song to its wailing music.

Love is a full red wine bowl

Passion the bubbles on its rim,

Drink deep down to the dregs, soul,

Heed not the froth on the brim.

Passion has wings like an eagle
    Love needs none; she is at rest--
Flood tide full--as the seagull
Drifts, the cold wave at her breast.

Love is the Lightless Ether
    Passion the star-shine it lets through
Building sense-worlds beneath her
    Love seeks not form, seeks not hue.

Passion has myriad senses
    Love has not voice, eyes, nor ears,
Space, Time, Life, Moods, and Tenses
    Chain not her Soul to the years.

Love is a sail, mid-ocean
    Losing itself in the Whole,
Passion the wavelets commotion
    Blurring the shores of the Soul.

    He ceased suddenly, and his whole face changed. The grave was filled up, the diggers were already passing stolidly back to the city. On the desert horizon the red sun had lost its warmth and was sinking coldly behind the gray verge.

    "Lo! I have done with Love," came the musician's mocking voice. "So take this, sister, and may it bring thee more luck than it hath brought Payandâr. For him only hate remains."

    When she looked up from her hasty glance at what he had thrust into her hand, the *rebeck* player was moving away rapidly after the grave-diggers and she was left alone, looking at the new-made grave, looking at the quaint green stone she had just been given.

CHAPTER XX

A trembling fell on mountain and on plain,
The earth, unstable as a juggler's ball,
Became a rolling sphere. The dust rose up
High to the collar of heaven. The clarion of the wind
Roused shock on shock, and from the valley's streams
The fish, out-cast, lay gasping. Lightning flash
On lightning flash split the wide sky; the sinking rocks,
Disjointed, filled with water, and the hills,
Clasping each other, squeezed themselves to death.

--NIZAMI.

Khodadâd Khan, Tarkhân, sate at the head of his supper cloth, with the dazed look of one who has taken drugs in his eyes. And in truth he had drugged himself body and soul to the uttermost. He had passed from one pleasure to another, and all the while he had raged inwardly at the necessity for seeking yet further forgetfulness; since after all what had he to forget? Only the shock of seeing deformity; for the rest was dead as the past years which had contained it. And yet he could not forget! Even as he had come hither to this last stimulant to jaded appetite--an *al fresco* entertainment out in the desert stretches beyond the city, where all the wallowing wickedness of humanity would show up the more alluringly vicious against that pure background of solitude and silence--even then he had shrunk back as from a snake before a glimpse that had come to him in the bazaar of a dead face. It could not be the same girl from whom he had turned horror-struck that morning, for his practised eye noted in a second all those graceful contours of budding womanhood, which showed above the shallow coffin. Besides, why should she die? He had barely kissed her, and--he laughed cynically, as the thought came to him--where was the woman who objected to a kiss, who was the worse for it? Were they not made for it?

He flung his arm round Yasmeena who lolled on the cushions beside him and kissed the heart-shaped curve of skin which her swelling, filmy bodice left exposed below her dimpled chin. She slapped him lightly on the cheek and the company laughed at his frown.

"None can escape
Wounds in the Red Rose garden where no Rose
But arms with thorns her Beauty"

quoted one of the guests. "My lord is over hasty. Our stomachs are not yet satisfied, though by the twelve Imâms, this saffron pillau of tender chicken filters fast to my vitals." He leered at Siyah Yamin, who threw up her dainty little head disdainfully.

"Keep thy spiced sentiment to thyself, fool," she replied archly, "I desire no forced feeling of fowl."

The laugh at her retort ran round boisterously, and even Khodadâd joined in it. But it was a mirthless laugh. Still as the hours went on the fun waxed fast and furious, and the stars above must have been glad of the widespread square canopy of tent which hid some of the doings of man from High Heaven. It was well on into the night ere the first guest, excusing himself, jingled in his palanquin back cityward. So, by ones and twos, the party dispersed until Khodadâd was left alone looking contemptuously down at Mirza Ibrahîm, whose senses had deserted him in the long orgie, and who lay helpless amid wine cups, torn shreds of muslin, and all the indescribable beastliness of uncontrolled amusement.

"Take the fool home, slaves," said the Tarkhân thickly, "And bring a bed here. I stop; the night air will cool my brain."

So in the midst of all the refuse of vicious humanity, they set a dirty string bed, and covered it with satin quilts. As he lay on it he formed fit matching to its hidden squalor.

It was now the hour before the false dawn; that hour of slumber even for wickedness and wrong. The servants, outwearied by long ministering to every whim of their masters, were soon asleep even while they simulated watchfulness.

But Khodadâd lay awake. Half-drugged, half-drunk though he was, his nerves tingled, he started at the least sound. Possibly some vague unacknowledged fear of what the darkness might bring had lain at the bottom of his resolution to sleep were he was, where none could know of his presence; yet everything disturbed him. A prowling jackal, a mere noiseless shadow in the moonlight, made him sit up and watch till it had slunk away.

How still, how horribly still the desert was! One could almost hear the soft patter of the birds' feet which would leave delicate tracery upon the sand for the dawn to discover. And then his mind flew back to another still, hot night in the past. Surely it must have been about this time of year? Perchance this was the very night. Was it so? His brain, reluctant yet insistent, traced back the past. Nay! it could not be--and yet-- Yet it was before that. Aye! and after that----

And by an odd chance, beyond a low thicket of caper bushes that bounded the desert to one side of the scene of past orgie, lay the little cemetery where Zarîfa slept so soundly. He did not know this but he lay awake, thinking of her.

Ye Gods! Why could he not sleep? What had he to fear; a Tarkhân in a strange country? Nothing. On the morrow he would be himself; free of all things--free to do as he chose.

And so suddenly with the comfort of the thought came slumber.

Was it for an instant or for an hour? He sate up, the sweat starting from him with causeless fear, to look about him.

He could see nothing. All was darkness itself. Then a sense of constriction about his forehead made him raise his hands to feel if aught were there.

God and his Prophet! He was blindfolded! He was on his feet in a second, but even as he rose, strong hands of iron grip closed round his and despite a wild struggle, he stood helpless, his arms fast pinioned to his sides.

"What is't?" he asked putting unfelt boldness into his voice; it sounded thick almost unintelligible.

"Dalîl, Tarkhân of the Royal House, thou art summoned to the Last Assize of thy Peers."

The answer came from close; so close that it seemed to knell in his ear as if it came from inside himself, and it brought a sudden throb of purely animal dread to his heart. But he essayed a laugh. This was not real; it was but a disordered dream, a nightmare due to the excesses of the day. His peers? Here in a strange land where were they?

"Wherefore?" he asked.

The answer was too swift for him to judge of the quality of his own voice; the other was resonant though still curiously personal, curiously close to him.

"Because the measure of thine iniquities is full at last! Mount the White Horse, and ride bravely to judgment, as thou hast ridden bravely to sin."

He felt himself half-forced forward, half-willingly yielding to unseen pressure, and he told himself again it was but a dream. The sooner through with it, the sooner to wake; it could not go on forever.

The warmth of the horse's body felt against him, brought another throb of fear. He heard its screaming neigh. Was it indeed, the Tarkhân's White Stallion of Death which he bestrode? Ah! if he could but see, could but move!

But his feet were fast bound beneath the warm breathing belly, his arms were close pinioned to his side. For an instant he thought of shrieking aloud--it might at least wake him; then something--perhaps pride of race and that admonition to bear himself bravely--held him back from cries.

Whither were they taking him? The way seemed endless, and he fought for bare breath between the mad throbbings of his heart; his very lips tingled and smarted as the life blood pulsed irregularly through them. Would that ceaseless strain and relaxation of muscle as the horse galloped on and on never end? Must he always wait and wait. For what? Something worse perhaps.

"Halt!"

He gave a convulsive gasp. The whole universe seemed to stand still. So an awful and intolerable silence settled down on all things.

"Who are ye!" he cried at last in desperation, and his voice rang out strident yet quavering, like an ill-tuned violin.

A low, reverberating roll of kettledrums was the only answer, and an uncontrollable shiver shook him, replying to the shudder with which they filled the air.

"Who are ye?"

This time the cry had a wail in it; but once again that roll of kettledrums was the only answer.

"Who are ye?"

It was a mere whisper, hoarse, half-choked; but this time a voice came instant, clear, in reply.

"Unbind his eyes, heralds, and let him see those who judge him."

The flood of moonlight seemed at first to blind him, and even after his eyes recovered sight a mistiness, a vagueness rested on all things. And yet he saw all things; aye! and recognised them, not from personal experience, for the Last Assize was even in those days fast becoming legendary, but from the racial experience which he could not escape.

Aye! Beneath him was the White Stallion of Death standing square upon the square of white cloth, whose purpose sent a shiver of horror through him. Those were the heralds masked, veiled, who rode on black horses beside him, and at their feet curled up, cowering like loathsome reptiles, he could see the two executioners, their long fingers clutching--at what?

Not a sword or a dagger. No! He knew what they held and with a wild hope of pardon, his strained eyes sought, beyond these nearer things, the semicircle of faces before which he stood. The moonbeams showed them clear yet blurred. How like himself they were, these chieftains of the Barlâs clan! And whence had they come? From the grave surely, some of them, or were they only simulacra? Was it indeed the race which sate in judgment on him? The race; and so himself. Ah! in that case what hope--what chance of life had he, Dalîl?

And then suddenly there leaped to clearness the figure which centred the wide semicircle of dim countenances.

It was dressed in regal robes, it wore the emeralds of Sinde, and there was no mistaking the face which stared at him with cold implacable justice.

"Payandâr!" he gasped--"hast come back from the dead to kill me?"

"From a life that has been a death I come to judgment," was the reply. "Chiefs of the Barlâs clan, assembled for this high purpose, listen! Listen to the record of this man's iniquities and say if the cup be full."

It was a long record, yet Dalîl's memory gave assent to all, and as each crime was counted a surging murmur of acquiescence came from those listening faces. It seemed to deaden the miserable man's senses, for after a time he forgot all things but that one accusing figure in its royal robes, and the hard, cold, accusing voice.

"It is but eight," he muttered hoarsely, "no Tarkhân can be condemned by eight----"

"Listen O Chief of the Barlâs clan," interrupted the accuser, "to the ninth crime. Yestermorn he did of vile licence kill with his lustful kiss----"

Khodadâd essayed a mocking laugh.

"With a kiss? What then? Lucky for any maiden to be so honoured by a Tarkhân; so much the more lucky for such a devil's mash of deformity."

"His own daughter," rang out the charge, harder, colder, crueller. "His daughter by the Rosebud of Love which he dishonoured. His daughter whom he called into being without cause, when he defiled her mother!"

Ah! now he knew! now he understood why--the thought came to Dalîl even as he fought blindly against it.

"Thou liest!" he murmured thickly. "She was Payandâr's spawn. He----"

"He is the accuser," returned the voice calmly, "and by his right of Tarkhân he swears it before the Last Assize. Speak, chiefs of the Barlâs clan, doth this man deserve sentence?"

Once again that surging assent mingled with the rolling of kettledrums, filled Dalîl's ears; but through it he heard the words:

"Executioners! open the veins of his neck and let the Barlâs blood go free of his vile body. Let him bleed to death while I, the king, mourn the spilling of good Barlâs blood."

Then from all around seemed to arise a low wailing, backed still by that quivering roll of the kettledrums. The veiled figures rose slowly; a blackness rose also obliterating all save awful fear. Ah! he knew what was coming! He knew. Was that the keen prick of a long lancet at his throat? Was that a warm stream trickling, trickling?

Oh! ye gods and devils! it was time to wake!

"Ohí my son! Ohí my brother!" The long-drawn wail rose louder and louder!

Wake! *Wake! Wake!* What a hideous dream it was. She was not--she could not be his----

An awful cry, half-choked, broke from him. It was bloodwarm blood--his own blood caressing his bosom, nestling at his heart ...

Wake! Wake!

"Ohí! my brother! Ohí! my son!"

Something surged in his brain. He heard no more.

*　　　*　　　*　　　*　　　*

It was dawn.

The delicate tracery of the desert birds' feet showed close up to the edge of the ruffled carpets whereon lay--hideously confused--all the indescribable refuse of sensuality which the mind has enabled humanity to bring to bear upon its pleasures. But he who had called all the past lust and licence into being, still slept peacefully on the squalid string bed beneath the rich satin quilts.

A servant or two wakened and yawned; then, seeing his services unrequired slept again. So, swiftly, the sun rose with a ruffling wind that followed the footsteps of the birds, in circling eddies, and passed on, leaving the sand without a sign of passage on it.

"He sleeps long," said one, a servant.

"Let him sleep," grumbled another, "when he wakes it will be but another service of sin for him and us."

But others needed the quick wit and relentless purpose of Khodadâd; so almost ere dawn had passed to day, two or three horsemen came galloping from the city intent on finding help from the arch-conspirator.

"God and His Prophet!" faltered Mirza Ibrahîm shrinking back from the shoulder on which he had laid an awakening hand, "he is dead!"

Dead and cold. There was no sign of violence upon him; only on his neck two blue marks, mere signs as it were, of scratches about half an inch long.

"He has died in the night," said Ghiâss Beg with a shiver. "No one is to blame. God send he had time for a prayer."

But Mirza Ibrahîm clutched the complacent Lord High Treasurer by the arm and gasped:

"Look! Look!"

In front of the tent just beyond the ruffled carpet lay a square of white cloth and on it as if in blood, lay clear, distinct, the red marks of a horse's hoofs.

"'Tis the sign," he whispered, his face ashen gray. "The sign that judgment has been passed by his peers."

CHAPTER XXI

No strength of Hand, no strength of Foot have I,
To reach the restful Heaven of Thy Throne;
Yet can my soul's eyes gaze upon the Sky
And finding dream there, dream the Truth mine own
Even while wearied by its ceaseless Strife
I watch the Shuttle in the Loom of Life.

--NIZAMI.

That self-same dawn Akbar the King sate alone, as he so often did, upon a large flat stone which lay in a lonely spot beside the Anup tank. He was dressed in the saffron sheet of an ascetic, and a fold of it, drawn across the lower part of the face, completely disguised him; though the few persons abroad at this early hour were not of the class from whom he could fear detection or even interruption--except perhaps a petition for a blessing. For this was the widows' hour; that strange hour in India, while the world still sleeps, when sorrowful womanhood works out the salvation of mankind. When dim, ghostlike in their white shrouding, figures creep out of the shadowy homes, burdened with the sins of men, and, after washing them away in the chill waters of dawn, creep back to the hearthstones, ere the sun rises upon the devoted drudgery of another widows' day.

The sight of these figures, the whole scene, unreal, mystical, had always had a fascination for Akbar, a curious almost angry interest. He felt himself helpless before it, King though he was. True! he had abolished *suttee* by a sweep of his pen. The swift cruel sacrifice of life he had checked; but this long-drawn agony was beyond him.

And what did it mean when all was said and done? His active mind, ever wrestling with problems of the psychic world, fought for a conclusion on this, the question which has puzzled so many inquirers.

"Whence and wherefore comes the sense of sin which in the woman lies ever at the root of sex, making her falsely modest or boldly brazen?"

How silent they were, these mateless, almost sexless bodies whose souls were seeking--through past æons, and for endless centuries to come-- salvation not for themselves but for their men folk! The very water slipped noiselessly over the shaven unveiled heads that slipped into it as noiselessly.

Sound only came when, on the red sandstone steps of the tank once more, they again drew their wet shrouds round youth and age alike.

Drip! Drip! Drip!

The water fell in blood-red tear drops beside the blood-red print of their bare feet upon the stones. A dolorous way indeed! a dolorous life.

A couple of gray-crested cranes, mates evidently, showed nestling side by side as they stood knee-deep in the gray levels of the tank; levels which brimmed up from the dim shadowy steps of the dim shadowy reflections in the water of the dim shadowy realities of stunted bushes and gnarled caper trees that rose against the dim gray of coming dawn.

Why was not humanity like the birds, accepting the Great Mystery of generation as differing not one whit from other functions of Life?

There lay the puzzle. What sin was it that the woman had committed in the dawn of days!

Yea! the dawn came fast! Below the distant verge of sight the bright-hued riders of the Day were galloping hard, each bringing his pennant to the battle of Light and Darkness.

Blue upon gray, violet tinting the blue, so passing to red, flaming to orange. Then with one throb of primrose----

Light!

He felt the thrill of it--that endless quiver of the ether waves passing on and on regardless of him, around him, through him, in him--felt it in a sudden answering shiver of nerve, and vein, and muscle, as he stood up, absorbed utterly in adoration.

"Thy blessing O my father!" came a voice beside him.

"May thy sacrifice be propitious O my daughter!" he replied mechanically.

"And may the King-of-Kings live forever! His slave kisses the dust of his footsteps."

He turned hastily, kingship coming back to him at once, to recognise Âtma Devi. Crouching at his feet, the wet folds of her widow's shroud clung to every curve of her supple body. After a night spent in fruitless inquiry she had come to the tank at the earliest point of dawn to wander fruitlessly in search round its shores; so after a hasty performance of her sacrifices, she was on her way cityward again when she had seen the solitary figure, and, guessing instinctively that it was the King--for his habits were known to all his people--had come to test her suspicion and so, perchance, gain direct speech of someone from whom, surely, she might hear the truth. But his first words checked her.

"I wist not, woman, thou wert widow," he said sternly. "As a rule thy dress----"

Thinking he blamed her--and blame from him meant all things--she was quick in explanation. "The Most-Auspicious is right," she almost interrupted, "but he to whom I was wedded as a babe proved vile; so my father--praise be to the Gods!--withheld me from him utterly. Yet these few years past, that the man's evil body is dead, I come hither to ransom his soul."

The answer fitting so aptly with Akbar's previous thoughts roused his instant curiosity.

"Wherefore?" he asked, his keen face lighting up with interest as he seated himself once more. "Sit yonder, sister, at my feet and tell me, wherefore?"

"Because he was my husband," came the almost aggressively quick reply. "And a wife is bound to her husband in Life and in Death."

Akbar smiled--the foibles of his world always amused him. "Not in Death, nowadays, my good woman," he cried lightly. "Akbar hath forbidden Death. Would that he could forbid this also."

He touched a fold of her wet shroud with his finger. A shiver shot heartwards from the contact. Was it merely the chill to his flesh warmed by his heart's blood, or was it--something he had told himself he had forgotten? He drew back in resentment. She also; but from his touch on what to her, as to most Hindu women, was the dearest privilege of her sex--the right to burn!

"The Most Excellent is a mighty King," she commented sarcastically, "but even he cannot stay the immortal man in woman from following man in death. We are not all cowards like she who sent yonder *râm-rucki* to the Most High."

She pointed with scorn to a slender, silken cord, behung with coloured tassels which the King wore on his wrist, bracelet fashion.

Akbar frowned.

"So. Thou knowest the story?"

"This slave knows all that concerns the Honour of the King," she replied proudly.

The frown grew.

"The King can keep his honour without thy help, woman! Aye! and his promises too; so this coward shall be saved." Then, as was so often the case with him, eager questioning swept away everything else. "Yet wherefore coward? Tell me that, thou, her sister in sex? Wherefore should a young girl not shrink from burning with an old profligate whose very age hath prevented natural fulfilment of husbandhood? By the sun, my very stomach turns at the thought of it; yet womanhood accepts it dutifully. Lo! couldst thou but tell me--but thou canst not--whence comes this sense of sin which makes women prostitute, and tempts men to be far worse than the beasts, I would give thee----." He paused, looking into her soft dark eyes whence the fierceness had died away giving place to wise surprise at ignorance.

"The Most Excellent must know," she replied. "Our mothers teach it to us. It is the love which seeks for pleasure, which forgets motherhood. Lo! in the beginning we were the nothingness which tempted form, even as Siyâla the courtesan sang; so we cannot live save through that which we create. We are 'thieves of form, and sanctuaries of souls,' even as the Princess Sanyogata told Prithvirâj. Aye! though she had lured him with the love that is illusion! But she was brave also. She left her womanhood to die, and followed the immortal in the man."

"Then this mortal love is woman's only?" he asked critically, eager as ever in argument.

"Aye!" she answered simply. "In the beginning it was so; but we have taught it to man; thus it returns to us again in every soul to which we give a body. Yea! it is so! Look how far we are, Most Excellent"--she pointed with slim finger to the distant cranes--"from yonder birds to whom pairing time is breeding time, who know not sex save for the life they have to give to the world."

She paused, and there was silence; for once again, the example she had chosen fitted in with past thoughts. Far away on the primrose verge a sword-shaped shaft of red-encircled cloud hid the rising sun.

"And there is no other Love?" he asked moodily, forgetful as ever of his *entourage* in the absorption of inquiry. Her face grew paler, her hand went up almost unconsciously to her throat round which the green stone of the *rebeck* player hung; but no essence of rose assailed her senses; or if it did she denied the fact strenuously.

"I know not, my King," she said quietly. "There be some who talk of it; but my father--he was very learned, Most High--held that Love, needing both subject and object" (she spoke quite simply of such abstruse idea as many a nigh naked coolie in India will do, if so be he is Brâhmin), "lay outside the Great Unity and so was illusion. Yet to me----" she hesitated and looked at him almost appealingly out of her large, dark, unfathomable eyes. "Lo! I am woman, so I cannot think--wherefore should not Love be all things?"

"Wouldst thou have it so, sister?" he asked, meaningly. She flushed faintly under her dark skin.

"Nay! Most High," she replied proudly. "For me honour is enough, since I guard the King's."

The words held something of self-revelation in them. He rose and wound his saffron veil closer. "So be it, sister! Guard the King's honour, aye! and his Luck too if thou canst!" he added with a smile as he moved away.

The word roused her to a sense that her chance was departing; she caught at his feet and bowed herself over them in the attitude which in India brings arrest to all in authority; for it is ultimate appeal.

"What is it, sister?" he queried almost mechanically.

"What--what, Most Excellent, of the King's Luck?" she asked tremulously. At the moment other, clearer words failed her.

"What?" he echoed perplexedly, wondering what the woman would be at. "Naught that I know of save that it shone when I saw it yester-evening, and that it will shine still more when the Feringhi jeweller hath spent his Western art upon it," he added with a smile.

"Yester-even," she could scarce speak for surprise, "then--then it is not stolen? The King's Luck is safe?"

"Stolen! Ye Gods, no!" His look of wonder changed to kindly compassion. "Go home, my sister," he said as he might have said to a child. "And dream not so much of the King and his Luck. He is not worth it! So farewell! Yet stay! I owe thee something once more for--thy treatise on Love! I gave thee thy father's titular office did, I not? Well! to-morrow take up his duties! Come to the Great Durbar in thy Châran's dress, and, for once, a woman shall challenge the whole world for Akbar. Lo! it will make some of the *durbaries* see Shaítan," he interpolated for himself light-heartedly. "But come and fear not--I will warn the Chamberlain to give thee place. So once more farewell, widow----"

Thus far he had spoken with a smile; now his face grew grave. "Lo! despite Akbar, methinks thou wilt die for some man yet; thou art of that quality. Heaven send he be worth the sacrifice!"

"I will die for the King's honour if need be," she muttered, true by instinct to her life-idea, even in the midst of her mingled joy and amazement. She sate for some time after Akbar left her, trying to piece together the tangled clues she held; but such intricate balancing of facts was beyond her. She lived only by what she felt, so she was without guide in following up the actions of others.

That the diamond had been stolen she knew; and now it was evident that Birbal had kept the knowledge of the theft from the King--doubtless to save him from distress. This latter thought leapt to her heart and found instant harbour there, so that she began to reproach herself with having gone so near to making such forethought of no avail; a forethought that had done its work too, since as the Most High had seen the diamond but the evening before it must have been recovered. The incident was therefore over--small thanks to her!

And yet the King had bidden her challenge the whole world on his behalf! She crept home and looked at her father's corselet and sword wonderingly. How had it come about that the Great Hope of her life was about to be realised, and she could scarce feel any joy in it?

Meanwhile Akbar was doffing his ascetic's robe, and donning the heron-plumed turban of empire. It was a change to which he was accustomed; but this morning, he felt that something of his interview with Âtma Devi lingered with him.

He paused for a moment as he passed to the Private Hall of Audience with Birbal to look out across the palace courtyard and so through the Arch of Victory to India stretching wide and far beyond it.

"If I leave this place," he said quietly, "as leave it surely I shall some day, thus condemning myself to sonlessness, I shall go down to the ages as one who failed--who built dream-palaces unfit for humanity; therefore fit home for the bats, the foxes, the hyenas."

"This will I warrant, sire!" replied Birbal, hotly, in instant defence of his master. "Let who will come to Akbar's Arch of Triumph in the future, it shall remain to them unforgettable, unforgotten, until Death kills memory!"

"The memory of a great defeat," continued the King shaking his head. "And to my mind a greater one if I remain!" He turned and laid his hand on Birbal's shoulder. "Yea! old friend. I have failed--why strain thyself to hide it? Wherefore--God knows! for I have striven." He paused, then went on, "There was a woman at the tank this morning who said that Love was all things. Is it so? Have I not loved enough? Is that the solving of the riddle-- is it the Master-Key?"

Birbal's face was a fine study in sarcastic disagreement. "Mayhap, my King! The poets have it so; though in God's truth this wondrous key has unlocked naught for me--save nothingness!"

"A perfect mating," went on the dreamer, absorbed in his own thoughts. "The Twain once more as One, sex and its vain search forgotten. Strange if it should be so! Strange if the finding of Self in the Giving of Self should bring back memory yet forgetfulness of that far beginning when the Ocean of Light everlasting, quiescent, stirred into ripples of Shadow, and the One became Two."

"The Audience waits, sire," said Birbal drily.

Akbar laughed, and went on. Yet he turned to Birbal swiftly half an hour afterward when, in the course of business, words were let fall which brought back the memory of this conversation.

It had been rather a disturbing audience and Akbar, ere he commenced it, had felt wearied beyond his usual measure.

So, as he sate below the throne, the position he invariably occupied as symbolising that he was but the representative of a higher power, he had listened with a certain sense of irritation, while a letter, which Father Ricci, the Jesuit, had left behind him, was read aloud by a slim white-robed man with a marked bend of the head and a kindly, patient face.

It ran as follows:

"To the Most Merciful and Most Illustrious King and Emperor Jalâl-ud-in Mahommed Akbar greeting, from his Father in God and Vicar of Christ, servant of the King of Kings: Whereas for long years past I have to the great injury of the cause of Christ, yet with the most pious hopes of eventual harvest, permitted that good servant of the Lord, priest Rudolfo Acquaviva to reside at the Most-Excellent's court in the hopes that by his godly example and teaching light might come to the eyes, and knowledge to the ears of the Emperor. Yet having, during my recent visit, seen with mine own eyes how small a part the great truths of the Church play in the life of the Most-Excellent, and having in view also the most great favour extended to heretick Protestants----"

Birbal's mime-like face puckered, he bent over the King.

"Said I not the reception of the English merchants would bring about greater zeal for Majesty's conversion?"

But Akbar checked him with a frown; so the long phrases of disappointment, partly pious, partly pique, went on and on. When they closed he turned swiftly to the reader.

"Be thou the arbiter, friend Rudolfo. Dost wish to go? Is Akbar not kind enough?"

Pâdré Rudolfo Acquaviva looked affectionately at the man whom he refused, almost to the point of insubordination, to count accursed.

"The King is not kind enough to himself," he said, his gentle face a benediction, as he noted the strain, the anxiety, which in all moments of rest sate on Akbar's countenance. "Wherefore should not weariness lay down its burden at the gracious command, 'Come unto me and I will give you rest'?"

For a second there was a pause. Then Akbar rose, and squared his broad shoulders. "I could not if I would, friend," he replied proudly. "A King's burden must be carried." So with a loud voice he cried:

"Has any or aught further need of the King's wisdom?"

There was no pause this time.

The Makhdûm-ul'-mulk, in his robes of chief doctor of the law, stepped forward hastily and began to read.

"Lo! Makhdûm-*sahib*," interrupted Akbar lightly yet impatiently, "Majesty hath listened to this before. The petition is dismissed. It hath seemed good to the Crown so to cement union with our Râjpût Allies, the marriage ceremonies are commenced, therefore this demand that the Heir-Apparent shall have his first wife one of his own faith is idle--and ill-timed."

"It hath the signature of fifteen thousand learned Ulemas of Islâm," continued the Makhdûm militantly.

"If it had fifty thousand----" interrupted Akbar again; this time sternly.

Ghiâss Beg, the Lord High-Treasurer flung himself, suddenly at the King's feet, and his example was followed by half a dozen of Akbar's most tried and trusted Mohammedan counsellors.

"If the Most-Auspicious will grant us private audience for a space, we will disclose that which may alter Majesty's opinion," said their leader.

Akbar frowned; Birbal and Abulfazl scenting some further conspiracy, stepped forward with instant excuse.

"It is not on the list, sire," said the latter. But the Emperor's sense of Kingship had been aroused, first by his reply to Pâdré Rudolfo, next by the Makhdûm's militant protest. So with a quaint admixture of pride and humility he set aside the Prime Minister's plea haughtily.

"Justice, Shaikh-jee, is not listed like an auctioneer's tale of goods. Ushers! clear the assemblage! My friends, farewell! I would be alone with these gentlemen for a while."

After the ceremonial salaamings, the rustle and glitter of retreating silks and satins had died away, he faced those few as he stood below the throne.

"Well," he said, "speak."

A little old man, poet as well as prince, prostrated himself, and so began with many flowers of speech, many ambiguities, and many quotations from Hafiz, on the story of Prince Salîm's sight of Mihr-un-nissa. "Thus O Most Illustrious King, O! Most Indulgent Father, Fate hath intervened and sent Love!" he concluded, adding in pompous monotonous chant the well-known lines:

He whose soul by Love is quickened, never can to death be hurled;
Written is his name immortal in the records of the world.

Then it was that Akbar turned and looked at Birbal. The latter was instant in reply to the unspoken questions.

"The love of a lad of eighteen, Most High, can scarce be counted love. And might we learn the honourable family of the lady? That hath been omitted."

Ghiâss Beg prostrated himself, "My daughter, sire! The shame of this plea overwhelms me, but in justice to Majesty, I cast away honour. My daughter, sire, a most excellent, admirable, and beautiful young lady."

"But surely," put in Abulfazl swiftly, suavely, "already betrothed to Sher Afkân, captain in the King's horse?"

Akbar frowned. "Is this so?" he asked and listened, the frown deepening, to the altercation that followed. Finally, he raised his hand.

"Enough," he cried, "that ends it. What is talked of is bespoken; and not even a King's son hath right to interfere."

The Makhdûm-ul'-mulk was the next to prostrate himself and speak. "True O Ruler of the Universe! but the Head of the Church hath ever had the right to annul such promises, and Majesty having assumed that title, might exercise the functions thereof." The suggestion was deft, but it failed.

"For my son's benefit," retorted Akbar "not so, Makhdûm-*sahib*. The office is held more incorruptible now."

"The August Pillar of Empire mistakes," put in a younger man, alert, intelligent. "It is for the good of Empire. Lo! we be here as humble friends, advisers, counsellors. With all duty be it spoken, the young Prince--may he live for ever!--hath given cause for anxiety. This chaste cupola of chastity of whom undesirable mention has been made, whose name my unworthy lips refuse to utter, hath a reputation for great wisdom as well as beauty. If then the Heir-Apparent were wedded to her, if love----"

Akbar raised his hand again sharply, and Birbal divining hesitation, whispered in his ear.

"Remember the Râjpût Allies sire; a hint of this----"

The King checked him haughtily, "Peace! That goes on as ever. I was but thinking--thinking of the boy and--and the girl." Then he raised his voice. "Gentlemen! I admit much of what hath been said. The Prince hath given cause for anxiety--he gives it still. And if Fate had been beforehand with fact, such might have been good solution for much anxiety. But she is behindhand. The wedding festivities of the Heir-Apparent have already begun----"

"The nuptials could be simultaneous, Most High," interpolated the younger man, who was court lawyer. "It is a royal custom----"

"And the young lady is already betrothed," went on Akbar inexorably. "That in itself is sufficient. The King's promise is given in the first, her father's in the second. Akbar will break neither." And then suddenly resentment, perhaps a faint regret, seemed to come to him and his voice rose. "Lo! have I ever broken faith? Has not my yea been yea, my nay, nay?"

"Of a truth it has, Great Sire," answered the court lawyer deftly as his forehead once more touched the dust. "Yea! even beyond the ordinary faith of kings, since Akbar hath not shrunk in the past from rescinding orders he hath made in error. Will he not do so now? Will he not bow to Fate?"

It was boldness beyond belief, and both Birbal and Abulfazl stood aghast. Yet it was a master-stroke, for Akbar paled and was silent.

"Fate," he echoed at last, and the tone of his voice brought Birbal's to his ear in earnest entreaty--but it was too late. "So be it! Fate shall be the arbiter for this boy and this girl. Let her see to it!" His eyes lit up, a certain buoyancy seemed to lift him above the dull world. "I, Akbar, challenge her! Ye say Fate hath intervened. Let her intervene! If in the hours from dawn to dawn, she can make the King go back from his word in one thing, to her the victory! If not, to me."

The words rang out through the maze of arches in the Diwan-i-Khas. Then there was silence, till on the silence the King's laugh rang out. "Look not so solemn, friends--and foes mayhap!--Akbar, like all things else is in the hands of Fate."

But as Birbal went out with Abulfazl, he cursed and swore. "Aye!" he assented "'tis true enough. All things are in the hands of Fate; but wherefore should the King be in the hands of his enemies? They will strain every nerve----"

"'Tis but for a short time--from dawn to dawn." put in Abulfazl consolingly, "and we must strain every nerve also." Then suddenly his face softened. "Lo! I would not have him otherwise, Birbal. He is like a racehorse! The least touch of the bit of Fate and--for all his words--he chafes against it. 'Tis not Acquiescence, it is Defiance that wings his challenge."

"Aye!" grunted Birbal with a whimsical smile, "and a half-hearted belief that Love is all things."

CHAPTER XXII

Take to the garden thy carpet of prayer
Wait, and watch how at God's command
The daffodils girdles of green prepare,
How sentinel straight the cypresses stand.
Forget thyself in the Path-of-Life
Plunge for a second in God's own Sea,
And the Seven Tides of the Water of Strife
Will never encompass thee.

--HAFIZ.

"Lo! I have prayed," said Auntie Rosebody, captiously, "and I have watched, but naught has come of it save a brow-ache. Truly Ummu, at my age, piety is fatiguing and 'tis better to trust the senses God gave than seek a new gift from him. Belike He is tired of old Gulbadan, and would as lief she took her rest decently in death like the rest of her generation. One cannot expect Him to count an old woman as worth so much to the world as a young one."

Little Umm Kulsum looked shocked.

"Nay, Auntie," she began, "are we not taught----"

"Taught," echoed the old lady tartly, "aye, we are taught much that is not true and more that is no use to us when we lose our way. But there! it serves me right! None lose themselves on a straight path; so mine--nay!--it is mine, child, not yours--hath been crooked, that is the truth. But I have made up my mind. The diamond shall go back to the jeweller from whom it was taken, for 'tis my belief that his Majesty the King knows naught about it. When I came from morning prayers and found him paying his respects to the Lady Mother, my conscience was exalted to the edge of confession and I began, as one does begin, to skirt round the subject--I never could abide, like my revered father--on whom be peace--to go head foremost into cold water. But the fount of my penitence soon ran dry in the parched desert of his ignorance. 'Tis useless telling a blind man that you have stolen his spectacles! So I gave over, came hither, and ordered a *do-piâza* with double spice of onions to it, for I was sick with fasting. And it hath cleared my brain. The diamond shall go back, and I will trust the red madwoman as thou didst suggest last night. For his Highness the Most-Auspicious spoke of her this morning to Lady Hamida, and bid us all look out to see this

Châran--forsooth!--at the Durbar to-morrow! Truly my august nephew hath a wit like a camel's cantrip; it leaves one uncertain whether to laugh or to weep! But he must hold her faithful, so I will write a letter to the Feringhi in a feigned hand, appointing time and place for restoration. This she shall take; and afterward I will lay strict oaths on her, such as not even a woman could evade, and she shall have the stone, and bring back receipt therefore. So that settles it, and may God forgive silly old Gulbadan!" She frowned fiercely. "Yea, grand-daughter, that is the sting in the scorpion's tail! For once Khânzâda Gulbadan Begum hath been a fool! She hath acted without counting the cost."

So, secretly and in haste, Âtma Devi was sent for and shewn into the little corbeilled balcony overhanging the lofty outside wall of the palace, where there could be no eavesdroppers save the purple pigeons that cooed and strutted on the wide cornices.

"The diamond!" she said incredulously. "Oh! Beneficent Ones! it is not stolen! Or rather it hath been given back. My lord Birbal must have replaced it, for the King knows naught about it."

"'Tis my lord Birbal who knows naught about it, foolish one," said Auntie Rosebody, peremptorily, "for he sent it back here safe sewn in the Prince's turban. Lo! unbeliever, look, and see if I lie."

Her small henna-tinged palm went into her bosom, and there, like a huge dewdrop among rose leaves, lay the gem.

"The King's Luck," murmured Âtma in stupefaction, "the King's Luck! And yet my lord Birbal knew--this slave knows that he knows, and the King does not know--this slave knows that he does not know."

"Oh cloud not perspicacity with noes and not noes!" cried Aunt Rosebody wrathfully and yet with a whimper in her voice. "If the Most-Excellent is ignorant--as I, too, believe him to be, and as I pray he may ever remain--that is the more reason why this should go back at once."

"Aye!" assented Âtma, her face scarcely less bewildered than little Umm Kulsum's as she sate rocking herself to and fro, mechanically repeating penitential verses of the Koran, "but my lord Birbal knew--wherefore?"

"Wherefore," echoed Aunt Rosebody vehemently protesting. "Lo! if thou wilt ask questions, I shall lose my way again. Remember the saying

'Ask not the road of twain
If one can make it plain.'

And for my part, I think the better of Birbal for his silence. If my nephew knew that his heir had filched his Luck from him----" and then suddenly she dissolved into tears, "Oh! Gulu! Gulu! beloved of thy father! why didst not think of this before, thou silly--old--fool?"

Umm Kulsum joined her in tears, only Âtma Devi sate calm, frowning. "Aye," she assented gravely, "I see. The Most High must never know. Therefore if the Beneficent Lady will give me the letter I will see it delivered, and when dark comes I can take the King's Luck to the place appointed."

Aunt Rosebody gave a sigh of relief. "Truly thou art not so bad, good red-woman. Ummu! my pen and ink. And we--we three will swear never to open our mouths concerning this again, least of all to the Most-Auspicious. No! not even as dying confession to ease our miserable souls."

"Lo! I promise," sobbed Umm Kulsum. "God gives the reward of silence."

"Yea! I promise," murmured Âtma softly.

And so it came to pass that just as Birbal had almost given up hope of coming even upon a trace of the lost diamond; when, thrown back upon himself, he was meditating the possibility of a private audience with the Beneficent Ladies, and a complete throwing of himself upon their mercy, he received a message to come down without delay to the Hall of Labour. He found William Leedes attempting to make out the meaning of a little scented note in a brocaded bag, which had been left for him at the outside door.

"A woman's writing for sure," said Birbal quickly at his first glance. "See how the curves are clipped showing lack of decision." He read the first words--"Ye Gods!" he muttered; so ran hastily through the few lines which appointed a place for the due restoration of the missing gem.

Then he refolded the letter, replaced it in its covering without a word, and stood silent, all the confident vitality gone from face and figure. Suddenly he sniffed at the brocaded bag. "Aye! violets!" he murmured. "The Lady Umm Kulsum's favourite flower! By heaven and earth, Birbal! thou art a fool!" He flung his arms out so recklessly that it seemed as if he would strike himself. "'Tis my mistake after all, sir jeweller! I must have confused the true and the false, for this is from the palace." he said bitterly, "and all my searchings, my chase after that vanishing quantity the harlot Siyah Yamin hath been lost time! I am a fool!"

It was a few minutes ere his quick brain had regained sufficient self-confidence to work; but then it worked rapidly. At nine o'clock--it was now six--by the large flat stone at the Anup tank, not only William Leedes must be in evidence, but he, Birbal, and a strong guard of deaf and dumb slaves must be concealed close by so as to prevent any possibility of treachery. For Birbal did not forget Akbar's curious challenge to his courtiers that day, or that the safe conduct given to the Englishman was a promise which an assassin's dagger might easily break. Ralph Fitch and John Newbery were too far away to be points of attack, but William Leedes must be guarded. Aye! and endless other possibilities must be foreseen, and precautions taken against defeat. For in this case defeat would mean a change in the King's whole line of policy. It is true that it would also, in all probability, mean his acceptance of practical politics and so bring him round to Birbal's point of view--namely that Kingship must follow certain definite and familiar lines; but Birbal's wholehearted love of his master could not brook defeat for him. What action he took must be free, not forced.

So in the interval between the time of receiving the notice of appointment and the appointment itself Birbal set seriously to work in consultation with Abulfazl.

"The hounds of hell will scour heaven and earth to find some pitiful failure," he said finally, almost grinding his teeth with impotent regret. "Lo! Shaikh-jee! What ails the King at times to give such handle to his enemies?"

"It is his sense of strength," replied Abulfazl calmly. "He feels like a God, and of a truth he is one." The Prime Minister's flattery had grown to be part of himself; he really thought of Akbar as he wrote about him.

"Perchance!" growled Birbal, "but he lives among men, and men know how to trick their gods. I can think of no more promises; if thou dost, guard against failure, for my leisure may be scant."

As he made his way to the appointment, he told himself that it might be scant indeed; since, somehow, he must recover the diamond that night. Despite his unbelief, his clear wit, his critical outlook on all things, he could not escape from the feeling that the best safeguard to his master would be the repossession of the lucky stone. Yes! he must recover it.

The night was dark, dark enough to favour the posting of men unseen in the shadow of the trees to the left of the big flat stone. So dark that even the still levels of the tank lay unrevealed, save here and there, where a feeble oil rushlight shone on the shore showing the little platter of food for the dead on which it stood, the fading chaplet of flowers twined around the offering.

So dark, so still, so quiet. No sign anywhere of movement.

Stay! up yonder where the steps might begin, a twinkling light. Was it some other bereaved woman coming to place her remembrance on the water's edge--or was it the messenger? By heaven! it bore to the left--just a twinkling light, no more. Birbal held his breath. And now, grown nearer, the faint circle of radiance showed a hand holding a little platter of offerings, and on the wrist a fold not of white but red drapery.

By all that was holy, Âtma Devi! Then she was at the bottom of it, after all!

The next minute he and his slaves were surrounding her and the dark figure of William Leedes, who had risen from the large flat stone where he had been waiting.

She stood quite still, apparently not much surprised, and her eyes met Birbal's without fear.

"Yea, kill me when I have fulfilled my errand," she said quietly, "but not till then. I have sworn to give it to none but the jeweller. Is he here?"

"Take it from her, sir jeweller," came the quick order. "I can settle with her afterward."

There was a pause as Âtma Devi appraised the Feringhi's strange dress, then from amongst the little pile of uncooked grain upon the platter of the dead, produced the diamond. It shone with a faint lambent glow in the flickering light of the oil lamp. A sigh of satisfaction came from Birbal, but William Leedes bent closer to look at what he held and his face as he raised his head showed ghastly gray.

"It also is false, master," he faltered. "See yonder is the scratch my tool made on it----"

"False," Birbal stood transfixed, feeling, even amidst his stupefaction, a quick sense of relief that after all he had made no mistake. "False," he echoed, and turned on Âtma Devi. She also stood surprised, so surprised that Birbal realised in an instant that she was innocent of all complicity in whatever had brought about this astounding revelation. So without a word, he drew out the other false gem which he had brought with him, and laid it beside its marrow on the jeweller's palm.

"There be two false stones, sister," he said striving to be calm, feeling that it was his only chance of getting any hint on which he could work from her, "but where is the real one; dost know?"

Her great, wide eyes roved helplessly from the twin stones to the jeweller's face, so back to his; then back again to the stones.

"Pooru must have made them," she said slowly, "but I wist not they were even made."

Then suddenly she threw up her arms and clapped her hands together high above her head. The platter of death offerings with its little lamp falling from her hold, dashed itself to pieces on the stones, and there was darkness. So from it came her wail--"Lo I have betrayed the King, I, his Châran! Yet I know nothing." She sank huddled in a heap upon the ground.

"There is no use wasting further time here," said Birbal roughly after several vain attempts to rouse Âtma Devi from ineffectual despair. "Leave her to her own condemnation. This points to deeper plotting than I dreamt of, and there is no moment to lose."

As he hurried off, he marshalled half a hundred theories before the judgment seat of his brain....

The biggest villain--who was the biggest villain? Khodadâd without doubt, but he was dead. Could *he* have had the diamond? It was becoming plain to Birbal that in this scheme of theft some one had played for the chance of the Great Diamond never coming again within reach of a jeweller's lathe. Someone had kept the real stone, and played off false ones upon the conspirators. He must search Khodadâd's house; aye even the corpse which still awaited the next dawn for burial. Then there was Siyah Yamin; but that devil's limb had once more disappeared. She would be found, of course--no power, not even fear, could keep a woman of her kidney quiet for long. But this was all in the future, and deep down in the cynical heart of the man lurked a clamour that his King, his master, should have the benefit of his luck stone within the next few hours. It must not be in the keeping of his enemies. It must be secure in the safe custody of a friend.

Yet he felt curiously helpless. Though he had ransacked Fatehpur Sikri, aye and Agra also, in search of the so-called Sufi from Isphahân--the mountebank, the juggler with men's senses, he had not come upon a trace of him. William Leedes was of no use, and the only other human being friendly to the King who knew of the diamond's loss, was the half-crazy woman whom he had left crushed in despairing remorse by the Anup tank. Most likely she would go home and kill herself with the death-dagger of her race.

Well she was of no use. From beginning to end, she had been a hindrance, not a help.

And Âtma, meanwhile, was feeling that the Seven Tides of the Waters of Strife had overwhelmed her.

What had she done? She had persuaded Diswunt to give the opportunity for the theft of the diamond, it is true; but only that she might take it--as she had taken it--to the keeping of the Beneficent Ladies. And they had given it back to her. She sate unconscious of the passage of Time, puzzling herself vainly to account for those twin stones which had lain shining in the jeweller's palm.

CHAPTER XXIII

Wash white the pages! In no book
Love's rule is written. Wherefore look
Not in my words for Flattery; nor dare
To claim me as thy rightful share.
Traced on my brow is Love--Fate wrote it there.

--HAFIZ.

The gongs striking eleven roused her. She stood up and looked about her, feeling lost, forlorn; and lo! she was in a world of stars. For it was the Night of the Dead, and every little hovel, every house, and homestead, and palace in the town behind her, glittered with the small lamps set to illuminate the feasts that are laid out for wandering spirits. And as she looked out over the unseen levels of the tank, the stars were there also, twinkling farther and farther away to the horizon in every hamlet and village. For an instant the inner vision of the soul was hers, and she saw, as it were a map stretched before her, the wide plain of India receding on and on into the darkness of the night, all sown with such stars in constellations.

And every star was the memory of some dear face; every star was set for some loved wandering soul!

She felt like a disembodied spirit herself as she looked down at her feet, remembering the little decorous platter in which she had hidden the diamond. Should she go back to the Beneficent Ladies and tell them what had happened? No! She had done her part toward them; she had given the gem they had given her into the jeweller's own hand as she had promised; so that was the end.

But it was not the True Luck; thus her duty, so far as she herself was concerned, still remained. She must try and find it, and if she failed there was always the death-dagger; for she must be true, though she was a woman.

"True! Aye! as true as it befits womanhood to be."

Who had said that?

Siyâla?

Then in a second she knew, and turning swiftly on her heel ran toward the town. Siyâl! Siyâla was the thief! She had the King's Luck. Ye gods! had it come to this. Her sister of the veil, the little dainty, delicate, perfumed piece of femininity which she had borne with, nay, had almost loved as a half-forgotten part of herself--she, and she only, was preventing her, Âtma, the representative of Chârans, from playing her man's part in Châranship. An uttermost loathing of herself, as woman, came to the mind that had been educated to believe in her womanhood as nothingness, the while she hurried through the full bazaars toward Satanstown. She almost had to fight her way through one portion where the crowd filled every inch of the roadway past Khodadâd's house. He was lying in state there with all the royal insignia of a Tarkhân about him. That had not saved his corpse, however, from quick searching by the hands of the city police (for treasonable papers was the excuse) but now that Birbal had come and gone unsatisfied, the professional wailers were once more skirling away their mercenary grief, and through the wide arches of the upper floor the swaying heads of the hired priests could be seen as they chanted their orisons for the dead.

"Who is't?" she asked, faint curiosity rising in her as she passed.

"Khodadâd, Tarkhân. Hast not heard?" answered someone. "They found him dead at dawn, the blood pouring from his veins, and the white horse from which he had fallen by his side."

"Aye! but thou forgettest neighbour!" said another eager voice "his hands were tied and----"

"God send his soul to the nethermost hell for treachery," broke in Âtma on the gossiping, as she fought her way on.

"Ari, sister! Have a care," protested the crowd. "Thou hittest like a man, and will hurt."

But she was gone ere the sentence ended in a broad laugh, and a rough jest on him who had such a termagant to wife.

Old Deena caught sight of her as she came breathlessly along the balconied lane. There were lights and to spare here, but Siyah Yamin's house stood a dark block amongst its radiant neighbours.

"Thou art too late, mistress most chaste," he called, "the singing bird is fled."

"Whither?" she gasped.

He shook his wicked old head and leered with his wicked old eye.

"No-whither so far as this world knows. A many have been after her, even my Lord Birbal, without success. She left for the desert to my Lord Khodadâd's devil's feast last evening and hath not returned. Now he is dead, and she hath disappeared! Belike the white horse carried her off too; or belike," he spoke in a lower voice, "the desert was but fair doubling ground for pursuit."

Âtma stared at him uncomprehending.

"But I need her," she muttered.

A hard metallic laugh rang from a neighbouring balcony.

"No woman needs woman!" came a coarse jeering voice. "But such a strapping wench could mayhap play a man's part. Play it, sister, and God go with you."

Âtma turned and fled from the burst of wild laughter that followed on the sally. There was nothing left now for her, truly, but the man's part. She must find the death-dagger of her race, and die as they had died.

But not for honour; for dishonour!

By the time she reached the winding tenement stair which led upward to her roof she had grown calm, and her mind, set loose from the urgency of the present, had begun to wander amid past scenes. Yea! yonder were the steps leading down to the cellar where the Wayfarer had lain asleep, half dead in dreams, with Zarîfa's face upon his bosom. A strange man indeed! What was it he had said about Love? Her hand sought her throat involuntarily and finding the quaint green stone clasped it.

Roses! Roses! Roses! Their scent bewildered her!

Then in a second she saw all, she understood all. Aye! she, the woman in her, had loved the King and she had been ashamed of it. But this--this was different. This was the mortal following the immortal! She was going to death as to a funeral prye, to find herself sexless, beyond the flames.

She stumbled on and on, up and up, every atom of herself forgotten save the deathless desire for Unity which lies behind sex, until, suddenly, some unfamiliarity beneath her feet made her pause.

Had she come too far? She stopped in the mirk darkness to feel the step on which she stood, so, groping felt the wall.

A nail. And something had caught on it. What?

A tiny scrap of fringe. And that was scent--not bewildering scent of roses; but bewildering scent of musk and ambergris--the essences of Satanstown!

Siyah Yamin's paradise!

The thought leaped to her brain; a second or so afterward she stood at the secret door. It was ajar.

But this time the darkness of the roof showed like a black shadow against the diffused radiance from the town below.

"Siyâla" she cried, but there was no answer. She moved forward a step; then, bethinking herself, turned back, locked the door and thrust the key in her bosom. If anyone were there, they would have to meet her face to face.

So, her eyes becoming accustomed to that outside radiance, that central shadow, she half-felt her way down the broad path from the door toward the place where, when last she had seen it, silken curtains had still hung, and the remains of feasting had still lain rotting--rotting surely, slowly by day and night.

But there was nothing now. Even the dead roses had disappeared and her feet as she walked sank softly in the carpet of sand and dust that covered all things. Was that a darker shadow flitting back as she advanced? She turned swiftly, heard an ineffectual rattle of the lock, and the next instant, in her haste, her outstretched hands pinned a slight figure to the door.

"Lo! Âto," came a petulant voice, "thou art rough as any man! I am here if thou needst me, so take thy big hands from my frail body and let me light a light. 'Twas thy step--manlike again--made me extinguish mine, for fear."

A spark from the tinder box showed small hands shaking; and the following light, a second too soon, found traces of sharp terror behind the mocking smile on Siyah Yamin's face. She was dressed as she had been before in man's clothes, but this time they seemed to sit ill on her shrinking figure; yet she strove hard for boldness.

"Well! what is't, Âto?" she went on recklessly as if trying to put off time. "Somewhat of the King I will go bail--the King thou dost not love! ha! ha!" Her jeering laugh roused a muffled echo from the low, empty walls.

"Yea, I love the King as woman loves man," replied Âtma gravely. "What of that. It is illusion. It will pass."

Siyah Yamin gave a little soft shuddering sigh.

"Come!" she said sharply, "we cannot talk so. Come! widow! follow thy lover, Sher Khân." She sprang forward light in hand, and her slender figure fled forward leaving darkness behind her; darkness through which her light song echoed.

What says philosophy
Love's an illusion!
Silly delusion!
Give me your lips
Take mine! Such sips
Prove Love felicity.
Wisdom is wearisome
Closer, my dearie, come
Let us find Unity--

"Peace Siyâl!" said Âtma, sternly interrupting the ribald verses.

"Peace? oh yea! let there be peace between us." laughed the courtesan, as she sank down on the dusty step of the dais, and put the light beside her. But her wide eyes belied her light words.

Fear sate behind their glitter, watching wickedly; and every subtle sense sought for some means of escape, some method of cajolery. "Wherefore not," she rattled on. "Lo! I give you in his Monkey-Majesty! He is not a man after my heart. Yet, I would not his enemies got the better of him, as they will do. What! hast not heard? He challenged them this day to write failure across a promise of his, or change across his mind. From dawn to dawn it was. And see you, Âto" the hurried palpitating voice steadied, as the wild search for some false trail happened upon one. "Thou art the King's Châran and must warn him! They have sent poison out to the paralysed profligate at Shâkin-garh--he will be burnt at dawn and with him the girl whose *râm-rucki* the King wears. There is small time to lose, Âto--I know it, I tell thee--I heard it from their lips--go thou, then, with warning."

She leant forward; her face full of guileful, beguileful beauty, close to the grave level brows that met in a steady frown.

"Aye! I will go, Siyâl--but not without the King's Luck. Give it me. Thou hast it in thy bosom--thy hand has hovered there. Give it me, I say." She essayed to grip those fluttering fingers but Siyah Yamin was on her feet in a second, and stood back, swaying unsteadily, one hand clasped to her heart.

"I--lo! it is not true. 'Tis something here that hurts"--she beat her breast sharply. "Be not so rough, Âto! Thou wert always rough as a man. Lo! in the old days it was I, little Siyâla who was to marry Âtma Singh, and now--now--Sher Khân." she paused, tore off her dandified turban, and let the great plaits and coils of her hair fall loose. "See I am woman again, and thou--thou art man! And, Âto, hist! Knowest thou why I came back here to-night?--would I had never come. It was to find the broken pieces of the glass goblet I broke." Her small face melted almost to tears, the babyish lips trembled over the words. "Yea! Yea! it is true. I came for them!--I was going away--for ever--and I remembered. Lo! Âto, a woman always remembers her first lover, even if she be courtezan. Yea! thou wilt remember the King, so have pity! What! dost not believe? Lo! I was looking when thou camest, and frightened me into putting out the light. See here if I lie." With her right hand she tore something out of her bosom and shifting it swiftly to her left held it out. It was a curved fragment of the blown-glass goblet which had fallen with a crash upon a rosebush, whose red wine of Shirâz had trickled thirstily to the rose's root.

Twined upon it in golden tracery lay part of its legend--

Take the cup of Life with laughing lip,
Forget the bleeding heart within.

She caught at the words hysterically. "So have I taken Life, Âto, as all women should; I have drunken heart's blood. Âto! touch me not! or before God I---- What dost seek, madwoman?

"The King's Luck, harlot! Thou hast it in thy bosom. Give it me, or----"

They were locked in each other's arms, but Âtma Devi was a second too late, for Siyah Yamin had drawn something besides a broken glass-sherd from her bosom, and her right hand with a flash of steel in it rose high, then fell on the Châran's broad breast. Âtma staggered under the blow, but the poniard blade crashing on the collar bone turned aside upward and cleft the muscles of the neck harmlessly. She had the weapon wrested from the small hand in a second, and her voice, breathless from exertion yet steady, went on relentlessly.

"Thou hast it, Siyâl! Thou didst steal it and betray--all men! Best give it to me--or--or I shall have to kill thee--sister of the veil."

But Siyah Yamin was true to her womanhood, and every atom of her fought for full possession as she struggled madly.

"It--it is mine." she gasped. "No one shall have it--I claim--I am the woman and I will have----"

Suddenly there was silence. Resistance melted out of Âtma Devi's arms; her insistent hand, still seeking, found what it sought. She gave a sharp cry of joy and relaxed her hold.

But the dainty figure her insistence had supported, doubled up limply and fell in a huddled heap upon the ground.

She sank beside it on her knees. She would have killed it, as she had said. Aye, killed it remorselessly! but surely she had not----

"Siyâl? Siyâla? Sister?"

But she called in vain. The very glare of hatred and fear was dying from the eyes over which the impenetrable veil of death was creeping.

She watched them for a second or two, then closed them, and stood up. She was not frightened nor remorseful at what had happened. Vaguely she felt relieved. It was womanhood which had died there on the roof in the Paradise of Lust. Now that she had time to think, she saw it all. It was so simple. Siyâla, beset by the desire of possession, had ordered the false gem maker to make two false stones, and palming them off on the conspirators had kept the real one, trusting to her luck that the one supposed to be the true gem would never again fall into the hands of the jeweller. But it had. The exchange of turbans had brought discovery close at hand, so she had meant to fly; and doubtless for once had spoken truly, when she said she had returned during the night to gather up the broken fragments of her first cup of joy.

So, quietly, methodically, Âtma straightened out the huddled figure that had held the *deva-dasi*, sister of the veil, daughter of the Gods, covering it decorously with the tinselled muslin scarf Sher Khân had worn in gay mockery of his sex. So it was pure Womanhood that lay there with face upturned to the dark. Then taking the light, Âtma searched under the rose-bushes for the broken cup. She found the bowl intact save for the one curved splinter Siyâla had gathered up. The stem, too, jarred and chipped, would still stand upright; so, making a little pile of dust she set them together beside the dead woman's hand, and left her lying there in the shadow, with the diffused light from the Lamps of the Dead below making a far-away halo to that central darkness.

Closing, and locking the door, she flung the key through a narrow loophole in the stairway, through which that same radiance of the Dead could be seen faintly; so passed down to her own door.

There was much to be done. The diamond, however, being so far safe, her first care must be to warn the King that the little coward of the *râm-rucki* was in imminent danger. For this she must make her way to the palace.

She made it quicker than she had thought for, since, as she unlocked her door, figures started out on her from the darkness below, and she felt what the Beneficent Ladies called an "all-over dress," being respectfully yet firmly pulled over her.

"By the King's command, bîbî," said the oily voice of a eunuch. "Thou hast been appointed of his household, and the Lord Chamberlain hath ordered us----"

She made no effort at escape, knowing herself helpless, but she could defend herself.

"The Lord Chamberlain, being here himself," she interrupted at a venture--and a faint stirring as if those around her turned to look at someone told her that her surmise was correct--"can take me prisoner if he choose; but let him remember that the King desires my presence as Châran at the Great Durbar. So let him treat me ill at his peril."

Mirza Ibrahîm who had, indeed, come to see his orders executed, said nothing; but he inwardly swore that the jade should repent her defiance. There were endless possibilities for a Lord Chamberlain once the wild-cat were fairly housed within reach.

Âtma meanwhile in her screened dhooli felt herself going palaceward contentedly enough. So far was good. But how to get her message conveyed to the King.

Yet conveyed it must be, and before long; for the soft radiance of the Lamps of the Dead had begun to die down. The wandering spirits had had their feasting; they must be in their graves by dawn.

Could she escape? Could she by good luck see a friend? bribe one of the bearers?

But time slipped by without opportunity and she found herself lodged at last in a very handsome apartment consisting of a room and beyond that a slip of roof with a latticed cupola before any chance had come of accomplishing her desire.

"Nay! no more! I need nothing more. I will call if so be," she said to the servants who fawned about her. "Go! I tell thee."

She must think, she must devise some plan. The room was well appointed; even a long pen-box with a quaint pot of glazy ink stood by a low stool, so she could write. Meanwhile she must have a few minutes in the open. The musk of the tented dhooli had almost been too much for her.

So, out on the roof of this cupola's bastion or turret, half way down the palace wall, she leant, her arms on the parapet, and looked downward and upward. Above, to one side, was the palace; but which part of it? Below her was one of the wide eaves so characteristic of Indian architecture, and it ran, after skirting the turret octagonally along the walls, into the darkness. There was foothold for one with a strong head, doubtless; but what then?

As she thought a sound of whirring ropes met her ear, and something dark slid down the wall from far above her.

The preacher's dhooli! Then the King's balcony was somewhere above her! Could she? How far did the eave run. It would need ten yards at least. And could she start the equipoise if once she got a hold on the ropes?

Stay! She would only have to signal.

CHAPTER XXIV

Oh clear the cushioned thrones from those who sleep
Preach thou the Truth, let the Untruth be dumb
Till gladsome voices once more fill both worlds
Freshen the universe--Be thou our soul
We are dead bodies. Bring us back to life
Thou art our guard, the caravan is lone.
Thou art our army, let thy standard wave.
Lo! the day steed is weary; the dim night
To all around us; bid thy seraphim
Herald the coming dawn, and wake us, Lord,
As helpless babes we sleep and sleep and sleep
Upon the threshhold of another world.

--NIZAMI.--A. D. 1140.

Birbal had been wakeful. The discovery of the second false gem had thrown him back on himself. At dawn all his energies must be turned toward making it impossible that the King's rash, almost incredibly rash challenge, should bring disaster on the policy of years; so ere that dawn came endless plans for the recovery of the missing jewel must be set in train. Then, if possible, he must find the juggler with men's senses, the man whose marvellous art had helped him before. There was a chance that King Bayazîd might know his whereabouts; so an hour or so ere daylight, all other things having been started, Birbal's swift-trotting bullocks drew up at the garden gate of the River Palace. All was dreamful as before. Here no lamps of the Dead shone in the wide arcades, only on the roof the light which burnt ever in Rupmati's shrine, showed the gaunt length of her lover asleep on cushions beneath it.

"The Sufi from Isphahân?" he said drowsily. "He who called himself the Wayfarer, pretended to be Payandâr, and *was* musician! Yea! he left a message for thee--that his work was accomplished. He whom he watched was dead, the danger was overpast; therefore he went, whither I know not. Neither do I care. He sang me a *ghazal* ere he left--it hath a good lilt to it."

And Birbal as he ran down the stairs again, heard that same lilt of it ringing after him.

A broken glass that held the red-wine of Strife,
The corpse of a man, besprinkled with essence of rose,
A child asleep on the threshold of larger life,
Such is thy dawn-wake, lover who seeks repose.
Lend, for the Love-of-God, to my thirsty heart thy bowl,
So with the dawn-waked winds He shall refresh thy soul.

He muttered a curse on Sufi nonsense, and flinging himself into the *râth* again, bade the servant return cityward. So, after a while he dozed, seizing on time for sleep when naught else could be done. He was aroused by a sharp jolt, a sudden drawing to one side on the part of the driver.

"What is't, fool?" he queried, sharply.

"Protector of the Poor" replied the man "It is the King!"

He was on his feet in an instant, rubbing his eyes in the gray dawn-light in time to see a rider whirl past alone.

The King undoubtedly; but his escort? Was this all? An old man bent with service, dropping farther and farther behind, not so much from any fault in his mount, but simply from lack of riding.

That anyhow could be remedied.

"Your horse!" he cried, and the old servitor, a tall, bony Mahommedan, recognising Birbal instantly, recognising also the advantage of the slim Hindu in a stern chase, obeyed.

"What is it? Where goes he?" asked Birbal briefly, hands busy shortening stirrups.

"Shakîngarh--to the burning. The Most-Auspicious slept when the madwoman--she who calls herself Châran came up in the Preacher's dhooli. Two horses are aye kept saddled in the yard below. The King was on Bijli in a twinkle, and I--there was none else--scrambled on Chytue shouting for some one to follow."

But Birbal had gathered up the reins and was off. Chytue lightened by the change of riders, sweeping on at a thundering gallop, lessening the distance at every stride between him and his stable companion.

Akbar looked round to frown; then to smile. "A race!" he cried gleefully. "How now Bijli?" The mare answering to the call shot forward like an arrow from a bow.

A race indeed! thought Birbal. A lost one, too, most likely, for the gray of the false dawn was passing into primrose.

How had they managed it--they must have killed the old man; and he would be burnt at sunrise, and then Akbar's promise to the little coward of a Râni--oh! curse all women!--

Fifteen miles good, though in the far distance behind him the low, jagged ridge of Sikri loomed like a cloud. One by one the mud mounds which tell of village sites, rose out of the treeless western horizon, showed silent, lightless, smokeless in the half-light, then sank, dwindled, to join that shadow of the ridge. How many more of them must be passed before dawn ... before dawn ...

So thought the rider behind, cursing himself as he rode, for having forgotten this easy-broken promise of his King.

But Akbar, riding ahead, had forgotten anxiety in determination, and as, at a deviating curve in the track, he struck boldly across country, his every vein thrilled with joyful excitement.

The dawn was coming! Under his horse's flying hoofs the interminable sequence of sandy by-paths through the sun-baked fallows chequered with fields of young millet and maize, seemed to slip past. As the light grew, the purple eyes of the feathery vetches seemed to look at him tear-drenched with dew, the goldy-green balls of the colocynth apples as they cracked under the thundering feet gave out a bitter, bracing, wholesome smell.

Down in an old backwater of the river which held a few acres of damper ground, a flight of cranes rose, to wing a wedge-shaped way to the west.

"Oh! for the wings of a dove."

That was what Pâdré Rudolfo sang.

Was that a spiral trail of smoke on the horizon? Aye; but from a village rubbish heap. After all, a funeral pyre was nothing more; a mere rubbish heap of accessories in which a soul had played its part.

Yea! but as when one layeth
His worn out robes away
And, taking new ones sayeth
These will I wear to-day.
So putteth by the spirit
Lightly its robe of flesh
And passeth to inherit
A residence afresh.

The words of the Bhagavad-Gita recurred to his mind, bringing with them as they do to every human mind that knows them, a sudden sense of companionship, of hand clasping in the wilderness of life.

The pale primrose of the dawn was reddening fast. A few more minutes and the sun's edge would for half a second sparkle like a star on the rim of the world; and then, with the coming of sunlight, the King's Shadow, swifter than the King himself would speed ahead, lengthening out, reaching, touching all things before he, the flesh and blood, could touch them!

Ah! The Shadow was the real man! He glanced backward. He had come fast. No one was in sight. Following the whimsey of his thought he told himself it was always so. Behind, out of sight, almost out of mind, rode the world, in front the Shadow--the Will, the Ideal, the Unattainable.

Faint and far on the horizon a square speck of light showed the tower of Shakîngarh, the Falcon's Nest. There was little time to spare then, for the sun shone on its battlements.

Little indeed! for as the gleam of the village clustering about the feet of the fortress rose to view, a sound of shawms and trumpets arose also. But there was no spiral of smoke as yet to tell of fire.

Bijli, responding to the spur, swept on over the more cultivated country. An old canal, dug hundreds of years before by some dead dynasty sent sinuous channels through the fields; high cactus hedges, shutting out the view, formed impenetrable barriers. With irritation at the delay, Akbar had to follow a winding cart track, deep-rutted beyond words--an old way-- the old way that made reform so difficult!

The sun at last! Akbar's shadow sped before him, climbing the thorn enclosures, which at a sharp corner barred the way.

If he himself could but so override difficulties.

Ye Gods! Smoke!

Bijli, at racing speed, was round the corner in a second. Before her lay a mud wall, beyond that an open space, a dense crowd encircling a huge pile of wood.

As she rose like a bird to the leap, Akbar saw nothing but a smoking flaming torch in a man's hand.

"Hold!" he shouted "Akbar the King forbids it."

Bijli, over the wall, was treating the crowd, as she was given to treating a squash at *chaugan* with kicks and bites, and an instant after, Akbar slipping to the ground, stood stern beside the pile.

There was a murmur of sheer surprise; but Akbar had no eyes for anything but the dulled, drugged, acquiescence of a girl's face as, dressed in bridal finery, she sate on the funeral pyre with an old man's head upon her lap.

"Unloose her! let her go!" came the order, bringing consternation; yet also relief. For half Shakîngarh knew the greed of land and gold which led to this enforced *suttee*. Briefly, the young wife had powerful friends who would claim her full widow's share; therefore she must die.

But a buxom woman, deep-breasted, arrogant, had seized the arrested torch from her husband and was brandishing it fiercely; for being wife to the old profligate's eldest son she had everything to gain by this getting rid of a rival.

"King?" she echoed, "By thine own word only! And even so King of men only! We women claim our right! She shall not be defrauded of it! Our father shall not go to the realms of Yama unattended."

"Then go thyself, woman," retorted Akbar peremptorily. "Thy part is done. Thy breasts have given suck to grown sons. Hers await an infant's lips! At thy peril, fool, or on thine own head be----."

He started forward to seize the torch she was in the act of thrusting into one of the firing places that were ready filled with resins, oil, and cotton wool.

To escape him she leaped nimbly to the pyre and with outstretched arm sought another feeder of the flames. As she did so, something that had lain like a withered branch moved and shot arrow-like at her bare ankle.

"Snake! Snake!"

Her yell of ultimate fear rang out and was caught up by the crowd. The torch dropped recklessly, she was down on her knees rocking herself backward and forward.

"A judgment! A judgment! Let her burn!" The cry of the crowd merged instantly into condemnation; but Akbar had leaped after her, dispatched the cobra--which hidden in some hollow log had doubtless crept out for warmth when the first sun rays had touched the pyre--and crushing out the torch flame with his heel, had his mouth on the woman's ankle.

To no purpose. Even in that brief second the poison had reached the heart, and after a few moans of agonised fear, merciful drowsiness invaded heart and brain, she breathed slowly and yet more slowly.

Akbar stood up and looked about him dazedly. This instant response of Providence in his favour filled him with exulting awe. The almost fanatical enthusiasm for himself, for his ideals, which so often possessed him, seized on him; and Birbal, riding up in weary haste, found him the centre of an enthusiastic crowd who, granting him supernatural power, were busy substituting a dead woman for a living girl, while the latter sate stupidly in the sunlight watching the flames blaze up round another victim with that burden of an old man's head upon her lap.

Anyhow, the promise was unbroken; but Birbal, as he rode back behind Majesty, told himself there was trouble ahead. Such incidents were not wholesome, especially when every effort must be made to keep the King down to practical politics. So little might make him break away.

"So, Shaikie, hath lost one chance of Love," said Akbar, suddenly, when after a long and silent ride, the towers of Fatehpur Sikri showed clear again.

"And Empire hath gained many chances of stability," replied Birbal drily. "With grandsons of Râjpût descent, Majesty may hand on the crown, when God's time comes, in security."

"Of what?" asked Akbar swiftly. "That my dream will be fulfilled--the dream of a King." And then suddenly he almost drew rein. "The woman must be rewarded, Birbal--she who came, God knows how, to warn me. I would not have her escape reward."

"As Majesty has bidden her act Châran at the Festival to-day," replied Birbal, still more drily, "there seems small chance of her escaping notice."

The King's face broke suddenly into charming, whimsical smiles. "Of a truth, friend! I must be a thorn in the flesh even to thee; and to those others. God knows how they bear with me."

"Or how they will bear with her," acquiesced Birbal, grimly. For all his liberal culture, his boasted freedom from prejudices, he was conventionality itself in somethings, and it irked him to think of a woman masquerading as a Châran.

And yet Âtma Devi looked her best when a few hours afterward she knelt on the floor below the short flight of steps on the second of which the Emperor sate on the royal yellow satin cushions, while the throne, a marvel of gold and gems, occupied the highest step. Her long black hair, unbound, encircled by a steel fillet, fell like a veil over her shoulders, but left her bosom half-hidden by a man's steel corselet bare. A cuirass of steel chains hanging below the corselet covered the muslins of her woman's drapery, and her shapely arms, strenuous under the weight of the huge straight sword, held hilt downward, balanced it straight as a die, steady as a rock, point skyward.

In truth, the whole scene was magnificent beyond compare. The ordinary reception was over, but there was to follow one of the great episodes of the gorgeous yearly round of splendid yet curiously imaginative festivals, which marked Akbar's court. That is to say, the Emperor having challenged his court to play chess with him, was to play the game with the living chessmen who stood duly ranged on the huge chequered board of black and white marble which still exists at Fatehpur Sikri, just beyond the flight of steps which leads downward from the Hall of Audience.

So Akbar alone, the empty throne above him, occupied those empty steps at the foot of which his challenger crouched. Opposite, on the other side of the marble board the court, a blaze of colour and gems--save for a knot or two of Ulemas in their dark robes--stood ranged; while between them, immovable as statues, waited the living chessmen. The very horses of the knights, black and white, scarce moved a muscle, and the unwieldy masses of the elephants, which in the Indian game do the bishop's duty looked carved of stone. Black and silver, white and gold, each and all ablaze with black and white diamonds. The pawns (peons, footmen) cased in gold or silver armour each carried a pennant in black or white velvet embroidered in gold or silver; and the great castles or forts--also of gold or silver--were worn as corselets by huge giants of men, who each held aloft a royal standard of the Râjpût sun or the crescent moon of Mahommed.

Overhead the hard, blue Indian sky; as a background rose-red palace or grass-green trees; and through it all insistent, never ceasing, like the shiver of cicalas on a summer's night a low tremor of muted strings, and deadened drums.

"Challenge for the King, O Châran!" came Akbar's voice and on it, almost clipping the last sound, followed a blaring clang, as the great steel sword sweeping forward hit the marble floor. The sound echoed and re-echoed through the arches, almost confusing the wild chant borne upon it.

Ohí! the King,
Challenge I bring
Let every man
In the world's span

Do what he can
To best the King.

A faint shiver ran through the crowding courtiers, and Birbal standing in a group composed of the King's greatest friends and allies, looked round anxiously. As a rule these contests were foregone conclusions. To begin with, the King was undoubtedly the best chess-player in his dominions; then as a rule the games were generally of the most *jejeune* description--mere spectacles of games. But to-day some new interest seemed to make the spectators' faces sharp, and though he could scarcely see how even defeat could be construed into such failure as Akbar had meant in his challenge, he felt vaguely uneasy.

"Thinkst thou they mean mischief?" he said to Abulfazl.

The latter smiled. "Mischief? not they! Mirza Ibrahîm hath as ever, forwarded the schedule and the King hath seen it"--he laughed,--"'Tis an irregular opening, but the onslaught is trivial--an elephant's charge----."

He paused, interrupted by the herald on the other side who took up the challenge on behalf of the Emperor's court.

Birbal looked over to his master. He could scarce tell why, but he was not satisfied. To begin with, that master's eyes were too dreamy. Had he perchance heard that Prince Salîm, seeking consolation from Love, had been found drunk in Satanstown that morning? As like as not; some of those sour-faced holy ones of set purpose had told him.

Ah! if the next few days were but over. If this Râjpût betrothal had but gone so far that there was no drawing back!

How many hours yet were there before this gnawing anxiety lest he should be overreached, and the King overpersuaded, should be past?

Akbar, nevertheless, showed intent enough upon his game. He was leaning forward his head on his hand, rapidly and in a low voice, calling out each move to the figure beneath him. And, ever, almost ere the tone ended, came that clash of steel on stone, that high strident cry "Ohí! The King! peon to *rukh's* fourth" and so on.

Yet in truth Birbal was right. Akbar was preoccupied. The morning's ride, with its hint of omnipotence, had, naturally enough, roused his physical and mental vitality to the highest pitch, and so dissociated him still further from his surroundings, and brought back the old question, "Why should he cling longer to the ancient pathways?" Being a King, accredited by God, seeing the truth clearly, why should he not cast aside old shackles, cease to attempt immortality through his unworthy sons, and achieve it for himself, by himself alone?

And something had happened that very morning which had almost driven from him all hope of one son at any rate. Not the escapade in Satanstown of which he had, of course, been informed. That was bad enough, bringing with it, as it did, scorn of a love which could so solace itself. No! it was not that! It was this: He had seen, being carried to a hospital almost lifeless, the body of a slave brutally beaten by Salîm's orders, before Salîm's eyes, and the sight had forced from Akbar's lips the bitter question as to how the son of a man who could not see God's littlest creature suffer without pity, could be so barbarous?

Would it not be better to give up the struggle?

All this was in Akbar's mind, as half-mechanically, working as good chess-players can with a portion of their intellect only, so that they can carry on many games at one and the same time, he marshalled his forces swiftly in these opening moves.

And now the board was clearer. Behind it on either side stood a long row of prisoners. The final onslaught was at hand.

"It is an elephant's attack" murmured Abulfazl and then checked himself--"they have changed it!" he exclaimed louder as the court herald cried.

"*Ghorah* (knight) to *badshad's* (king's) seventh."

"Wherefore not?" sneered one of the Mahommedan faction who stood hard by. "There be many alternatives in a game of chess."

Birbal looked hurriedly round him. There was evident eagerness on the very faces where he expected to find it; aye! and there was anticipation in many more. Then he glanced at the board, seeing in an instant that this move altered the whole defence: but even as he recognised this, and recognised that an answering change would make it strong as ever, the Châran's cry rang out.

"*Badshah's rukh* takes *wazir*" (Queen).

Akbar had let the move slip--had evidently been in a dream, was still in one! Yet it would need skill now to extricate himself for by God! he, himself, had not seen that before! It would be checkmate in two moves if the *rukh* were moved. The only defence--what was the defence?

"*Wazir's rukh* takes *peon*."

Inexorably the Court-herald's voice echoed through the arches and out into the garden. It was followed by a little tense murmur from the crowd.

Ye Gods! what was the defence? *Ghorah* to---- No! that was fatal. The king of course! The king one step backward and the game was won!

Would Akbar see it?

His attention had anyhow been aroused. He had leant forward, his elbow on his knee, his brows bent. The question was--*how much of his mind had been withdrawn from dreams.*

"He is not here!" murmured Abulfazl hurriedly, "but surely they cannot----"

"They can and dare all," interrupted Birbal "Oh! devils in hell."

For clear from the King's lips came the words, "*Ghorah* to----"

This time, however, that clang of steel on stone blurred the closing tones of the King's lips and the Châran's rose on it clear.

"*Badshah* to his eighth."

Birbal gasped, the King started, the courtiers stirred swiftly. But Birbal's quick wit was the first to recover from surprise.

"Repeat the move, O Châran of Jalâl-ud-din Mahomed Akbar, Emperor of India! It hath not been fully heard!"

Instantly the clang repeated itself, and the words followed high, strident, unmistakable.

"By the order of the King, *badshah* to his eighth."

"But we protest," cried the Makhdûm-ul'-Mulk, finding voice, and Akbar rising, looked angrily downward and prepared to speak.

"Great sire!" interrupted Birbal advancing on the very board itself--"we protest also against disorder. A Châran's voice duly challenged, is the voice of the King. Naught can alter it, save treachery. Where is the treachery here? He speaks that which he hears. Question the woman. Ask her what she heard?"

A great wave of sudden curiosity swept over the King's mind. What would this woman say? So far Birbal was right. She could be punished for treachery--but----

"Speak, Âtma Devi, Châran of Kings. What didst thou hear?" His voice was strangely soft, but so clear that it could be heard by all.

There was not a quiver in the straight-held sword of steel, no tremor in the firm mouth that gave the answer.

"I heard what I spoke!"

There was an instant's pause; she sate motionless, her face impassive, the half-shut eyes gleaming coldly out at all the world. Then Birbal laughed, a quick cackling laugh.

"The move is played, messieurs! Answer, it if ye can!"

And then he looked admiringly across at Âtma Devi; in truth she was man indeed, in woman's--nay! by the Gods! she was man altogether--a man amongst men; for that was checkmate--checkmate to the King's enemies.

CHAPTER XXV

'Tis Eve O Sakil fill the wine cup high
Be quick! the clouds delay not as they fly.
Ere yet this Fading World to Darkness goes
My senses darken with thy wine of Rose,
Till Fate makes flagons of my worthless clay.
Then fill my empty skull with wine I pray
So neither Death nor Judgment shall be mine
The Grave a brimming cup of Limpid Wine.

--SA'ADI.[114]

_Âtma, back in the palace, was once more racking her mind what to do about her remaining responsibility, the diamond. So far Fate and the Gods had guided her aright. She had managed to give the King timely warning that the little coward would claim his promise (better, sure, if she had burned!) then, having little time for thought, and knowing, in truth, that she had no chance of escaping unmolested through the strictly guarded entrances to the King's private apartments, she had returned by the swinging dhooli to her own, thus for the time keeping her method of escape secret from her gaolers. So, immediate urgency being over, she had set to work first to conceal what till then she had hidden in the dark braids of her hair; for she guessed at once, by the luxury with which she was surrounded, that tirewomen would appear in the morning, that every temptation would be plied to make her yield to Mirza Ibrahîm's lawless desires. She smiled at the thought. Yea, let him come; but not till after she was prepared. So she deftly cut a snippet of brocade from a hanging, and greasing it in an oil lamp rolled the diamond and the Wayfarer's square stone together, so as to form a fine large packet, stitched it together with gold thread she found ready on an embroidery frame, and hung it once more on the greasy black skein, telling herself none would interfere with so palpable a talisman. For the rest she had the Death-dagger of her race, which she hid until dressing-time was over in a woman's work-basket; though nothing, she told herself, would happen before her appearance at the Festival as Châran. So, seeing always but a short space into the future, she lay down and slept.

When she had wakened, servants had been ready to fly in lawful command, to temporise soothingly with unlawful ones, and she had smiled grimly, telling herself they were afraid of her, and that when the end came, she need only fear the violence of poison.

But that again was not yet.

Even after the Festival was over, after she had lied so calmly to save the King's honour, she had hours to spare. The Mirza would need darkness for his proposals; so she had quite smilingly put on the gorgeous dress of a court lady which on her return from the Audience was all she had found in the place of her own old red garments. What did it matter? The steel hauberk of her father's, the circlet, and the sword were still hers. These she had worshipped, these would look down on her death for honour. So if her white robe trailed on the ground and was sewn with stars, if her jewelled bodice flashed under the light folds of a saffron pearl-set veil, what was that to her, the King's Châran, who carried a death-dagger in her waistband?

Nothing mattered so long as her hardly-thought-out project for the delivery of the King's diamond could be brought about. If the message could be sent--if old Deena the drum-banger would take it, then the jeweller might come disguised as a Sufi in the Preacher's dhooli, and she could fulfil her promise; she could give it into his very hands--yea even if she had to yield, before that, to the Lord Chamberlain's desires.

Even this supreme sacrifice she was prepared to make if they failed to send Deena, or if the Feringhi failed to come. For she must have time.

She leant listlessly on the steps below the cupola toying idly with a scrap of silk-made writing paper and pen and ink. A slave-woman, gaoler, duenna--whom Âtma had sent from her very side on plea of chilliness, was standing a little way apart, making believe to drive away the sunset-time mosquitoes with a peacock's feather fan; in reality watching every movement of her charge.

Would Deena come? She had sent for him calmly to drum to her rhythm of pedigrees. That was her right, and he was so far a hanger on of the Mirza's that they might count him of themselves; yet he might be true to her also.

"The drumbanger waits," said a eunuch at the door, and her heart leapt to her mouth.

"Lo 'tis luscious as honey to a bee; lascivious to the liver, as saffron pillau to the stomach!" ejaculated the old man admiringly, In truth Âtma looked superlatively handsome amid the fine feathers of silken carpets and satin cushions.

"Thy liver, and thy stomach, sinner!" retorted Âtma carelessly, as she crumpled up the scrap of paper and flung it into the lacquered pen-tray.

"But come! to work! Since I am here as King's woman I may be called on any moment to sing in the harem; and I sing few women's songs: none of the modern style."

She broke into the high trilling commencement of a not over-respectable ballad of the bazaars.

Deena's wicked old face took on an air of outraged virtue, his hands refused to touch his drum.

"Nay! mistress most chaste," he protested in an injured tone, "salvation comes not that way to old Deena. He can get drumming and to spare of that sort elsewhere."

Âtma stared at him, and held his eyes with her large meaningful dark ones.

"'Tis not drumming, but deeds, that count, sir sinner," she said slowly. "As King Solomon said to the peacock who remained to salaam by drumming his wings, while the hoopoe gained his golden crown by running a message."

Deena's old face set instantly like a stone. No muscle quivered, but his wicked old eyes twinkled. He understood in a second what was wanted of him, for intrigue was his very food and drink. It made him feel years younger to carry a love letter. This would have naught to do with love of course; but the joy was in the deception. Happen he meant to help, happen he did not, it was all one to him; it meant the deceiving of a duenna.

"Shall I then take a message for the mistress most chaste?" he asked hardily, winking the while at the latter as if taking her into his confidence.

"Message?" echoed Âtma scornfully "Nay! no message! My lord Ibrahîm, my lover, will come when he thinks fit, and go when *I* choose, like a cur with his tail belly-wards!"--she had been full of such jibes all day--"So let us to work; the song of the Tale of the Wisdom of the Princess Fortunata can hurt no woman folk! But take heed to the time!" She broke at once into irregular chanting.

Listen women! I pray to the wise
Sanyogata, the Queen's advice
To Prithvi on courage and cowardice.

Then she changed rhythm and the words swept on like a torrent.

What fool asks woman for advice--The world
Holds her wit shallow. Even when the truth
Comes from her lips, men stop their ears and smile
And yet without the woman, where is man?
We hold the power of Form--for us the Fire
Of Shiv's creative force flames up and burns;
Lo! we are Thieves of Life, and sanctuaries of souls

     And sanctuaries of souls! of souls!

There was a sudden check of irritation; the singer interrupted herself to complain of lack of accord; then continued:

Vessels are we of Virtue and of Vice
Of knowledge and of utmost ignorance
Astrologers can calculate from books
The courses of the stars; but who is he
Can read the pages of a woman's heart?
Our book hath not been measured, so men say
"She hath no wisdom" but to hide their lack
Of understanding. Yet we share your lives,
Your failures, your successes, griefs, and joys.
Hunger and thirst, if yours, are ours, and Death
Parts us not from you; for we follow fast
To serve you in the mansions of the Sun

     The mansions of the Sun.

Yet once again some discord in voice and music seemed to rouse ire.

"Fool!" cried Âtma, "hast no sense! Thou art like a sitting hen with thy cluck, cluck, cluck, all out of tune! Take a paper if thou canst not remember and set it down in notation. See there is a bit yonder."

She pointed to the pen-tray and Deena with contrite face took the crumpled scrap, smoothed it out on the top of his drum and thereinafter, with some slight exaggeration in displaying a fair white surface, proceeded to write down quaint musical hieroglyphics. Then folding it, notation uppermost, stuck it into the drum-brace.

"Now let us try again, mistress most chaste," he said cheerfully. "For old Deena never failed a woman yet; least of all one who hath oft times stood between him and damnation."

There was a faint tremble as of relaxed tension in Âtma's voice as she went on:

Love of my heart! Lo! you are as a swan
That rests upon my bosom as a lake,
There is no rest for thee but here, my lord!
And yet arise to Victory and Fame
Sun of the Chanhans! Who has drunk so deep
Of glory and of pleasure as my lord!
And yet the destiny of all is Death.
Yea! even of the Gods! And to die well
Is Life immortal. Therefore draw your sword,
Smite down the Foes of Hind. Think not of Self,
The garment of this Life is frayed and worn--
Think not of me--we Twain shall be as One
Hereafter and for ever. Go! my King.

We Twain shall be as One, as One!

The nicest musical ear might have detected small change in Deena's accompaniment, but Âtma professed herself satisfied.

"And now," asked the old go-between, as she leant back wearily, "What next?"

"Nothing," she answered. "One is enough for a day. Thou canst come to-morrow--for reward or punishment."

"And the mistress hath no orders, no message?" he asked, winking at the duenna elaborately.

"Nothing; save to get thee gone as quick as may be. See him out, woman!"

That faint tremor of voice only betrayed that her nerves were almost at breaking point; that she felt the need of solitude for a second.

When it came she passed swiftly to the sword of her fathers and kissed it passionately. Then flinging her arms on the parapet she gazed out over the plain scarce seeing the pageantry of sunset that was being enacted on the distant horizon.

What had she written on that scrap of paper? It had necessarily to be guarded--but had she said enough?

"To the Feringhi jeweller! Come disguised as a Sufi in the Preacher's dhooli to-night at one o'clock. Âtma Devi will give thee the luck thou desirest."

After all it did read like a love letter. So much the better perhaps, with Deena as messenger. Anyhow the message was sent.

What, therefore, lay before her? Within measurable distance of probabilities now, she could face them. Supposing the Mirza came that night? Oh! where was the use of considering what at the worst she might have to do, in order to secure leisure at one o'clock! For, that *had* to be gained. Aye! even though before that hour, say at eleven, she had to----

One, and eleven! Her mind, unaccustomed to strain, circled vaguely. There was only a pin's-point difference between the two hours on paper, just a mere scratch, a duplication and yet--mayhap!--between them, tonight, a whole life--1 and 11--Strange! so little difference!

"Why didst thou lie to-day, woman?" said a voice beside her, "to save my honour?"

She turned with a cry and fell at Akbar's feet. He had met Deena's outgoing, had sent the duenna packing by a word backed by the display of the ring which was Royalty's sign manual in all matters pertaining to the women's apartments; so entering, had flung aside his muffling shawl and for the last few seconds had been watching Âtma. For a sudden new perception of her beauty had come to him, perhaps with the sight of her in a dress familiar to him, since it is generally some such subtle hint which, at first, makes a man's eyes differentiate one woman from another.

Down at his very feet, Âtma's voice was yet proud. "To save the honour of the King."

Akbar was quick in comprehension--"Who never dies--Not to save Jalâl-ud-din-Mahomed Akbar! Still, thou needst not have lied."

"This slave only said what the King would have said."

A quick frown flew to his keen face. "Thou speakest bravely woman! But 'tis true. Akbar's brain was clouded. How came thine to be so clever?"

"My father was a chess-player," she said simply. "He taught me. And it was not difficult, Most High. It was trivial."

For a second he looked really angry; then said quietly. "True again, O Châran. Stand up, woman! Wherefore shouldst thou grovel before-- triviality?"

Standing there beside her their eyes met, and his showed admiration.

"So thou didst not lie, because the King can do no wrong. Then art thou, woman, to be judge? thy thought, thy standard, always to be right?"

"It--it was to-day, Great King," she said gravely.

He laughed outright.

"This is wholesome as a draught of bitter apples! Lo! Chāran, thou didst give me a lesson in love last time we met. Give me one in tactics to-day! Not tactics in chess--that is past praying for--but in Kingship."

She looked at him with pitiful humility. "This slave knows not, she is only woman!"

"And yet thou didst come at dawn to save me from a broken promise! I have not thanked thee yet for that; but in truth"--here his voice grew softer, and leaning his elbow on the parapet, he looked into her eyes, "thanks being all on one side----" Then suddenly curiosity beset him. "How didst thou come?"--he looked down rapidly--"not by yonder projecting eave? not by that, surely? Why! even my head----" He paused a while, and her silence assuring him, murmured: "And thou didst that *for me?*"

"For the King, Most-High!" she protested in a low voice as she clutched convulsively at the talisman. For through her swept with tumultuous force her first real knowledge of what her womanhood might hold. Ye Gods! have pity! she must not lose herself. The King's Luck must be safe first. He must never know the tale.

He looked at her curiously. Her lips were parted her breath came fast.

"Thou hast the nerve of ten," he said rapidly, "thou couldst walk yonder ledge where I--even I--might fear to fall, and yet----" His hand, reaching out as they stood close together by the parapet, caught her wrist swiftly, and clasped it. "Yet now thou art afraid--afraid of what?"

Her pulses bounding under his cool, firm touch seemed to suffocate her.

"Aye," she admitted, turning her mind frantically to excuse, "I fear--I fear the night, alone in a strange place."

In truth she did fear it. Her soul shrank now, knowing what she might have to sacrifice. But for the blind, half-confusing memory of one o'clock she would have fallen at his feet and begged for freedom. She might have done so had she had time to count the cost.

"Strange?" echoed Akbar, haughtily. "Dost forget it is the King's house?--that the King is guardian? Though in truth," he added with a smile "Jalâl-ud-din Mahomed Akbar sleeps to-night in his pitched camp beyond the gates." The memory seemed to obsess him with other ideas, for he turned away gloomily.

"Farewell, widow. Akbar will strive to be King--thou hast done thy best to make him one, anyhow," he added almost angrily. But as he went, something in her face and form recalled his youth, and he hesitated. Then drawing off a ring hastily he strode over to her, and taking her hand roughly, slipped it on her finger.

"Yea, thou hast done many things for me," he said proudly, "so let me do one for thee. This ring, the Signet of the Palace, may calm thy fears for to-night. None dare harm its possessor without my order. At thy peril, use it not unworthily. I----" He paused, drew his shrouding shawl round him, and corrected himself--"It will be reclaimed at dawn."

The dusk had died down almost to dark, the stars grew clearer and clearer on the growing violet of the sky. Âtma stood gazing with unseeing eyes over the wide plain that was losing itself rapidly in shadow. She was scarcely thinking at all. She was only feeling how increasingly hard it was becoming to dissociate Akbar from the King, Love from Love.

"The Lord High Treasurer hath called to inquire and craves admittance."

She awoke to realities at the duenna's voice, but with a new element in her outlook on the future--a palpitating horror at the thought of the sacrifice she had faced calmly but an hour ago.

"He--he is welcome," she said faintly. There was no use shirking, and she might be able to put him off till after one.

But his first words told her theirs was a fight for life in the present.

"All in the dark!" he said lightly, "so much the better mayhap, mistress, for Ibrahîm's peace of mind, seeing that he hath but a few hours to count his own. The jackal hath to eat his bones betimes."

"What meanest my lord?" she asked hurriedly.

"That his Majesty the King will feast on the flesh," he replied recklessly. "Ah I have heard He hath been here this last half-hour. In troth, but that he interferes with my quarry, I would say thank God the anchorite *hath* found his meat. As it is, I have come earlier to handsel my share." Then he turned swiftly to the duenna. "Leave us for a while. I would speak alone with this lady."

When she had gone he said curtly. "Thou hadst best sit down. I have much to say."

"Say on," replied Âtma laconically, as without the faintest sign of trepidation she sate herself calmly down amid the silken carpets and cushions; for behind her propped against the marble pilasters, were the hauberk, the sword of her fathers, to give her courage. It was the Mirza who showed uneasiness. He walked up and down as if uncertain how to begin.

"Well," she asked with a scornful smile as she played idly with the pens in the open pen-box, "what hast thou to say?"

He cast aside doubt at her words, flung himself on the steps, and leaning forward peered through the dusk into her eyes. "What thou wilt not care to hear; so brace thyself--if thou canst, woman! Thou didst send by Deena----"

"He has betrayed me," she exclaimed involuntarily.

"Or died! Take it as thou willst. The letter was sent to its destination anyhow, for it served our purpose. Thou knowest the King's challenge? Well, we have sought all day to get hold of the Feringhi jeweller, so that his death might break the King's safe conduct. But Birbal hath been too quick for us. He hath him safe cooped up in his house. But *thou* hast called the man here."

Âtma, with a cry, rose to her feet. "I meant but----" she began.

"What thou didst mean matters not now, though I have my suspicions," broke in the Mirza brutally. "Sit down, I tell thee, and listen. Whether thy call be, as I hold it to be, one that even Birbal would admit, time will show. But if this doubly damned infidel be found within the palace precincts it is death. And see here"--he held out a paper.

"I cannot see," she murmured dully. "It is too dark." And in truth, even as she spoke, the palace gong sounded one stroke.

How often it sounded one she thought as the Mirza struck a light. But this time it meant half-an-hour beyond eight. One, yes--it was the knell of doom.

The spark had come to the tinder-roll, and now a sputtering oil lamp in the sevenfold cresset showed her the writing on the paper. "To the Sergeant of the Palace watch. At one of the clock, guard the Preacher's dhooli and enter the apartment of Âtma Devi. Her lover will be there."

"He is not my lover," she began.

"But he will be there at one." He laughed devilishly, "Now listen. None but me know of this--as yet. Âtma," his voice took on urgency, almost appeal, "grant me thyself--and this paper shall be destroyed."

So it had come. She was the price of honour. Would it not be the simplest way?

"It must be to-night," he whispered hoarsely, "Tomorrow the King----"

She could have struck him full upon the mouth, but she sate trembling with tense desire to do so.

"If I promise," she asked firmly, "may this paper be mine?" She had noticed that it was signed and countersigned by the captain and commandant of the guard. If she had it, it might be difficult to get another. Anyhow it would show good faith.

Ibrahîm's face grew hard. "Nay, fair one," he said, "hardly till the promise is fulfilled. I must have due security."

And she must have it also, she thought fiercely. Aye, she knew him, devil-spawn, vile utterly. He meant to take all from her and send the order too. She might give him everything at eleven and yet at one--eleven and one!--11 and 1!

She glanced hastily at the paper; then sate silent her face hardening, her hands still playing idly with the pens in the pen bag.

"Think over it, bibi" he said insinuatingly for even the faint lamp light showed her bewilderingly beautiful. "It is not so much to ask! I am no ill-favoured churl, and before heaven, I love thee. Then, surely, thou wouldst not betray the King."

Betray the King! No! that must never be. She had thought of a way to prevent that.

"And--and if I give the audience thou desirest at--at eleven?" she began slowly.

He fell at her feet rapturously. "Âtma! I swear!"

She stilled him with a wave of her hand. "I must think," she cried, and rising, walked to the parapet. Only however, to return after a second.

"I consent," she said quietly. "At eleven be it--thou wilt not send this?" She showed the paper she still held.

"Nay," he replied with a bow as he took it from her. "I will keep it ever next my heart as security for happiness--at eleven."

When he had gone she broke into a sudden, wild laugh, and flung the pen she held concealed in her right hand into the pen tray.

"Only a fly's foot on the paper, but it will show truth or untruth!" she muttered.

Then she sate down and waited; there was nothing else to be done. She dare not use the King's signet--if indeed this token of mere personal safety to herself would be of any avail--since that might lead to his discovery of the diamond's theft. And that (this had grown to an immutable creed) must never be!

"Light not so many lights," she said to the servants who came in with long garlands of flowers and coloured lights; but they went on with their work. It was by the Lord Chamberlain's orders they said. And they brought her new jewels, and scattered rose-oil-water about the cushions, and spread a low stool-table with fruit, and goblets, and wine flagons.

She sate and watched them, interested as she would not have been but for the awakening of her womanhood under the King's touch. Now she understood; now for the first time she realised the philosophy of Siyah Yamin.

So Ibrahîm, coming in early--she smiled mysteriously at his haste-- found her watching the slave-women who were reaching up to place coloured lights amongst the roses twined round the cupola, and as they worked they sang in a quaint roundel:

Shine earthen lamps, outblaze the stars
So cold, so white, so far.
Shine little lamp, hide Heaven's light
Love comes to Love to-night.

"Bid them remove them, my lord," she said eagerly. "Lo! they are garish. Are not mine eyes and the stars sufficient for--for lovers?" She hung her head and looked at him. Her cheeks showed a crimson flush beneath the corn-coloured skin, her eyes blazed, indeed, like many stars.

He gave the order instantly, and as it was being executed walked to the parapet whence he could feast his eye upon the picture she made as she sate in the cupola, the rose garlands bending to touch her, the light of the seven-lamped cresset on the step below her shining full on her face, and glinting behind her on cold steel of sword and hauberk. Aye! she was right. The coloured lights were garish; she was colourful enough herself; she needed no adventitious aids to passion; that hint of cold steel was enough! His blood rose to fever heat.

"Quick slaves! quick!" he cried. "Are we to be kept waiting all night."

Her laugh rang out provocatively. "My lord is before his time. It is not yet eleven! Drink to our love, Mirza--or stay! Let us drink to the truth between us!" She filled two goblets of the good red wine and passed him one. "So! to the truth between us," she cried; then, as she drained the glass flung it far into the darkness of the night. It showed curving comet-like, then sank, a distant tinkle telling where it had smashed to atoms. "Thine also! Thine also! Ibrahîm!" she cried. "To the Truth between us!"

He muttered something unheard, flung his glass away, then essaying a laugh caught up a lute and began to sing in high airy trills:

Lo! the green-hued sea of heaven
And the crescent moon its ship
Bear me, dearest, to the haven
Where Love's Anchor I may dip
In the harbour of thy bosom.
Find in shelter of thy lip
Kisses seven! Kisses seven
Oh! what nectar--One more sip
Surely thou wilt be forgiven
Even angels sometimes trip.

As he stood there dressed in white from head to foot, becurled, bescented, bedandyfied, Âtma thought of the man who had stood there before, and something purely savage crept into her smile.

"Lo! thou singest well" she said. "So do I, give me the lute?"

The servants had gone. He crossed to her, passion in his eyes. "I came not here for lutes." he cried almost brutally, "I came for love!"

She motioned him back with her hand. "It is not yet--eleven! And I will sing--of--of--love."

He drew a long breath. She was surpassing beautiful with that enticing smile. Why should he be greedy of his pleasure?

Love of my heart, bring blushes to my face,
Seek not at wisdom's hand, excuse or grace.
Speed thou my blood in passion's tireless race
Till lip meet lip, and arm with arm embrace
For the love of the heart has no end----

"Âtma! I love thee!"

His quick cry sank before her steady voice:

But the grave
But the cold, cold grave
But the grave!

He gave a slight shiver and drew back; then threw himself beside her. "Come!" he said, "there is life before the grave!"

She shook her head playfully. Not even Siyah Yamin with all her knowing wiles, could have played her part better.

"It is not yet--eleven" she answered and if her face showed haggard it was belied by her gay laugh. "Lo! keep to compact, Mirza Sahib. There is another verse; by then, it may be--eleven!"

She paused a second as if her keen ears had caught some faint sound, then she swept the strings with a resounding force that echoed and re-echoed through the roof, drowning all else.

Love of my soul, bring courage to my heart
Seek not at passion's hand her lure and art.
Claim thou the whole of me and not the part
Though Death meet Death and Life from Life depart
For the love of the soul has no end in the grave.

In the cold, cold grave.
In the grave.

A crashing chord, dissonant, fierce, overbore all things, and out of it rose mellow the first chime of eleven.

She leant forward, her eyes full of allure, on his. "Out with the lamps, Love needs no light," she quoted rapidly.

"One!" Her curved red lips smiled, parted, and one of the cressets was gone. Its dying breath exhaled perfumes of musk.

Again the mellow note rang out.

"Two," she whispered and again a cresset flickered, went out.

"Three."

"Four." This time the Mirza seemed to be listening.

"It will be counting kisses by and by when light fails," she suggested gaily, pointing to the three remaining lamplets.

"Five--"

There were but two now. She was leaning closer to him, his arm had stolen round her waist.

"Six--"

Something made her glance hastily to the door, but the bounding blood in his pulses seemed for him to have invaded the whole world, and he heard nothing.

"*Seven!--*"

It was dark now, and from the darkness came the long-drawn sound of a kiss; then of another.

*Eight--Nine!--*The chiming hour went on.

His arms were round her. Aye, but hers were round him also. Arms like iron, lips like steel upon his mouth.

"*Ten!*"

"Die dog!" she whispered with the kiss. "Nay, thou shalt take it."

He struggled fiercely.

Eleven!

"Die in mine arms, for thine untruth, traitor!"

"Help!" he choked feebly. "Harlot! let me go!"

But it was too late. The palace guard under orders for eleven, not for one, had found their quarry in the dark. Had found him in a woman's arms, and swift daggers did their work.

There was not a quiver in Mirza Ibrahîm's body when, turning it over, they discovered by a lantern's light their mistake and started back in horror.

"Yea, he is dead," said Âtma as she stood, fast held for future punishment. There was sombre menace in her voice, her eyes blazed with a cruel fire. Then she turned on her captors.

"Loose me, slaves. I carry the Signet of the King. Seek his orders concerning me."

It was true. The signet was on her finger. So releasing her, they double-guarded the door, while, with the dead body of the Lord Chamberlain as witness, they sought superior wisdom.

Left alone, Âtma found the old sword as solace and clasped it to her bosom. She had but killed for the King; a? her fathers had killed many a time.

CHAPTER XXVI

'Twas in the bath a piece of perfumed clay
Came from my loved one's hands to mine one day
Art thou then musk or ambergris? I said,
That by thy scent my soul is ravished.
"Not so," it answered, "naught but clay am I,
But I have kept a rose's company."

--SA'ADI

It was nigh twelve of the night, and Akbar was awake. He sate on the low divan which served him as a bed, and in a measure as throne also, when he was in camp; but there was little else about the magnificent apartment in which it stood to suggest the smallest withdrawal of luxury, still less of comfort. The walls were of the finest Kashmir shawls draped in panels between the parcel-gilt tent poles, and the floor was covered with strangely-glistening silken carpets from Khotan. A marvellous lustre of precious stones hung from the roof, and beside the divan stood the seven-light cresset stand, the golden and gemmed scent brazier, and the clepsydra with its lotus bowl, without which the King spent no night.

He was alone for the time, though countless guards doubtless stood in the vast city of huge tents which formed the King's camp. Weary work indeed, is it to even read the catalogue of such a camp. Of the hundreds of tents of scarlet cloth bound with silken tapes, fitted with silken ropes, some of which would seat ten thousand people. Of the great circle of double-storied screen around the "Akass-deva" lamp--the King's lamp that showed the way to God's Justice. Then the dais for Common Audience with its avenue of five hundred feet by three hundred broad, and its great circular enclosure of over one thousand feet diameter. Truly the mind wavers over the tremendous size of it, and refuses to grasp the possibility of a pavilion with fifty-four rooms in it!

Such, nevertheless, was the camp in which Akbar sate alone awaiting a favoured visitor.

For he had made up his mind to see this little "Queen of Women" with whom his son was said to have fallen in love.

It was easy. She was but a child, and he the father of his people. So he had ordered Ghiâss Beg to bring her to the camp privately at twelve of the night, when all was quiet.

Then, he felt, he would be able to judge aright. Since what was this challenge of his but mere childishness? Everyone, even Birbal, was keen to win or lose; but if he lost or won, how did that affect the truth?

Was Love powerful enough to wean Salîm from his life of debauchery? The idea of it had not been; but the compelling force depended on the woman. Was this child of twelve----? Pshaw it was impossible.

Yet he must see her, he felt; for it was a momentous decision, not to be made lightly.

He rose, and walking over to the clepsydra, watched the lotus cup sinking with the weight of time.

So sank beauty under the weight of years.

And then, suddenly, to him came the remembrance of Âtma Devi. Ye Gods! if from the beginning he had had a mate such as she--a woman to whom the honour of the King outweighed the honour, nay, even the love of the man, he need not now have stood uncertain, hesitating whether to leave all, even his sons, to wallow in the mire of conventionality--to leave all, and dream out his dream of Empire in his own way. For he would have had not only sons, but heirs.

Should he so leave all? Should the morrow see the camp no more spectacle to the wedding festivities, but a real departure?

He could take her with him as an inspiration--the sudden unlooked for thought caught him unawares, left him surprised.

"The Captain of the Palace Guard without and the Chief Eunuch have urgent news," came the obsequious voice of a page.

"Bid them in," he replied, returning to the divan, almost glad of an interruption to what was disturbing in the uttermost.

"Dead!" he echoed incredulously to the news they brought. "The Lord High Chamberlain dead--by whose hands?"

"By mine, Most High," answered a trembling voice as the Sergeant of the Guard fell at the King's feet. "We had warning that the English jeweller was to be in Mistress Âtma Devi's rooms to-night at eleven. We went. All was dark. We found him as we thought, in her very arms. Yet when Justice was done and we brought the light, it--it was Mirza Ibrahîm."

"In whose apartment?" Akbar's voice was very cold, very quiet.

"In the Châran-woman's, Most High! Lo! there is some mistake, doubtless. Yet she was brought in by the Mirza's orders--she had the fairest apartment set apart for her and--and he visited her this evening--just after Majesty, so the woman said."

Akbar rose to his feet fiercely.

"What has that to do with it, slave?" he interrupted, his voice full of swift sudden anger, "go on with the noisome tale!"

"Of a truth, sire, there is no doubt lamps were lit and wine brought. So he deserved death, and the woman too----"

"Aye!" assented the King, "she deserved it more! Didst kill her too?" He felt outraged beyond words; every atom of his manhood rose in hot anger against the woman who had dared--aye! dared to make him think of things he had forgotten, when she herself---- Ah! it was past mere anger.

"Nay! Most High. She--she showed us the Signet of Majesty and so----"

Under his breath a curse broke from Akbar's lips. Aye! he remembered now! He had given her the ring, and with the memory came back such an impotent flood of pure savage rage as never before in all his life had he felt. The Mogul scratched showed the Tartar; for an instant not even his ancestor Timur could have felt more bloodthirsty. The shame of it alone cried for instant revenge.

The thought brought him outward calm.

"She dies at dawn," he said quietly. "As women do who sin in God's night. Bring her here, *then*. She shall affix the seal to her own death-warrant. Write it now, and lay it on yonder desk so that it may be ready."

"And till then, Most High?"

"Leave her where her lover died; being Hindu she may learn to follow him without fear."

For already bitter anger was passing; inflexible justice taking its place.

"His Highness the Lord Treasurer waits without with a dhooli," said the page once more.

"Close the screens, let no one enter. Bid the Lord Treasurer bring the dhooli to the outer tent and remain there himself." The order was given calmly, but he who gave it was in a whirlwind of passionate protest.

And this woman--this common strumpet of the bazaars--had talked to him of Love; had, in reality, set him on the first step which had led him so far from common-sense; which had brought him here to an interview with a chit of a child at dead of night!

A slim white figure parting the curtains which separated this inner pavilion from the one beyond, brought him back to his bearings. It was not the child's fault; she must be courteously dealt with.

"Wilt not unveil, my child?" he said gravely, "there is none to fear----"

"And Mihr-un-Nissa fears none," came the reply, as the cloud of white drapery thrown back, fell on the ground, and the girl stepping forward lightly from the billowy folds, stood to salaam.

There was a moment's pause; then eager, warm, came Akbar's verdict. "By all the Gods of Indra! by Allah and his Prophet! thou art beautiful indeed, my daughter."

A deeper flush tinged the rounded cheeks, but the girl looked frankly into the admiring eyes.

"I am glad."

Something in her conscious unconsciousness made him ask quickly, "Wherefore?"

"Because they call me Queen of Women, sire, and the Queen should please the King," she answered demurely.

"Thou hast a ready wit, child. Dost wish to be a Queen?"

There was not a trace of sauciness in her quick reply. "It depends, sire, upon the King."

Akbar felt completely taken aback; he recognised in this slender little maid-ling of twelve, the germs of something that might grow to greatness indeed.

"I am a churl, lady," he said at last, "to keep Beauty standing. Seat yourself so, beside me, and we can talk. Or stay!" A whimsical smile irradiated his face, he put out his hand to lead her to the throne-divan. "Sit thou upon the seat of Majesty, and I will sit at Beauty's feet. I have much to learn from it."

She did not even protest. She took her place with childish dignity, and waited for him to speak. Frankness seemed the only possible approach, so he plunged at once in *medias res*.

"Lady, dost thou love my son Salîm?"

The cupid's-bow of her lips smiled over a cold definite "No."

Akbar's parental pride rose instantly.

"And why, prithee?"

The answer was nonchalant, uncompromising.

"I like not his looks."

"Yet he is not ill-favoured," protested the proud father, beginning to feel injured, "he is stalwart and young, hath fine eyes, and----"

"He is not so good looking as his father is--even now," said Mihr-un-nissa, sagely nodding her head.

"But for that 'even now' fair daughter," said Akbar nettled, "your compliments might make one shy! Then thou lovest Sher Afkân?"

The flush came again. "He is a brave soldier, anyhow," said the little maiden holding her head high.

"A brave soldier, indeed!" assented Akbar gravely, yet feeling inclined to smile, "but as for looks, hath he not a scar upon his face?"

"'Twill be a place whereon a wife may lay her kisses," retorted Mihr-un-nissa hastily, then grew crimson with shame at having inadvertently used an argument which had evidently done duty in sparring matches on the subject with her mother.

Akbar laughed out loud, then grew grave. "Of a truth Mistress Quick-wit, women are beyond men's comprehension! But we have been playing with words hitherto. Now let us be serious--let me see thy mind. Why dost not like my son?"

Instant, clear, decisive, came the reply.

"Because he doth not love his father."

"Wherefore does he not love him? What proof hast thou?" asked Akbar hotly.

Mihr-un-nissa's face had no pity, even in its deep unfathomable eyes.

"Because, Great King, he seeks ever to betray Jalâl-ud-din Mahomed Akbar. Oh!"--the words once started rushed out now like a torrent--"I know they say it is better Akbar should not know! I know how they all--even my Lord Birbal--keep things back, saying the King's mind should be tranquil. But it is not so! Kingship is the truth! Kings must know all things! There is the diamond--They have kept that back, I dare swear. It was stolen, Most High----"

"Stolen!" echoed Akbar stupidly, "who was it--who spoke of that before?" Then memory returning, impotent rage once more rose in him. "Well, what then?" he queried roughly.

"I say the King should know!" came the high girlish voice. "Pain is but a safeguard from ill. He should know, aye, and use his knowledge that it was stolen for the Prince--that he wore it in his turban and, that if it hath gone back to safekeeping 'tis not because of remorse upon the Prince's part, but because the King exchanged the Turban of Brotherhood----"

"It is not true," muttered Akbar, hiding his head in his hands. "Child-- say it is not true." Something in him told him it was true, therefore he fought against it all the more fiercely.

"Will saying it alter fact?" went on the inexorable young voice. "My King, the knowledge of all this is to be King; ignorance is--is foolishness!"

She stood up, a startled look in her eyes. "Have I, have I made thee cry?" she said solicitously. Then she burst out fiercely, "Oh, if I were Queen I would have no son, no husband. I would be Queen indeed."

Akbar had stood up also, his face blurred by emotion, but strong and stern.

"I have to thank thee for the Truth. Strange I have had to learn it from a little maid's lips. Lo! Mihr-un-nissa, wilt thou not love my son?"

She shook her head, "Had he been more like----" she paused, and hung her head, shy for the first time.

He took her little hand, and stooping, kissed it. "And had the Queen of Women but been fifteen years older--thou art sure, child, thou wouldst not care to be Queen?"

Her face grew grave, the perfect features took on dignity. "Queen I shall be. The crystal says so. But not now, for I am too young and he would break my heart. Why should I give up youth?" Then suddenly recollecting her rôle of virtuous wisdom, she added solemnly, "But God alone knows what the future may hold."

When she had gone Akbar sate down, feeling dazed by the many unlooked for buffettings which Fate had given him that night.

To begin with, he had been within an ace of dishonour himself. Aye! there was no use denying it. It must have been unrecognised passion in himself which had led him into this childish, unkinglike challenge. And now had come this dishonour of degenerate heirs; for what use was there in dissociating Salîm from Murâd, Murâd from Danyâl? His sons were all alike--were they indeed his sons, these dissolute drinking louts?

He paced the tent almost in despair. Pride, anger, love, justice, tearing at his heart.

Yes, he must go! He must leave his City of Heirship for ever. He must cast off earthly shackles and live only for the immortal dream.

Birbal's slim figure stealing through the curtains roused him to instant anger, almost as instant patience; since how could he judge of those bound by conventional standards?

"What now?" he asked briefly. Something uncompromising in his tone made the minister begin an excuse. He had been close by, and hearing that Majesty waked----

Akbar walked up and laid his hand on Birbal's shoulder.

"Lie not, friend," he said, "hath the stolen diamond been found? Sh! hold thy peace. I know the tale. A queen of common sense hath told it to me; and rightly told it. What, she said, was pain but a warning against evil. That is truth; but is the stone found? That is what I ask."

Birbal, whose jaw had almost fallen in his blank surprise, was on his knees, instinct telling him to attempt no excuse.

"Sire! I have it with me now. The madwoman Âtma Devi----"

"What of her?" asked Akbar fiercely.

Truth was the only resource, so Birbal told it. "She sent a message to bid William Leedes come to her at one o' the night in the Preacher's dhooli; and I, fearing treachery--for I never trusted woman yet without regretting it--went myself. For the safe-conduct given by Majesty to these strangers was a fertile field for the breaking of promise."

Akbar interrupted him impatiently.

"And she met you, where?"

"In truth where there was scant foothold for a goat," said Birbal glibly, trying to get through with confession lightly, "on the wide eave of the turret. Belike she heeded not the danger, being as she said, under sentence of death at dawn. And it was that made her yield the gem to me--'twas her last chance--for she held fast to her promise to give it to none save unto the jeweller's own hand. So she stood there, with death in a falter, administering fearful oaths and----" He had been feeling in his breast and now held forth the Luck of the King "here it is, sire."

In the light of the cressets, the gem glowed familiarly like soft moonshine; but Akbar peremptorily set it aside.

"Thou art under oath to deliver it to none but the jeweller. Traitor! are women to be more faithful than men?"

Birbal grovelled at the King's feet, but Akbar did not notice him.

He was dully trying to piece the parts into a whole, telling himself he would hear the truth when Ātma Devi should be brought to him at dawn.

CHAPTER XXVII

Look lover! Now indeed Love endeth right
This is the only road. Oh, learn of me
That Death shall give thee Love's best ecstasy
Oh! If thou be'st true lover wash not hand
From that dear Stain of Love; from worldly brand
Of Wealth and Self-love wash it. At the last
Those win who spite of Fortune's tempests stand
Glad to wreck all for Love--I say to thee
I, Sa'adi, launch not on Love's boundless Sea
But, if thou puttest forth, hoist sail, quit anchor,
To Storm and Wave trust thyself hardily.

--SA'ADI[15]

"The Woman-Châran waits without under guard."

"Bid her in--alone!"

Akbar had been awaiting this it seemed to him for hours. Now that it had come he would have delayed, if he could.

The tent was still dark, but as the outer screen was lifted something paler, grayer than murk-night showed in faint square, grew blurred with moving shades, then disappeared altogether. The cresset light scarce reached into the shadowy corners of the tent, where hung faint clouds of scented smoke; but Akbar's keen eyes pierced the gloom clearly.

"What? Have they bound thee? I meant not so," He stepped to the tall dim figure and unloosed the cord with which its hands were tied.

"Come hither, woman."

The kindly office done, he was back on the throne, his face showing stern in the cresset light. As she came forward she stumbled slightly in her walk. They must have tied her feet also, when they were bringing her to the camp and she was numb and stiff. His heart went out to her in swift pity, then returned to him in swifter justice.

"The ring, woman! The signet that I gave thee," he said peremptorily. Until that was gone from her finger, even he could not touch her for harm. She held it out to him without a word, then sinking to her knees crouched at his feet. The folds of her star-set skirts clung round her closely, the saffron, pearl-sewn veil hardly hid her beauty of strong supple curves. She had begged to be allowed to die in the steel hauberk of the Châran, but they had jeered at her, saying the race was well quit of such representatives as she. So in her final arraignment she stood as simple woman.

Perhaps by so doing she gained advantage. Anyhow, Akbar who had meant to be sternly judicial, felt, now they were alone together, that this was no question of Culprit and Judge, but of a man and a woman. And with the feeling came, to his surprise, a sense of keen personal injury.

"Why hast thou done this thing?" he asked bitterly.

The long tension of the night, the sight of the man she knew she loved, the very touch of his hands as he undid the knot which had bound her, and now the regret, the pain of his voice, all conspired against calmness, though she fought for it desperately. There was but one refuge--the refuge of race.

"I--I did it for the King," she said mechanically, not realising the full meaning of her words.

He caught at it in a moment. "For the King? Then *thou* art true."

She gave no answer. What was the use of explanation when she could not explain? When the King must never know aught concerning the theft of the diamond. Silence was better. God gave the reward of that.

"Âtma"--she shivered at the name, at the tone, of the King's voice--"I command thee, as King, answer truly. What was there betwixt thee and the Mirza?"

She sighed faintly. By forgetting what really mattered in the purely personal, he had enabled her to obey.

"That which is ever between a man and woman when they both need somewhat, my liege," she said simply. "So now I must die. It will be better."

She had told herself this a hundred times that night. She had done her work. Life might bring difficulties. Death was the only remedy. But she over-reached herself in self-sacrifice.

"Oh! let me die, my liege," she cried kissing the dust of his feet. "Majesty will forget." This hope was also in her blurred mind.

"It will not forget," he cried passionately, "unless it knows the truth. Speak! woman--Blazon out thy shame if shame there be, else I call Birbal with the diamond he took from thee----"

She was on her feet trembling with anger, outraged utterly.

"What! he hath told the Most-High! Oh! traitor, coward! And he swore--he bade me never tell----"

Akbar gave a sigh of relief. He understood now. This woman had been in the conspiracy of silence; and she would have kept that silence until death.

"Sit thee down again, King's Châran," he said almost with a smile. "The King was not to know. Aye! but he does know, so silence is of no avail. He knows all--how the Luck was stolen for the Prince Salîm, and how he, deceiving his father----"

Âtma gave a little cry and crept closer, almost as it were consolingly, to his feet.

"He is but young, my liege, he did not think," she pleaded. "Truly he loves his father--there is no cause for pain----"

In the slight pause Akbar's eyes showed suspiciously as if they held sudden tears. "Not so spoke she who told me," he said, his voice bitter. "Yet she also was woman!"

Âtma's slow brain busy over that "she" broke in on the silence.

"Was't Khânzada Gulbadan or Umm Kulsum?" she asked naïvely.

Akbar frowned quickly. "I wist not *they* were in the scandal," he said quite petulantly. "But what matters it if all the world knew--save only the King! Leave that alone, for God's sake, and tell me truly what lay between thee and Ibrahîm?"

To him so near desire, that was the fateful question.

To her also, for dimly she saw ahead. "Silence is best," she said obstinately. "It does not injure Truth, *whose hiding place is immortality, whose shadow, death.*"

The well-worn quotation fell from her lips like the juice of poppy, restful, soothing, opiate; but Akbar was in no mood of acquiescence. He bent hastily and seized her by the wrist, fiercely, tenderly. All his blood was stirring in him as it had not stirred for years.

"I tell thee thou shalt answer! I, the King, command thee, Châran. Nay I, Jalâl-ud-din Mahomed Akbar, as man, command thee as woman. Tell me the truth----"

She shrunk back--looked into his eyes, whence peace and dignity had fled, leaving naught but man's passion--then gave a little sob, feeling her effort had failed. He was man, not King.

"Yea! I will tell thee, Jalâl-ud-din Mahomed Akbar!"

So she told him dully, piteously, of her treachery concerning Diswunt, of her immediate repentance, of her much searching. Of the Wayfarer and his strange gift that she wore even now around her neck and how it had helped her, until as she spoke a scent of fresh roses seemed to fill the tent where those two sate hand in hand; for the grip on wrist had slackened and her fingers now lay in his willingly, confidently. Then she told him of Mihr-un-nissa and the Beneficent Ladies, of the false gems and the true one hidden in a harlot's bosom, until interest growing in Akbar's eyes, she forgot herself in her story, as she told of the Mirza and his uttermost deceit. Her very hand withdrew itself unnoticed as she described the fly's foot upon the paper which had altered the hour, and her voice rang defiant as she gave her challenge for the Truth. So, instinct with the mere drama of the deed, she sprang to her feet and made as if she flung the goblet, curving like a comet, into the night. And Akbar sate and watched her with ever growing admiration as, action by action, she followed her own words.

It became breathless, palpitating--the seven lamped cresset--the chiming gong--even the long-drawn kisses----

Akbar's cheek paled--this was more than womanhood--this was his dream of it----!

"Die dog! Die for thine untruth!"

Her passion had risen to its height; she staggered, for it was Akbar whom she found within her clasp.

But it was Akbar who held her close, as men hold women whom they love, who strained her to his breast, murmuring, "Nay! thou shalt live, live for thine uttermost Truth."

The excitement died from her face in a moment, she drew back from him in deadly fear.

"My liege--my liege--not so--it cannot be--for pity sake, my liege."

"Cannot?" he echoed with an exultant laugh. "Wherefore can it not be. Am I not the King?"

"It is because the Most High *is* the King" she began--"Remember, my liege--the death warrant."

He had forgotten it; but he passed rapidly to the desk whereon it lay.

"That is easy remedied," said he seizing on it and making as if he would tear it up.

"Hold!" she cried peremptorily.

"Wherefore?" he asked as peremptorily.

She drew herself up to her full height. "Because I am keeper of the King's honour, and I forbid it."

"Again, wherefore?" Checked in his immediate intention his temper rose.

"Does my liege forget," she said and her voice was calmness itself, "that it is not yet Dawn? That to destroy that paper is failure?--that the King's enemies will triumph? It is not yet Dawn and *that*"--she pointed to what he held--"belongs to To-day."

There was an awful silence. Akbar stood blinded by the truth. It was as she had said; to annul the death-warrant was to confess failure.

So, after a time his voice--or was it not his voice--sounded through the tent.

"It is not sealed. Thou hadst the ring--therefore it doth not count"

She had taken a step or two nearer to him as if to beg the paper of him, now she shrank back as from a snake, frozen with fear.

"What!" she whispered and her voice was close on tears. "Shall Kingship stoop to Craft--Leave that to the King's enemies."

But Akbar was past reproach; passion had mastered him and his hands instinct mobile with fierce life, met and parted again and again until the death-warrant torn to shreds lay in his clasp a mere handful of waste paper. "Lo!" he cried joyfully, "Let Kingship go! Jalâl-ud-din is man--he will reap man's harvest of love."

He flung what he held from him with the action of a sower who sows. The light scraps of paper hung in the air for a second then fell steadily, softly, like seed grains. Some of them fell on Âtma's white star-sewn skirts.

She stooped slowly to raise one and hold it up menacingly.

"Not a grain of the sheaves of life is stored by one who has trod
The furrows and fallows of passion, and sown no seed for God."

But Akbar had drifted too far from philosophy for such hoarded wisdom. He was back beside the speaker his arm around her.

"It is idle, Âtma I tell thee naught shall stand between us. Let Kingship go--thou art my Queen!"

She fought frantically against him and his claim.

"Sire, bethink you, if the challenge be lost?"

"What care I--thou lovest me--dare not to say thou dost not----"

"Yea! Yea! I love thee oh Jalâl-ud-din," she cried pleading with him, for himself, "but thou art the King. Thy faith must not fail."

"My faith in thee will never fail," he replied, "naught else matters."

"Not mine in thee? Not mine, the Châran's in the King? Nay, it shall not be so Âtma the Châran dies!"

Her hand which had snatched out the death-dagger of her race held it high above her head; but Akbar was too quick for her. His was on hers; so arrested, it remained, bringing her face closer to his.

"Nay, my Queen!" he said and the softness of his voice sent despair and delight through her veins. "Thou hast said thou lovest me, as I do thee. Is that not enough for poor mortal man? What is Kingship compared to it? Let it go! Kiss me, sweetheart--kiss me but once, and thou wilt learn----"

She lay passive on his shoulder, her eyes, full of the fire of love immortal, found and held his.

"What shall I learn, Great King?" she whispered falteringly.

"To take even love from my hand," he said, bending closer.

Her whole body seemed to yield to him, she nestled closer, finding soft rest in his strong arms.

"Yea!" she whispered, raising her lips for the kiss. "I will take--all things from the hand of the King."

So, ere he could prevent it, ere, taken by surprise, his iron muscles could counteract the strong downward sweep of her right hand, his, clasping hers, followed the flash of the death-dagger of her race.

It found fit sheathing close to her heart.

"Âtma," he whispered sinking to his knees with the dead weight he held. "Âtma!"

He did not call her love or queen; he knew too well that she was slipping away from such empty titles.

A low murmur made him bend his ear closer.

"May the--Gods pity--us Dreamers--who--dream----"

The old refrain. The first words surely he had heard from her lips. But at least she still lived.

Gathering her in his arms he carried her to the divan; then knelt supporting her on his breast. If she died she should die as a queen--in the King's clasp--upon his throne.

So there was silence.

The dawn was coming fast. It showed in streaks of shimmering gray light between the dark screens.

"Âtma!"

There was no sound.

Then suddenly gay, light-hearted as a bird, a bugle rang out; followed by another, and another.

The dying woman stirred.

"The--the dawn has come!" she whispered to herself. And then, suddenly, as if galvanised to an instant's life, she sate up and the tent rang with her cry.

Ohí! The King, The King,
Challenge I bring
Ohí! The King--the----

The last word never came. In her effort to rise she overbalanced and slipped in a huddled heap at Akbar's feet.

He stood quite still. He knew that she was dead; that nothing but worthless clay lay there; the deathless spirit--the dreamer that never dies-- had fled--whitherward? His way, surely!

So as he stood, he felt Kingship rise in him, as he had never--no not even he the prince of dreamers--felt it before.

Ohí! The King the King!

He stooped, gathered the dead thing in his arms, and laid it on the low throne. He did not even kiss the dead face, though the scent of roses clung round her. For an instant he felt inclined to take the gift of the Wayfarer from her as a remembrance. Then he remembered himself.

Such things might be for Jalâl-ud-din the man. He was the King. She should take Love with her.

Outside the bugle notes were echoing each other merrily through the camp. All things were astir with the dawn.

And he, the King was needed elsewhere. He called, and a servant entered.

"Lo! I have killed the woman," he said pointing to the divan briefly. "Give her fit burning, at once, ere the sun rise. She is *suttee*--she hath died for a man."

So he strode through the screen to the larger tent, and gave the signal for the uprising of Majesty.

In a second the huge weighted curtains at the end had swung to their high looped places, and advancing, he took his seat upon the canopied dais behind them. On the far level horizon the pearl gray of dawn was changing to primrose, darkening even as it changed to rosy-red; for Dawn comes swiftly in the cloudless skies of India. Before him, thronged with courtiers, circled the vast enclosure of the Inner Audience, opening out into a wide avenue wherein, drawn up on either side, stood soldiers in battalions. Their spear points struck at the sky; for beyond was nothingness. Only a wide, empty plain reaching up to a wide, empty sky.

ALLAH-HU AKBAR!

The cry rose from a thousand throats.

Akbar was indeed the King.

His enemies had failed.

Yet there was one thing which must be done before the dawn, if all was to be well, and Birbal looking somewhat crestfallen, stepped forward at a signal from the throne; behind him came William Leedes the jeweller.

The latter was saying "Ave-Mary's" under his breath, partly from pure fear of evil, partly from thanksgiving for delivery from evil.

"Mirza-Râjah Birbal," came the King's voice clear and resonant, to be heard of all men. "Deliver up the diamond called the King's Luck which was stolen, but which the King's Châran Âtma Devi hath died to restore" (Birbal started, then hung his head). "Deliver it up to the Western jeweller, William Leedes, in accordance with the oath by which she bound you."

Then turning to the Englishman the royal voice became less stern.

"And you--who are without blame--take it once more to thy lathe. Akbar's will hath not changed. His Luck shall shine. Aye! and his empire shall shine--as *he chooses*; let subjects, princes, friend--yea--even sons, say what they may!" Then changing gravity for cheerfulness he called down the line of soldiery: "Gentlemen! make ready for your march! Akbar goes forward! He leaves this Town of many Tears and Lack of Water behind him for ever!"

As he spoke the curved edge of the sun showed like a star for a second across the waste of desert that stretched as a sea before him, and from behind, from the Darkness of the Tents, from the Shadows of Man's Habitations, came the Procession of the Hours. In rosy pink like Dawn-Clouds, the pair of little children, no longer wide-eyed and solemn, danced at the head; and behind them, radiant with smiles followed the choric singers each with an unlit taper, singing the Song of the Dawn that has been sung in India since the Dawn of Days.

Many-tinted Morn! Th' immortal daughter of heaven
Young, white-robed, come with thy purple steeds
Follow the path of the dawning the world has been given
Follow the path of the dawn the world still needs.

From behind came quaint interludes that sounded like the carolling of birds, the whisperings of wind among the corn, the lowing of cattle--all the sounds of waking life upon the earth; and three of the taper holders advancing placed a taper, one on each side of the dais, one in the middle; so stood beside it still singing:

Darkly shining Dusk, thy sister has sought her abiding,
Fear not to trouble her dreams! Daughters ye twain of the Sun,
Dusk and Dawn bringing Birth. Oh! Sisters your path is unending!
Dead are the first who have watched. When shall our watching be done?

Once again three taper bearers bore their burdens to the appointed places.

Bright luminous Dawn; rose-red, radiant, rejoicing,
Show the traveller his road; the cattle their pastures new,
Rouse the beasts of the earth to their truthful myriad voicing,
Leader of Lightful days, softening the soil with dew.

The semicircle round the dais was almost complete now. It needed but three more tapers, and once again the voices rose exultant!

> Wide expanded Dawn: Open the gates of the Morning
> Waken the singing birds. Guide thou the truthful light
> To uttermost shade of the Shadow, for see you! the dawning
> Is born white-shining out of the gloom of the night!

As one, the twelve camphor candles flashed into white light, that shone for a second, then grew pale and cold, as the sun, heaving his mighty shoulder out of the dust haze that hung on the horizon, flooded the wide earth with his shine.

There was a pause. Akbar was about to rise, so ending the ceremony, when down the wide centre, betwixt the serried ranks of the soldiers, showed a man.

He walked slowly, his head was bent, and on his right arm was knotted a blue handkerchief.

"News of death!" commented the soldiers, quickly recognising the emblem--"Whose?"

"Whose?" asked the courtiers rapidly, while Akbar stood arrested.

"Whose?" queried Birbal quickly. He had been busy all night; had heard nothing.

"His half-brother of Kabul," said Abulfazl sadly. "The runner came in but half an hour agone; and this seemed the best way of breaking it; the shock will help----"

"Now heaven be thanked!" cried Birbal. "Not that I do not grieve--for the King; but this may make his decision less final. He *must* go now for the sake of Kingship--but His Dream in Red Sandstone may see him yet once again!"

L'ENVOI

O Gardener wide open the gate of the garden.
Let in the rose from her long winter sleep;
Bid the tall cypress stand sentinel-warden,
Spreading soft shade where the narcissus keep
Heads drooping down in their slumbering deep.
Bid the shoot harden,
Bid the sap leap!

Gardener! array all with manifold flowers.
Figure the garden like damask of old,
Tell of its hues in the turtledove's bowers,
Gild the bare ground with the pansies of gold
Pomegranate lips, stained with wine have you told
"These are the rose hours
Nightingale bold!"
Lo! she returns with bud-cradle of birth
Rose of the wine-house she brings to the earth,
Drink to the Spring time, to Love, and to Mirth.

--NIZAMI.

Four years had passed away and the Dream in Red Sandstone still waited for the Dreamer: waited, as it still waits, deserted but not ruined, the Great Arch of Victory remaining as Birbal had prophesied, that which no man having once seen, can ever forget.

But Birbal himself had passed into the unknown; almost into the forgotten save for his master's undying affection which, even after two years, still scanned the earthly horizon eagerly looking for news, at any rate, of his lost friend; since Birbal's actual death is one of those things of which neither past or present hold any knowledge. He disappeared in the mountains of Swât whither he had gone in the vain effort to translate one of Akbar's dreams into terms of reality.

For the Great Mogul, Emperor of India, had dreams of conquest, not by sword, not even by religion, as his great forerunner the Emperor Asoka had had in the years before Christ--but by common sense; that is the voluntary submission of the individual to a collective policy which makes for peace and prosperity to the mass of the people.

Deprived of latter-day delusions, modern foolishnesses, Akbar's dream was Socialism. Not the Socialism which proclaims the right of the individual, which presses that home against all other considerations, but the Socialism which sweeps all things, individual poverty as well as individual wealth into the Great Mill of God for the good of the race; which holds personal comfort unworthy of consideration.

It was not, perhaps, a policy suited to the most turbulent tribes upon the Indian Frontier. Still Kabul had been annexed almost without a blow, Kashmir brought into the Imperial net by a peaceful demonstration, and, but for Sinde, the Imperial armies would scarcely have struck a blow during these years of Imperial aggrandisement.

Anyhow, the experiment, one after Akbar's own heart, was tried; and Birbal went with the forces as a counterpoise to the old Commander in Chief (he was the Wellington of Akbar's reign) and his more antiquated methods of suasion. They drew lots, those two friends of the King, Abulfazl and Birbal, which should take the onerous post; and the lot fell on Birbal. It is said that the King hesitated to let him go; but behind friendship lay Kingship.

So he went, and disputes soon arising between the policy of pike and cannonade, as against a mere display of force, Birbal, left in the lurch, disappeared for ever with fifteen hundred picked men amid the peaks and passes of the Alai Mountains.

It had been a great blow to Akbar; he had, indeed, refused to believe in his friend's death, and still looked for him to return--even if from the Other Side--in obedience to his promise.

But now, this 10th of May, 1590, he was pausing a little below the top of the Pir Panjal Pass on the way to Kashmir, awaiting the arrival of William Leedes, the English jeweller, who all these years had been engaged in cutting the Great Diamond of India.

It was ready now, and Akbar was eager to see it. But the little party escorting the jeweller and his charge had not arrived that morning, so Akbar had come out alone to a favourite vantage point below the actual snows, whence the whole Panjab plain rising an almost incredible height in the sky, could be seen.

It was like a shield, he thought suddenly, as he noted the palpable curve of the horizon; higher in the middle, lower at the sides. That was the curve of the world's surface, of course; still it reminded one of the curve of a great shield set between these holy snows of Himâlya and the world beyond. Aye! for the blue of that distant plain was darker nowhere, was lighter nowhere; and everywhere alike it was damascened with threads-- broader, narrower--of gold.

The land of the Five Rivers! A fair land indeed! A broad battle shield to the rest of India.

"Lo! there is gran'dad!" came a voice from behind him, and he turned at the sound of little pattering feet to see his grandson, a child of about two, stumbling swiftly over the broken ground toward him.

"Have a care Fair-face," (Khushru) he called, holding out his arms, and the child with a laughing crow, hurrying still harder, almost fell into their shelter.

"Truly! thou art as two peas in one pod," gasped a breathless voice, as Auntie Rosebody, completely done by hurrying up the hill, flung herself on the ground beside her nephew. She looked not a day older with her gray hair stuffed away into a Mogul cap, her petticoats tucked away into full Mogul trousers. So, had she roamed the hills, as a girl, with her father Babar, and now, in her old age, she set an example to all other ladies of the camp. Umm Kulsum, ever her close companion, followed on her heels, dressed in like manner, and stood looking down on the little family party.

"Lo! nephew! at times it takes me," said the old lady, nodding her head sagely, "to leave the scapegrace--who hath, nathless been behaving more reputably of late--out of the bargain altogether! The boy is more like Jalâl-ud-din Mahomed Akbar than Salîm ever was, and that is a fact! But"-- seeing a frown come to Akbar's face--"I am not here to fashion likeness, but because," here she drew her face into a decent pucker of sorrow, "having been--God forgive me--Aye! and Umm Kulsum too--part responsible for its theft--truly, nephew, your old aunt feels ever about her neck the bowstring that should have been drawn, and was not, thanks to---- "

Akbar interrupted her with patient gloom. "We have talked this out many times, oh! most reverend aunt. After all there was no mischief done." He thought ever as he spoke of that Arch of Victory standing deserted on the Sikri Ridge.

"But there might have been," interrupted Aunt Rosebody, hotly. "Take not penitence from my soul, nephew. 'Tis good to have sins to repent when one grows old and there are no more to commit. So, having been in the tale at the beginning----"

Akbar looked pathetically at Umm Kulsum, who had sunk to her knees in contrition.

"It is because, Highness," she answered as if to a question, "the jeweller is arrived, and is even now on his way hither."

Akbar sprang to his feet, light as a boy. Dressed in hunting leathers with the close Mogul cap crested with a heron's plume, he looked not a day older, though his short hair above his beardless face had grown almost white.

"Here!" he cried, and even as he spoke a party of three or four showed rounding the rocky path.

A few minutes later Akbar stood holding the diamond, half its original size, but brilliant exceedingly in the hollow of his right hand.

"For my part," sniffed Auntie Rosebody, "I liked it better as it was. True, it dazzles the eyes, but to look at it much would be to court blindness. Lo! it gives *me* the browache. Come Ummu, let us on our way. I have promised Hamida, rhubarb-stew to her dinner and we must climb to the snows for that."

But Umm Kulsum lingered for consolation since, in truth, the stone bewildered her. "True, *chachaji*" (maternal uncle), she said softly, "I am not clever enough for it. There be so many sides, and each seemeth different."

Aye that was it! So many sides, thought Akbar, as, after dismissing the jeweller and his escort for refreshment, he sate on that pinnacle of rock almost overhanging the Panjab plain, and looked at the Luck which he had had cut in Western fashion.

His fowling piece--for he had been on his way to one of his long solitary rambles--lay beside him and on the polished steel of its lock the brilliant sunshine glinted, sending reflected light to touch and make visible the almost microscopic fruition of a tiny lichen on the rock.

But how much more brilliant was the light that sparkled from the diamond!

A hundred suns in one? No it was a hundred worlds--worlds unseen till then.

What would it--what might it not--what ought it not to make manifest?

So once more as he sate holding his luck in his hands, holding it between him and the river-damascened shield of the wide Panjab plain, the Self that is behind Self found eyes and saw.

What did he see? Did he see the Shield of India stand in the forefront of battle for the principles he preached, as it did in Mutiny time? Or did sight pass beyond that, and did he see the East, intoxicated by the errors of the West, aping the horrors of a civilisation which has missed its way, which has forgotten that Socialism is Despotism--the Despotism of Fate whose eye is fixed, not on the equality of the individual, but the ultimate outcome of Race?

Who knows?

For as the morning sun rose to power, vapoury mist-clouds gathered on the damp mountain sides below, and crept up and up, hiding all things, obscuring all things.

The wide shield of the Land of the Five Rivers went first. Bit by bit the hurrying mists obscured it, the damascening disappeared until high upon the sky only a clear blue curved rim remained--an arch of victory that stretched over the visible world.

Then the mist claimed Akbar's outstretched hand; so, rising, rolling over on itself, almost playing with the short flower-set turf, patched here and there with melting snow, and nestling into the crannies of the rock, it shrouded the King from his Kingdom, the Man from his World--and the Dreamer was alone with his Dream.

He was asleep, his head resting on a tuft of those tiny blue poppies which grow on the peaks of Holy Himâlya--poppies of heavenly rest whose petals look as if they had been cut from the sky--when Aunt Rosebody's voice roused him. The sun, having overcome the mists, was shining brightly.

"Lo!" she exclaimed, "the King hath been delayed no doubt, but high up where we were seeking rhubarb it was like the Day of Resurrection to see the mists tear themselves to shreds in rage as the Sun caught them. So goes Ignorance before Wisdom. And little Fair-face hath found his granddad a *nârgiz*--present it, child, though 'tis late for a New Year offering. Lo! he is the spit of my father--on whom be peace--no flower escapes him."

"And I have found violets for the King," smiled Umm Kulsum, comfortably. She was more than ever a Mother of Plumpness in her stuffed Mogul costume.

"Ps'sh" commented Auntie Rosebody scornfully. "What are flowers to rhubarb? And I have enough for two stews, so Râkiya Begum may lay her tartness to that--if she will eat of it, though mayhap at her age she hath forgotten her youth. As for me, 'twill be a Day of Resurrection indeed to taste of it again, for I have dreamt of it all these years."

Akbar caught up the child with a sudden laugh, and setting him astride his shoulders began the descent to the camp below.

"'Tis as well, most reverend," he said "that some dreamers dream true."

Did he think as he spoke of a woman who had dreamed her dream through to the Truth, *whose hiding place is immortality, whose shadow is death?*

Perhaps he did. Perhaps, even now, on those misty spring mornings when the sun chases the snow vapours over the blue gentians and rosy alpine primulas that edge the snow patches on the peaks of the Pir Panjal, the Self that lay behind the Self that was called Akbar sits, enshrouded by the mists and looks out over the Empire of the Great Mogul.

What does the Prince of Dreamers think of it?

F. A. Steel.

28th January, 1908.

FOOTNOTES

Footnote 1: Memoirs of Gulbadan Begum.

Footnote 2: New Year.

Footnote 3: Two opposing sects of Mahommedans.

Footnote 4: Two opposing sects of Mahommedans.

Footnote 5: The Châran bard and champion is a hereditary office held very sacred by the Râjpûts.

Footnote 6: Favourite supper dishes on account of their supposed qualities.

Footnote 7: Copy of real letter.

Footnote 8: The ordinary outside-veil with eye-holes in it.

Footnote 9: This is a fair translation of the name Payandâr.

Footnote 10: The Syeds as lineal descendants of Mahommed.

Footnote 11: A very dreadful female ghost.

Footnote 12: A tribe who have the gift of (to use theatrical parlance) "making up" to perfection.

Footnote 13: The two Recording Angels.

Footnote 14: Sir Edwin Arnold's translation.

Footnote 15: Translated by Sir Edwin Arnold.